An Introduction to Object-Oriented Programming with Visual Basic .NET

DAN CLARK

Apress™

An Introduction to Object-Oriented Programming with Visual Basic .NET
Copyright ©2002 by Dan Clark

ISBN (pbk): 1-59059-015-5

Printed and bound in the United States of America 12345678910

Trademarked names may appear in this book. Rather than use a trademark symbol with every occurrence of a trademarked name, we use the names only in an editorial fashion and to the benefit of the trademark owner, with no intention of infringement of the trademark.

Technical Reviewer: Jon Box
Editorial Directors: Dan Appleman, Peter Blackburn, Gary Cornell, Jason Gilmore, Karen Watterson, John Zukowski
Managing Editor: Grace Wong
Project Manager: Alexa Stuart
Copy Editor: Kim Wimpsett
Production Editor: Kari Brooks
Composition: Impressions Book and Journal Services, Inc.
Indexer: Valerie Robbins
Cover Designer: Kurt Krames
Manufacturing Manager: Tom Debolski
Marketing Manager: Stephanie Rodriguez

Distributed to the book trade in the United States by Springer-Verlag New York, Inc., 175 Fifth Avenue, New York, NY, 10010 and outside the United States by Springer-Verlag GmbH & Co. KG, Tiergartenstr. 17, 69112 Heidelberg, Germany.
In the United States, phone 1-800-SPRINGER, email orders@springer-ny.com, or visit http://www.springer-ny.com.
Outside the United States, fax +49 6221 345229, email orders@springer.de, or visit http://www.springer.de.

For information on translations, please contact Apress directly at 2560 9th Street, Suite 219, Berkeley, CA 94710. Phone 510-549-5930, fax: 510-549-5939, email info@apress.com, or visit http://www.apress.com.

The source code for this book is available to readers at http://www.apress.com in the Downloads section. You will need to answer questions pertaining to this book in order to successfully download the code.

To my wife, Angie. Without her immense support and patience, this book never could have been written.

Contents at a Glance

About the Author ....*xii*

About the Technical Reviewer ....*xiii*

Acknowledgments ....*xiv*

Introduction ....*xv*

Part One: **Object-Oriented Programming and**

Design Fundamentals *1*

Chapter 1   Overview of Object-Oriented Programming *3*

Chapter 2   Designing OOP Solutions:

Identifying the Class Structure *13*

Chapter 3   Designing OOP Solutions:

Modeling the Object Interaction *41*

Chapter 4   Designing OOP Solutions: A Case Study *77*

Part Two: **Object-Oriented Programming with**

Visual Basic .NET *101*

Chapter 5   Introducing VB .NET *103*

Chapter 6   Creating Classes *135*

Chapter 7   Creating Class Hierarchies *155*

Chapter 8   Implementing Object Collaboration *187*

Part Three: **Developing Applications with**

Visual Basic .NET *221*

Chapter 9   OSO Application Revisited:

             Implementing the Business Logic *223*

Chapter 10   Developing Windows Applications *269*

Chapter 11   Developing Web Applications *317*

Chapter 12   Wrapping Up and Reviewing *367*

Appendix A   Fundamental Programming Concepts *373*

Appendix B   Exception Handling in VB .NET *393*

Index *399*

Contents

About the Author ....*xii*

About the Technical Reviewer ....*xiii*

Acknowledgments ....*xiv*

Introduction ....*xv*

Part One: Object-Oriented Programming and Design Fundamentals...*1*

Chapter 1: Overview of Object-Oriented Programming *3*

The History of OOP *3*

Why Use OOP? *4*

The Characteristics of OOP *6*

The History of Visual Basic *9*

Summary *11*

Chapter 2: Designing OOP Solutions: Identifying the Class Structure *13*

Goals of Software Design *14*

Understanding the Unified Modeling Language *15*

Understanding Class Diagrams *28*

Summary *38*

Chapter 3: Designing OOP Solutions: Modeling the Object Interaction *41*

Understanding Scenarios *41*

Introducing Sequence Diagrams *43*

Using Collaboration Diagrams *59*

Understanding Activity Diagrams *61*
Exploring GUI Design *71*
Summary *75*

Chapter 4: Designing OOP Solutions: A Case Study *77*

Developing an Office-Supply Ordering System *77*
Avoiding Some Common OOP Design Pitfalls *99*
Summary *100*

Part Two: Object-Oriented Programming with Visual Basic .NET *101*

Chapter 5: Introducing VB .NET *103*

Goals of the .NET Framework *103*
Components of the .NET Framework *106*
Understanding Assemblies and Manifests *109*
Referencing Assemblies and Namespaces *110*
Compiling and Executing Managed Code *110*
Using the Visual Studio Integrated
     Development Environment *111*
Summary *132*

Chapter 6: Creating Classes *135*

Introducing Objects and Classes *135*
Defining Classes *136*
Using Constructors *143*
Using Destructors *144*
Overloading Methods *145*
Summary *153*

Chapter 7: Creating Class Hierarchies 155

Understanding Inheritance 156
Overriding Methods of the Base Class 164
Overloading Methods of the Base Class 176
Using Shadowing 176
Implementing Interfaces 177
Understanding Polymorphism 178
Summary 185

Chapter 8: Implementing Object Collaboration 187

Object Communication through Messaging 187
Event-Driven Programming 190
Understanding Delegation 197
Handling Exceptions in the .NET Framework 203
Accessing Shared Properties and Methods 207
Asynchronous Messaging 213
Summary 220

Part Three: Developing Applications with Visual Basic .NET 221

Chapter 9: OSO Application Revisited: Implementing the Business Logic 223

Revisiting Application Design 224
Introducing ADO.NET 225
Working with Data Providers 226
Working with DataSet Objects 240
Building the OSO Application's Business Logic Tier 253
Summary 266

Chapter 10: Developing Windows Applications *269*

Windows Forms Fundamentals *269*
Working with Form-Based Inheritance *287*
Creating and Using Dialog Boxes *290*
Data Binding in Windows Form-Based GUIs *300*
Creating the OSO Application's Windows
    Form-Based GUI *306*
Summary *315*

Chapter 11: Developing Web Applications *317*

Web Form Fundamentals *317*
Web Server Control Fundamentals *319*
Understanding Web Form and Web Server Control Inheritance
    Hierarchy *320*
Using the Visual Studio Web Form Designer *322*
Handling Web Form and Control Events *325*
Understanding Application and Session Events *329*
Storing and Sharing State in a Web Application *338*
Data Binding in Web Form-Based GUIs *341*
Creating the OSO Application's Web Form-Based GUI *354*
Summary *366*

Chapter 12: Wrapping Up and Reviewing *367*

Improving Your Object-Oriented Design Skills *368*
Investigating the .NET Framework Namespaces *368*
Becoming Familiar with ADO.NET *369*
Moving Toward Component-Based Development *369*
Finding Help *370*
Joining a User Group *370*
Getting Certified *370*
Please Provide Feedback *371*
Thank You and Good Luck *371*

Appendix A: Fundamental Programming Concepts 373

Working with Variables and Data Types 373
Understanding Elementary Data Types 374
Introducing Composite Data Types 376
Looking at Literals, Constants, and Enumerations 378
Exploring Variable Scope 379
Understanding Data Type Conversion 381
Working with Operators 383
Introducing Decision Structures 385
Using Loop Structures 388
Introducing Procedures 390

Appendix B: Exception Handling in VB .NET 393

Managing Exceptions 393
Looking at the .NET Framework Exception Classes 395

Index 399

About the Author

DAN CLARK IS A MICROSOFT Certified Trainer, a Microsoft Certified Solution Developer, and a Microsoft Certified Database Administrator. For the past seven years, he has been developing applications and training others how to develop applications using Microsoft technologies. Dan's teaching experience runs the gamut from training beginners on object-oriented programming to training experienced developers on the nuances of COM programming. He finds particular satisfaction in turning new developers on to the thrill of developing and designing object-oriented applications. When not training, writing, or programming, Dan can be found stinking up the house brewing his next batch of beer.

About the Technical Reviewer

As a solutions architect at Quilogy (`www.quilogy.com`), Jon Box has advanced experience in multiple technologies with a solid background in infrastructure, application development, data access, and a host of other technologies. He serves an important role in evangelizing the business value of new technologies to Quilogy clients and has served in diverse roles as an architect, trainer, author, project manager, and general manager at Quilogy. He is currently part of Quilogy's Atomic education team, where he is focusing on authoring and developing advanced .NET training courses and technical content for the Atomic Web site (`atomic.quilogy.com`).

Jon is a Microsoft regional director for Memphis, Tennessee, and serves on the MSDN Customer Council. He is a noted speaker on Microsoft emerging technologies and an active participant in the Memphis technology community. He also founded the Memphis .NET User Group (`www.memphisdot.net`). Jon frequently speaks at DevDays and recently conducted an MSDN Webcast on the Microsoft Mobile Internet Toolkit. Jon's credentials include Microsoft Certified Solution Developer and Microsoft Certified Trainer.

Acknowledgments

A SPECIAL THANKS TO THE following people who made this book possible:

- The team at Apress, who have made writing this book a truly positive experience

- Alexa Stuart, for keeping track of the madness

- Jon Box, for the unenviable task of wading through the code and activities to ensure accuracy and clarity

- Kim Wimpsett, for her ability to clarify my thoughts and fix the incomprehensible styling tags in the copy I gave her

- Dan Appleman, for being the catalyst who got the ball rolling

- Angie, for filling the void

- Greg, Morgan, and Noah, for keeping me on task

- Mom and Dad, for being there

Introduction

It HAS BEEN MY EXPERIENCE as a Visual Basic trainer that most people do not have trouble picking up the syntax of the language. What perplexes and frustrates many people are the higher-level concepts of object-oriented programming methodology and design. To compound the problem, most introductory programming books and training classes skim over these concepts or, worse, do not cover them at all.

My goal in writing this book is to provide you with the information needed to understand how one goes about architecting an object-oriented programming solution aimed at solving a business problem. As you work your way through the book, first you will learn how to analyze the business requirements. Next, you will model the objects and relationships involved in the solution design. Finally, you will implement the solution using Visual Basic .NET. Along the way you will learn the fundamentals of software design, the Unified Modeling Language (UML), object-oriented programming, and Visual Basic (VB) .NET.

Because this is an introductory book, it is meant to be a starting point for your study of the topics presented. As such, this book is *not* designed to make you an expert in object-oriented programming and UML; be an exhaustive discussion of VB .NET and the .NET Framework; nor be an in-depth study of Visual Studio .NET. It takes considerable time and effort to become proficient in any one of these areas. It is my hope that by reading this book your first experiences in object-oriented programming will be enjoyable, comprehensible, and instill a desire for further study.

Target Audience

The target audience for this book is the beginning VB .NET programmer who wants to gain a foundation in object-oriented programming along with the VB language basics. Programmers transitioning from a procedural-oriented programming model to an object-oriented model will also benefit from this book. In addition, there are many pre-.NET VB programmers who do not have a firm grasp of object-oriented programming. Now is the time to become acquainted with the fundamentals of object-oriented programming before transitioning to VB .NET. Because the experience level of a "beginner" can vary immensely, I have included a primer in Appendix A, "Fundamental Programming Concepts," which discusses some basic programming tenets. I would suggest you review these concepts if you are new to programming.

Organization of the Book

This book is organized into three parts:

Part One delves into object-oriented programming methodology and design—concepts that transcend a particular programming language. The concepts presented are important to the success of an object-oriented programming solution regardless of the implementation language chosen. At the conclusion of this part, a case study walks you through modeling a "real-world" application.

Part Two looks at how object-oriented programming is implemented in Visual Basic .NET. You will look at creating class structures, creating hierarchies, and implementing interfaces. This part also introduces object interaction and collaboration. You will see how the object-oriented programming topics discussed in Part One are transformed into Visual Basic coding constructs.

Part Three returns to the case study introduced and modeled at the end of Part One. Using the knowledge gained in Part Two, you will transform the design into a fully functional VB .NET application. This includes designing a graphical user interface, implementing the business logic, and integrating with a relational database to store data. Along the way you will be exposed to the .NET Framework classes used to work with data, create a Windows-based user interface, and finally a Web-based user interface.

Activities and Software Requirements

One of the most important aspects of learning is doing. You cannot learn to ride a bike without jumping on a bike and you cannot learn to program without "cranking out" code. Any successful training program needs to include both a theory component and a hands-on component. I have included both components throughout this book. It is my hope that you will take these activities seriously and work through them thoroughly and even repeatedly. Contrary to some students' perception that these activities are "exercises in typing," this is where the theory becomes concrete and true simulation of the concepts occurs. I also encourage you to play during the activities. Do not be afraid to alter some of the code just to see what happens. Some of the best learning experiences occur when students "color outside the lines."

You can download the starter files referred to in this book from the Apress Web site at www.apress.com. The UML modeling activities in Part One are for someone using Objecteering's UML Modeler. I chose this program because of

its simple user interface and the fact it can be downloaded for free at
`www.objecteering.com/us/produits_pe.htm`. You do not need a CASE tool to complete these activities; a paper and pencil will work just fine. You can also use
another CASE tool such as Visio to complete the activities. The activities in Part Two
require Visual Studio .NET with Visual Basic .NET installed. I encourage you to
install the help files and make ample use of them while completing the activities.
You can find a trial edition of Visual Studio at `msdn.microsoft.com/vstudio/pro-
ductinfo/trial.asp`. The activities in Part Three require Microsoft SQL Server 7.0 or
2000 with the Pubs and Northwind databases installed. The case study application's database needs to be hosted in Microsoft SQL Server 2000. You can find a trial
edition of this at `www.microsoft.com/sql/evaluation/trial/2000/default.asp`. The
activities in Chapter 11, "Developing Web Applications," require the Microsoft IIS
5.0 Web server be installed and configured with FrontPage Server Extensions. You
can find more detailed instructions and requirements at the Apress Web site.

> **NOTE** *The Web addresses mentioned are subject to change without
> notice. Check the Apress site (`www.apress.com`) for any updates.*

Part One

Object-Oriented Programming and Design Fundamentals

CHAPTER 1

Overview of Object-Oriented Programming

To SET THE STAGE for your study of object-oriented programming and Visual Basic .NET, this chapter will briefly look at the history of object-oriented programming and the characteristics of an object-oriented programming language. You will look at why object-oriented programming has become so important in the development of industrial-strength distributed software systems. You will also examine how Visual Basic has evolved into one of the leading business application programming languages.

After reading this chapter you will be familiar with the following:

- The history of object-oriented programming

- Why object-oriented programming has become so important in the development of industrial-strength applications

- The characteristics that make a programming language object-oriented

- The history and evolution of Visual Basic

The History of OOP

Object-Oriented Programming (OOP) is an approach to software development in which the structure of the software is based on *objects* interacting with each other to accomplish a task. This interaction takes the form of messages passing back and forth between the objects. In response to a message, an object can perform an action, or *method*. If you look at how you accomplish tasks in the world around you, you can see that you interact in an object-oriented world. If you want to go to the store, for example, you interact with a car object. A car object consists of other objects that interact with each other to accomplish the task of getting you to the store. You put the key in the ignition object and turn it. This in turn sends a message (through an electrical signal) to the starter object, which interacts with the engine object to start the car. As a driver, you are isolated from the logic of how the objects of the system work together to start the car. You just initiate the sequence of events by executing the start method of the ignition object with the key. You then wait for a response (message) of success or failure.

Object-oriented programs consist of objects that interact with each other to accomplish a task. Like the real world, users of software programs are isolated from the logic needed to accomplish a task. For example, when you print a page in your word processor, you initiate the action by clicking a print button. You are isolated from the internal processing that has to occur—you just wait for a response telling you if it printed. Internally, the button object interacts with a printer object, which interacts with the printer to accomplish the task of printing the page.

OOP concepts started surfacing in the mid-1960s with a programming language called Simula and further evolved in the 70s with advent of Smalltalk. Although software developers did not overwhelmingly embrace these early advances in OOP languages, object-oriented methodologies continued to evolve. In the mid-80s there was a resurgence of interest in object-oriented methodologies. Specifically, OOP languages such as C++ and Eifle became popular with mainstream computer programmers. OOP continued to grow in popularity in the 90s, most notably with the advent of Java and the huge following it attracted. And in 2002, with the latest version of Visual Studio, Microsoft introduced a new OOP language, C# (pronounced *C-sharp*) and revamped Visual Basic so that it is truly an OOP language.

Why Use OOP?

Why has OOP developed into such a widely used paradigm for solving business problems today? During the 70s and 80s, procedural-oriented programming languages such as C, Pascal, and Fortran were widely used to develop business-oriented software systems. Procedural languages organize the program in a linear fashion—they run from top to bottom. In other words, the program is a series of steps that run one after another. This type of programming worked fine for small programs that consisted of a few hundred code lines, but as programs became larger they became hard to manage and debug.

In an attempt to manage the ever-increasing size of the programs, structured programming was introduced to break down the code into manageable segments called *functions* or *procedures*. This was an improvement, but as programs performed more complex business functionality and interacted with other systems, the shortcomings of structural programming methodology began to surface:

- Programs became harder to maintain.

- Existing functionality was hard to alter without adversely affecting all of the system's functionality.

- New programs were essentially built from scratch. Consequently, there was little return on the investment of previous efforts.

- Programming was not conducive to team development. Programmers had to know every aspect of how a program worked and could not isolate their efforts on one aspect of a system.

- It was hard to translate business models into programming models.

- It worked well in isolation but did not integrate well with other systems.

In addition to these shortcomings, some evolutions of computing systems caused further strain on the structural program approach:

- Nonprogrammers demanded and were given direct access to programs through the incorporation of graphical user interfaces and their desktop computers.

- Users demanded a more-intuitive, less-structured approach to interacting with programs.

- Computer systems evolved into a distributed model where the business logic, user interface, and backend database were loosely coupled and accessed over the Internet and intranets.

As a result, many business software developers turned to object-oriented methodologies and programming languages to solve these problems. The benefits included the following:

- A more intuitive transition from business analysis models to software implementation models

- The ability to maintain and implement changes in the programs more efficiently and rapidly

- The ability to more effectively create software systems using a team process, allowing specialists to work on parts of the system

- The ability to reuse code components in other programs and purchase components written by third-party developers to increase the functionality of their programs with little effort

- Better integration with loosely coupled distributed computing systems

- Improved integration with modern operating systems

- The ability to create a more intuitive graphical user interface for the users

The Characteristics of OOP

In this section you are going to look at the some fundamental concepts and terms common to all OOP languages. Do not worry about how these concepts get implemented in any particular programming language; that will come later. My goal is to merely familiarize you with the concepts and relate them to your every-day experiences in such a way that they make more sense later when you look at OOP design and implementation.

Objects

If you think about it, you live in an object-oriented world. You are an object. You interact with other objects. To write this book I am interacting with a computer object. When I woke up this morning I was responding to a message sent out by an alarm clock object. In fact, you are an object with data such as height and hair color. You also have methods that you perform or are performed on you—for example, eating and walking.

So what are objects? In OOP terms, an object is a structure for incorporating data and the procedures for working with that data. For example, if you were interested in tracking data associated with products in inventory, you would create a product object that is responsible for maintaining and working with the data pertaining to the products. If you wanted to have printing capabilities in your application, you would work with a printer object that is responsible for the data and methods used to interact with your printers.

Abstraction

When you interact with objects in the world, you are often only concerned with a subset of their properties. Without this ability to abstract or filter out the extraneous properties of objects, you would find it hard to process the plethora of information bombarding you and concentrate on the task at hand.

As a result of *abstraction*, when two different people interact with the same object, they often deal with a different subset of attributes. When I drive my car, for example, I need to know the speed of the car and the direction it is going. Because the car is an automatic, I do not need to know the RPMs of the engine, so I filter this information out. On the other hand, this information would be critical to a racecar driver, who would not filter it out.

When constructing objects in OOP applications, it is important to incorporate this concept of abstraction. If you were building a shipping application, you would construct a product object with attributes such as size and weight. The color of the item would be extraneous information and filtered out. On the other hand, when constructing an order-entry application, the color could be important and would be included as an attribute of the product object.

Encapsulation

Another important feature of OOP is *encapsulation*. Encapsulation is the process in which no direct access is granted to the data; instead, it is hidden. If you want to gain access to the data, you have to interact with the object responsible for the data. In the previous inventory example, if you wanted to view or update information on the products, you would have to work through the product object. To read the data, you would have sent the product object a message. The product object would then read the value and send back a message telling you what the value is. The product object defines what operations can be performed on the product data. If you send a message to modify the data and the product object determines it is a valid request, it will perform the operation for you and send a message back with the result.

You experience encapsulation in your daily life all the time. Think about a human resources department. They encapsulate (hide) the information about employees. They determine how this data can be used and manipulated. Any request for the employee data or request to update the data has to be routed through them. Another example is network security. Any request for the security information or a change to a security policy must be made through a network security administrator. The security data is encapsulated from the users of the network.

By encapsulating data you make the data of your system more secure and reliable. You know how the data is being accessed and what operations are being performed on the data. This makes program maintenance much easier and also greatly simplifies the debugging process. You can also modify the methods used to work on the data, and if you do not alter how the method is requested and the type of response sent back, then you do not have to alter the other objects using the method. Think about when you send a letter in the mail. You make a request to the post office to deliver the letter. How the post office accomplishes this is not exposed to you. If it changes the route it uses to mail the letter, it does not affect how you initiate the sending of the letter. You do not have to know the post office's internal procedures used to deliver the letter.

Polymorphism

Polymorphism is the ability of two different objects to respond to the same request message in their own unique way. For example, I could train my dog to respond to the command bark and my bird to respond to the command chirp. On the other hand, I could train them to both respond to the command speak. Through polymorphism I know that the dog will respond with a bark and the bird will respond with a chirp.

How does this relate to OOP? You can create objects that respond to the same message in their own unique implementations. For example, you could send a print message to a printer object that would print the text on a printer, and you could send the same message to a screen object that would print the text to a window on your computer screen.

Another good example of polymorphism is the use of words in the English language. Words have many different meanings, but through the context of the sentence you can deduce which meaning is intended. You know that someone who says, "Give me a break!" is not asking you to break his leg!

In OOP you implement this type of polymorphism through a process called *overloading.* You can implement different methods of an object that have the same name. The object can then tell which method to implement depending on the context (in other words, the number and type of arguments passed) of the message. For example, you could create two methods of an inventory object to look up the price of a product. Both these methods would be named getPrice. Another object could call this method and either pass the name of the product or the product ID. The inventory object could tell which getPrice method to run by whether a string value or an integer value was passed with the request.

Inheritance

Most objects are classified according to hierarchies. For example, you can classify all dogs together as having certain common characteristics, such as having four legs and fur. Their breeds further classify them into subgroups with common attributes, such as size and demeanor. You also classify objects according to their function. For example, there are commercial vehicles and recreational vehicles. There are trucks and passenger cars. You classify cars according to their make and model. To make sense of the world, you need to use object hierarchies and classifications.

You use *inheritance* in OOP to classify the objects in your programs according to common characteristics and function. This makes working with the objects easier and more intuitive. It also makes programming easier because it enables you to combine general characteristics into a parent object and inherit these characteristics in the child objects. For example, you can define an employee object that defines all the general characteristics of employees in your company. You can then define a manager object that inherits the characteristics of the employee object but also adds characteristics unique to managers in your company. The manager object will automatically reflect any changes in the implementation of the employee object.

Aggregation

Aggregation is when an object consists of a composite of other objects that work together. For example, your lawn mower object is a composite of the wheel objects, the engine object, the blade object, and so on. In fact, the engine object is a composite of many other objects. There are many examples of aggregation in the world around us. The ability to use aggregation in OOP is a powerful feature that enables you to accurately model and implement business processes in your programs.

The History of Visual Basic

By most accounts, you can trace the origins of Visual Basic to Alan Cooper, an independent software vender. In the late 1980s Cooper was developing a shell construction kit called Tripod. What made Tripod unique was it incorporated a visual design tool that enabled developers to design their Windows interfaces by dragging and dropping controls onto it. Using a visual design tool hid a lot of the complexity of the Windows Application Programming Interface (API) from the developer. The other innovation associated with Tripod was the extensible model it offered programmers. Programmers could develop custom controls and incorporate them into the Tripod development environment. Up to this point, development tools were, for the most part, closed environments that could not be customized.

Microsoft paid Cooper for the development of Tripod and renamed it Ruby. Although Microsoft never released Ruby as a shell construction kit, it incorporated its form engine with the QuickBasic programming language and developed Thunder, one of the first Rapid Application Development (RAD) tools for Windows programs. Thunder was renamed to Visual Basic, and Visual Basic 1.0 was introduced in the spring of 1991. Visual Basic 1.0 became popular with business application developers because of its ease of use and its ability to rapidly develop prototype applications. Although Visual Basic 1.0 was an innovation in the design of Windows applications, it did not have built-in support for database interactivity. Microsoft realized this was a server limitation and introduced native support for data access in the form of Data Access Objects (DAO) in Visual Basic 3.0. After the inclusion of native data support, the popularity of Visual Basic swelled. It transitioned from being a prototyping tool to being a tool used to develop industrial-strength business applications.

Microsoft has always been committed to developing the Visual Basic language and the Visual Basic Integrated Development Environment (IDE). In fact, by many accounts, Bill Gates himself has taken an active interest in the development and growth of Visual Basic. At one point, the design team did not allow controls to be created and added to the Toolbox. When Bill Gates saw the product demo, he insisted that this extensibility be incorporated into the product. This extensibility brought on the growth of the custom control industry. Third-party vendors began to market controls that made programming an application even easier for Visual Basic developers. For example, a Resize control was marketed that encapsulated the code needed to resize a form and the controls the form contained. A developer could purchase this tool and add it to the Toolbox in the Visual Basic IDE. The developer could then drag the resize control onto the form, and without writing any code, the form and the controls it contained would resize proportionality.

By version 6.0, Visual Basic had evolved into a robust and industrial-strength programming language with an extremely large and dedicated developer base. But as strong as Visual Basic had become as a programming language, many programmers felt it had one major shortcoming. Visual Basic was considered by many to be an object-like programming language—not a true object-oriented programming language. Although Visual Basic 4.0 gave developers the ability to create classes and to package the classes in reusable components, Visual Basic did not incorporate such basic OOP features such as inheritance and method overloading. Without these features, developers were severely limited in their ability to construct complex distributed software systems. Microsoft has recognized these shortcomings and has changed Visual Basic into a true OOP language with the release of Visual Basic .NET.

Summary

In this chapter you became familiar with the following:

- The history of object-oriented programming

- Why object-oriented programming has become so important in the development of industrial-strength applications

- The characteristics that make a programming language object-oriented

- The history and evolution of Visual Basic

Now that you have an understanding of what constitutes an OOP language and why OOP languages are so important to enterprise-level application development, your next step is to become familiar with how OOP applications are designed. Successful applications must be carefully planned and developed before any meaningful coding takes place. The next chapter is the first in a series of three aimed at introducing you to some of the techniques used when designing object-oriented applications. You will look at the process of deciding what objects need to be included in an application and what attributes of these objects are important to the functionality of that application.

CHAPTER 2

Designing OOP Solutions: Identifying the Class Structure

THE FIRST STEP in developing an object-oriented program is to turn the system's functional requirements into a model of the classes that will implement the required functionality. It is important to incorporate a well-organized approach to system design when developing modern enterprise-level object-oriented programs. Most software projects you will become involved with as a business software developer will be a team effort. As a programmer on the team, you will be asked to interpret the design documents into the actual application code.

Therefore, a software developer must be familiar with the purpose and the structure of the various design documents. Because the design of object-oriented programs is a recursive process, designers depend on the feedback of the software developers to refine and modify the program design. As a result, it is also beneficial for software developers to have some knowledge of how these documents are developed. As you gain experience in developing object-oriented software systems, you may be asked to sit in on the design sessions and contribute to the design process.

This chapter is the first in a series of three chapters that introduce the concepts involved in designing object-oriented software solutions. This chapter introduces you to the some of the common documents used to design the static aspects of the system. Chapter 3, "Designing OOP Solutions: Modeling the Object Interaction," details how the dynamic aspects of the system are modeled. In Chapter 4, "Designing OOP Solutions: A Case Study," you will develop the design documents introduced in the previous chapters. The chapter introduces a limited case study to illustrate the processes involved in object-oriented design.

After reading this chapter you should be familiar with the following:

- The goals of software design

- The fundamentals of the Unified Modeling Language

- The purpose of a Software Requirement Specification

- How use case diagrams model the services the system will provide

- Interpreting class diagrams notation to model the classes of objects that need to be developed

- Analyzing class diagrams to determine the relationships required between the different classes of the system

Goals of Software Design

The design phase is one of the most important in the software development cycle. You can trace many of the problems associated with failed software projects to poor upfront design and inadequate communication between the system's developers and the system's consumers. Unfortunately, many programmers and program managers do not like getting involved in the design aspects of the system. They view any time not spent cranking out code as unproductive.

To make matters worse, with the advent of "Internet time", consumers expect increasingly shorter development cycles. So, to meet unrealistic timelines and project scope, developers tend to forgo or cut short the time involved in system design and testing. This is truly counterproductive to the system's success. Investing time in the design process will achieve the following:

- Provide an opportunity to review the current business process and fix any inefficiencies or flaws uncovered

- Educate the customers as to how the software development process occurs and incorporate them as a partner in this process

- Create realistic project scopes and timelines for completion

- Provide a basis for determining the software testing requirements

- Reduce the cost of and time required to implement the software solution

A good analogy to software design is the process of building a home. You would not expect the builder to start working on the house without detailed plans (blueprints) supplied by an architect. You would also expect the architect to talk to you about the home's design before creating the blueprints. It is the architect's job to talk to you about the design and functionality you want in the house and convert your requests to the plans that the builder uses to build the home. A good architect will also educate you as to what features are reasonable for your budget and projected timeline.

To successfully design object-oriented software, you need to incorporate a proven design methodology. This methodology must incorporate a set of guidelines and notation used to transform the business requirements of the system into the code used to implement the system. The methodology must also be consistent with the concepts associated with the various object-oriented programming (OOP) languages. One of the most common design methodologies used in OOP today is the Unified Modeling Language (UML).

Understanding the Unified Modeling Language

UML was developed in the early 80s as a response to the need for a standard, systematic way of modeling the design of object-oriented software. It consists of a series of textual and graphical models of the proposed solution. These models define the system scope, components of the system, user interaction with the system, and how the system components interact with each other to implement the system functionality. Some common models used in UML are the following:

- **Software Requirement Specification (SRS)**: A textual description of the overall responsibilities and scope of the system.

- **Use Case**: A textual/graphical description of how the system will behave from the users' perspective. Users can be human or other systems.

- **Class Diagram**: A visual blueprint of the objects that will be used to construct the system.

- **Sequence Diagram**: A model of the sequence of object interaction as the program executes. Emphasis is placed on the order of the interactions and how they proceed over time.

- **Collaboration Diagram**: A view of how objects are organized to work together as the program executes. Emphasis is placed on the communications that occur between the objects.

- **Activity Diagram**: A visual representation of the flow of execution of a process or operation.

The first step in the design process is to develop a SRS.

Developing a SRS

The purpose of the SRS is to do the following:

- Define the functional requirements of the system

- Identify the boundaries of the system

- Identify the users of the system

- Describe the interactions between the system and the external users

- Establish a common language between the client and the program team for describing the system

- Provide the basis for modeling use cases

To produce the SRS, you interview the business owners and the end users of the system. The goal of these interviews is to clearly document the business processes involved and establish the system's scope. The outcome of this process is a formal document (the SRS) detailing the functional requirements of the system. A formal document helps to ensure agreement between the customers and the software developers. The SRS also provides a basis for resolving any disagreements over "perceived" system scope as development proceeds.

In the following sample SRS you can see that several succinct statements define the system scope. They describe the functionality of the system and identify the external entities that will use it.

Investigating a Sample SRS

The owners of a small commuter airline want customers to be able to view flight information and reserve tickets for flights using a Web registration system. After interviewing the business managers and the ticketing agents, a SRS document was drafted that lists the system's functional requirements. Some of these requirements are the following:

- Nonregistered Web users can browse to the Web site to view flight information but not book flights.

- New customers wanting to book flights must complete a registration form providing their name, address, company name, phone number, fax, and email.

- A customer is classified as either a corporate customer or a retail customer.

- Customers can search for flights based on destination and departure times.

- Customers can book flights indicating flight number and the number of seats requested.

- The system sends customers a confirmation email when the flight is booked.

- Corporate customers receive frequent flier miles when their employees book flights. Frequent-flier miles are used to discount future purchases.

- Ticket reservations can be canceled up to one week in advance for an 80-percent refund.

- Ticketing agents can view and update flight information.

As this partial SRS document illustrates, a series of succinct statements should identify the proposed functionality of the system. These statements describe the functional requirements of the system as viewed by the system's users. It is important to note that the SRS does not contain references to the technical requirements of the system.

Once the SRS is developed, the functional requirements it contains are transformed into a series of use case diagrams.

Introducing Use Cases

Use cases describe how external entities will use the system. These external entities can be either humans or other systems and are referred to as *actors* in UML terminology. The description emphasizes the users' view of the system and the interaction between the users and the system. Use cases help to further define system scope and boundaries. They are usually in the form of a diagram along with a textual description of the interaction taking place. Figure 2-1 shows a generic diagram that consists of two actors represented by stick figures, the system represented by a rectangle, and use cases depicted by ovals inside the system boundaries.

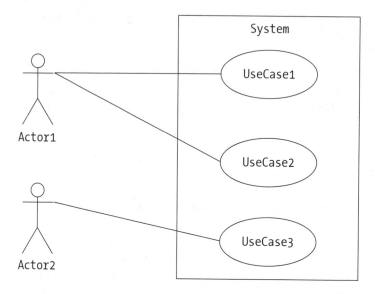

Figure 2-1. Generic use case diagram with two actors and three use cases

Use cases are developed from the SRS document. The actor is any outside entity that interacts with the system. An actor could be a human user (for instance, a rental agent), another software system (for instance, a software billing system), or an interface device (for instance, a temperature probe). Each interaction that occurs between an actor and the system is modeled as a use case.

The example use case shown in Figure 2-2 was developed for the flight booking application introduced earlier. The following statement has been developed into the use case diagram: "Customers can search for flights based on destination and departure times."

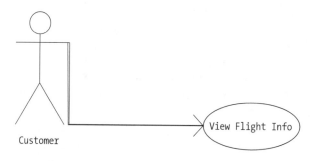

Figure 2-2. View Flight Info use case

Along with the graphical depiction of the use case, many designers and software developers find it helpful to provide a textual description of the use case. The textual description should be succinct and focused on *what* is happening and not on *how* it is occurring. Sometimes any preconditions or postconditions associated with the use case are also identified. The following text further describes the use case diagram shown in Figure 2-2:

- **Description**: A customer views the flight information page. The customer enters flight search information. After submitting the search request, the customer views a list of flights matching the search criteria.

- **Preconditions**: None.

- **Postconditions**: The customer has the opportunity to log in and proceed to the flight booking page.

As another example, take a look at the Reserve Seat use case shown in Figure 2-3.

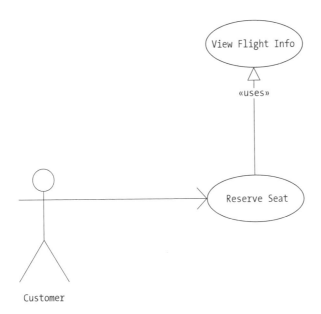

Figure 2-3. Reserve Seat use case diagram

The following text further describes the use case diagram shown in Figure 2-3:

- **Preconditions**: The customer has looked up the flight information. The customer has logged in and is viewing the flight booking screen.

- **Description**: The customer enters the flight number and indicates the seats being requested. After the customer submits the request, some confirmation information is displayed.

- **Postconditions**: The customer is sent a confirmation email outlining the flight details and the cancellation policy.

As you can see from Figure 2-3, certain relationships can exist between use cases. The Reserve Seat use case includes the View Flight Info use case. This relationship is useful because you can use the View Flight Info use case independently of the Reserve Flight use case. This is called *inclusion*. You cannot use the Reserve Seat use case independently of the View Flight Info use case, however. This is important information that will affect how you model the solution.

Another way that use cases relate to each other is through *extension*. You might have a general use case that is the base for other use cases. The base use case is extended by other use cases. For example, you might have a Register Customer use case that describes the core process of registering customers. You could then develop Register Corporate Customer and Register Retail Customer use cases that extend the base use case. The difference between extension and inclusion is that in extension the base use case being extended is not used on its own. Figure 2-4 demonstrates how you model this in a use case diagram.

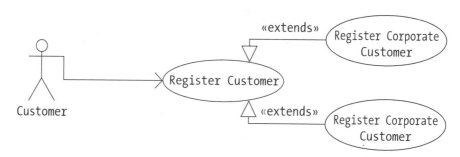

Figure 2-4. Extending use cases

A common mistake when developing use cases is to include actions initiated by the system itself. The emphasis of the use case is on the interaction between external entities and the system. Another common mistake is to start including a description of the technical requirements of the system. Remember, use cases are not focusing on how the system will perform the functions but rather on what functions need to be incorporated in the system from the users' standpoint.

ACTIVITY 2-1. CREATING A USE CASE DIAGRAM

After completing this activity you should be familiar with the following:

- Producing a use case diagram to define a system's scope

- Using UML Modeler to create and document a use case diagram

Examining the SRS

The software user group you belong to has decided to pool its resources and create a lending library. Lending items include books, movies, and video games. Your task is to develop the application that will keep track of the loan item inventory and the lending of items to the group members. After interviewing the group's members and officers, you have developed a SRS document that includes the following functional requirements:

- Only members of the user group can borrow items.

- Books can be borrowed for four weeks.

- Movies and games can be borrowed for one week.

- Items can be renewed if no one is waiting to borrow them.

- Members can only borrow up to four items at the same time.

- A reminder is emailed to members when an item becomes overdue.

- A fine is charged for overdue items.

- Members with outstanding overdue items or fines cannot borrow new items.

- A secretary is in charge of maintaining item inventory and purchasing items to add to the inventory.

- A librarian has been appointed to track lending and send overdue notices.

- The librarian is also responsible for collecting fines and updating fine information.

The next step is to analyze the SRS to identify the actors and use cases:

1. By examining the SRS document, identify which of the following will be among the principal actors interacting with the system:

    *   Member

    *   Librarian

    *   Book

    *   Treasurer

    *   Inventory

    *   Email

    *   Secretary

2. Once you have identified the principal actors, the next step is to identify the use cases for the actors. Identify the actor associated with the following use cases:

    *   Request Item

    *   Catalog Item

    *   Lend Item

    *   Process Fine

ACTIVITY 2-1 ANSWERS *Step 1: The actors are Member, Librarian, and Secretary. Step 2: The Request Item use case goes with Member, the Catalog Item use case goes with Secretary, the Lend Item use case goes with Librarian, and the Process Fine use case goes with Librarian.*

Creating a Use Case Diagram Using UML Modeler

Although it is possible to create the UML diagrams by hand or on a whiteboard, most programmers will eventually turn to a diagramming tool or a Computer-Aided Software Engineering (CASE) tool. CASE tools help you construct professional-quality diagrams and enable team members to easily share and augment the diagrams. There are many CASE tools on the market, including Microsoft Visio. Before choosing a CASE tool, you should thoroughly evaluate if it meets your needs and is flexible enough. A lot of the advanced features associated with "high-end" CASE tools are difficult to work with, and you spend more time figuring out how the CASE tool works than documenting your design.

A good CASE tool to learn on is UML Modeler from Objecteering. It enables you to create UML diagrams without adding a lot of advanced features associated with the higher-end CASE tools. Best of all, you can download a free personal version from Objecteering's Web site (www.objecteering.com). After downloading and installing UML Modeler, you can complete the following steps (if you do not want to use a CASE tool, you can create the following diagram by hand):

1. Start UML Modeler. Choose File ➤ New. Change the project name to **UMLAct2_1** and click OK.

2. Locate the Properties Editor along the left side of the screen (see Figure 2-5). On the left side of the Properties Editor, click the Create a Use Case Diagram button.

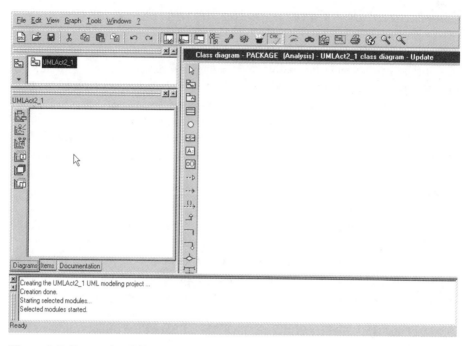

Figure 2-5. Properties Editor

3. You will be presented with a design surface in the main editor window. Along the left side of the window are shapes used in creating use case diagrams. Click the Create an Actor button (see Figure 2-6). Draw the Actor shape on the design surface. Change the name of the Actor shape to **Member**.

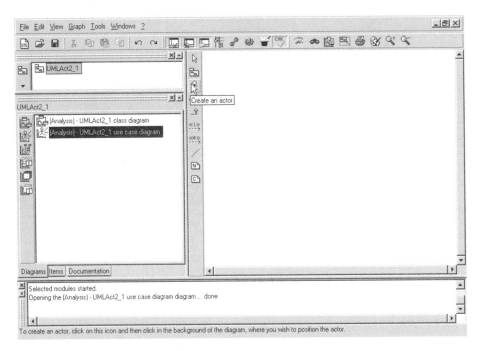

Figure 2-6. Adding an Actor shape

4. Right-click the Member shape on the design surface and choose Modify. You will be presented with the Actor dialog box. Under the Notes tab, click the Add button. Under the Type drop-down list, choose Description. In the Contents textbox, enter **A dues-paying member of the software users group.** After entering the description, click OK (see Figure 2-7). Click OK again to close the Actor dialog box.

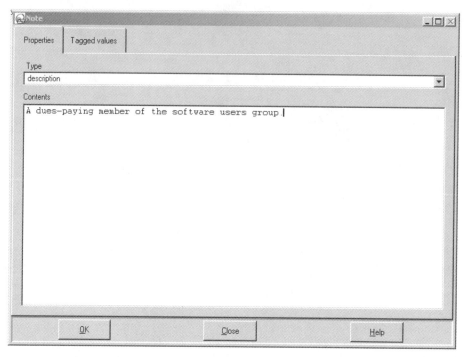

Figure 2-7. Adding a description

5. Repeat the procedures to add a Secretary and a Librarian actor.

6. From the Shapes toolbox, choose the Use Case shape and draw a Use Case shape on the design surface. Right-click the Use Case shape on the design surface and choose Modify. (This can be tricky; make sure you click the oval shape and not the rectangle shape.) You will be presented with a Use Case dialog box. Change the name of the use case to **Request Item**. Under the Notes tab, add the following description: **A Member views a list of items, chooses an item from the list, and submits a request for the item.** After entering the description, click OK. Click OK again to close the Use Case dialog box.

7. Repeat step 6 for two more use cases. Include a Catalog Item use case that will occur when the Secretary adds new items to the library inventory database. Add a Lend Item use case that will occur when the Librarian processes a request for an item. These will be added to the system rectangle created when you added the first use case.

8. From the Shapes toolbox, choose the Communication Link shape and draw a Communication Link shape on the design surface. Attach end 1 to the Member shape and end 2 to the Request Item shape.

9. Repeat step 8 to create a Communication Link shape between the Librarian and the Lend Item shapes. Also create a Communication Link shape between the Secretary and the Catalog Item shapes.

10. From the Shapes toolbox, choose the Extension Relationship shape and draw an Extension Relationship shape on the design surface. Attach end 1 of the Extends arrow to the Lend Item use case and attach end 2 of the arrow to the Request Item use case.

11. Your completed diagram should be similar to the one shown in Figure 2-8. Choose File ➢ Save and then exit UML Modeler.

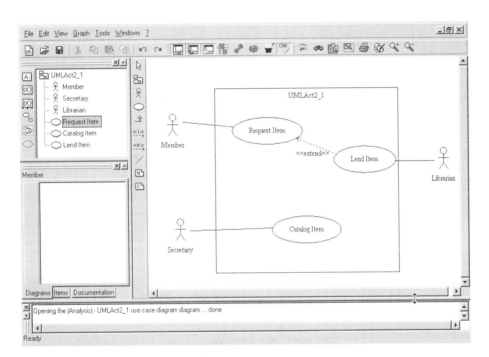

Figure 2-8. Completed use case diagram

After you have developed the use cases of the system, you can begin to identify the internal system objects that will carry out the system's functional requirements. You do this through the use of a class diagram.

Understanding Class Diagrams

The concepts of classes and objects are fundamental to OOP. An *object* is a structure for incorporating data and the procedures for working with the data. These objects implement the functionality of an object-oriented program. Think of a class as a blueprint for the object. A class defines the structure and the methods that objects based on the class type will contain. A potential list of classes that will need to be developed is identified from the SRS and the use case diagrams. One way you identify the classes is by looking at the noun phrases in the SRS document and the use case descriptions (more about this later in Chapter 4, "Designing OOP Solutions: A Case Study"). If you look at the documentation developed thus far for the airline booking application, you can begin to identify the classes that will comprise the system. For example, you can develop a Customer class to work with the customer data and a Flight class to work with the flight data.

A *class* is responsible for managing data. When defining the class structure, you must determine what data the class is responsible for maintaining. The class attributes define this information. For example, the Flight class will have attributes for identifying the flight number, departure time and date, flight duration, destination, capacity, and seats available. The class structure must also define any operations that will be performed on the data. An example of an operation the Flight class is responsible for is updating the seats available when a seat is reserved. A class diagram can help you visualize the attributes and operations of a class. Figure 2-9 is an example of the class diagram for the Flight class used in the flight booking system. A rectangle divided into three sections represents the class. The top section lists the name of the class. The middle section lists the attributes of the class. The bottom section lists the operations performed by the class.

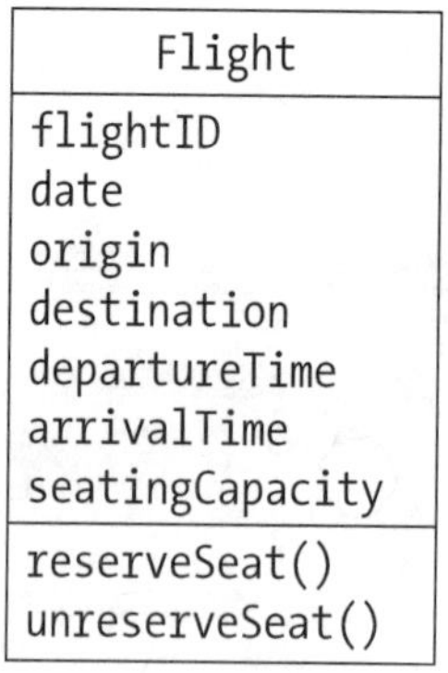

Flight
flightID
date
origin
destination
departureTime
arrivalTime
seatingCapacity
reserveSeat()
unreserveSeat()

Figure 2-9. Flight *class diagram*

In OOP, when the program executes, the various objects work together to accomplish the programming tasks. For example, in the flight booking application, in order to reserve a seat on the flight, a Reservation object has to interact with the Flight object. There exists a relationship between the two objects, and this relationship has to be modeled in the class structure of the program. In OOP terminology, these relationships between classes are called *associations.* The associations among the classes that make up the program are modeled in the class diagram. Analyzing the verb phrases in the SRS often reveals these relationships (this is discussed in Chapter 4, "Designing OOP Solutions: A Case Study"). The following sections examine some of the common associations that can occur between classes and how the class diagram represents them.

Association

When one class refers to or uses another class, the classes form an association. You draw a line between the two classes to represent the association and add a label to indicate the name of the association. For example, a Seat is associated with a Flight in the flight booking application (see Figure 2-10).

Figure 2-10. Class associations

Sometimes a single instance of one class associates with multiple instances of another class. This is indicated on the line connecting the two classes. For example, when a customer makes a reservation, there is an association between the Customer class and the Reservation class. A single instance of the Customer class may be associated with multiple instances of the Reservation class. An asterisk placed near the Reservation class indicates this multiplicity (see Figure 2-11).

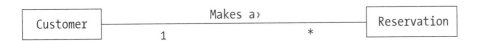

Figure 2-11. Indicating multiplicity in a class diagram

A situation may also exist where an instance of a class may be associated with multiple instances of the same class. For example, an instance of the Pilot class represents the captain while another instance of the Pilot class represents the co-pilot. The pilot manages the co-pilot. This scenario is referred to as a *self-association* and is modeled by drawing the association line from the class back to itself (see Figure 2-12).

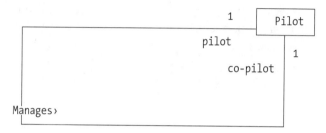

Figure 2-12. A self-associating class

Inheritance

When multiple classes share some of the same operations and attributes, a base class can encapsulate the commonality. The child class then inherits from the base class. This is represented in the class diagram by a solid line with an open arrowhead pointing to the base class. For example, a CorporateCustomer class and a RetailCustomer class could inherit common attributes and operations from a base Customer class (see Figure 2-13).

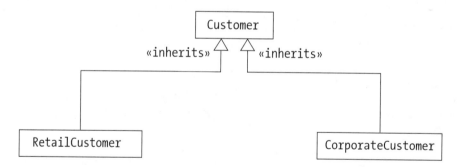

Figure 2-13. Documenting inheritance

Aggregation

When a class is formed by a composition of other classes, they are classified as an *aggregation*. This is represented with a solid line connecting the classes in a hierarchical structure. Placing a diamond on the line next to a class in the diagram indicates the top level of the hierarchy. For example, an inventory application designed to track plane parts for the plane maintenance department could contain a Plane class that is a composite of various part classes (see Figure 2-14).

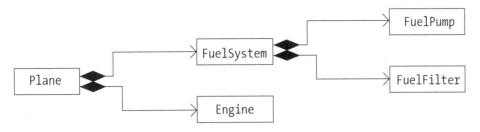

Figure 2-14. Depicting aggregations

Association Classes

As the classes and the associations for a program are developed, there may be a situation where an attribute cannot be assigned to any one class but is a result of an association between classes. For example, the parts inventory application mentioned previously may have a Part class and a Supplier class. Because a part can have more than one supplier and the supplier supplies more than one part, where should the price attribute be located? It does not fit nicely as an attribute for either class, and it should not be duplicated in both classes. The solution is to develop an association class that manages the data that is a product of the association. In this case, you would develop a PartPrice class. The relationship is modeled with a dashed line drawn between the association and the association class (see Figure 2-15).

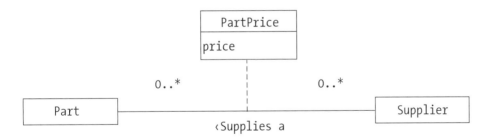

Figure 2-15. An association class

Now that you have looked at some of the notations that you can incorporate into a class diagram, it may be helpful to see what a complete class diagram looks like. Figure 2-16 shows an example of a class diagram for the flight booking application.

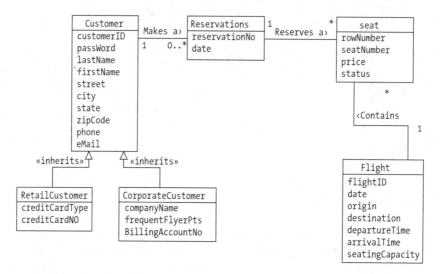

Figure 2-16. Flight booking class diagram

After completing this activity you should be familiar with the following:

- Determining the classes that need to be constructed by examining the use case and the system scope documentation

- Using UML Modeler to create a class diagram

Identifying Classes and Attributes

Follow these steps to identify the classes and attributes:

1. Examine the following scenario developed for a use case from the user group library application:

    After viewing the list of available loan items, members request an item to check out on loan. The librarian enters the member number and retrieves information about outstanding loans and any unpaid fines. If the member has fewer than four outstanding loans and does not have any outstanding fines, the loan is processed. The librarian retrieves information on the loan item to determine if it is currently on loan. If the item is available, it is checked out to the member.

2. By identifying the nouns and noun phrases in the use case scenario you can get an idea of what classes you must include in the system to perform the tasks. Which of the following items would make good candidate classes for the system?

    *   Member

    *   Item

    *   Librarian

    *   Number

    *   Fine

    *   Check out

    *   Loan

3. At this point you can start identifying attributes associated with the classes being developed. A Loan class will be developed to encapsulate data associated with an item out on loan. Which of the following would be possible attributes for the Loan class?

    *   MemberNumber

    *   MemberPhone

    *   ItemNumber

    *   ReturnDate

    *   ItemCost

    *   ItemType

ACTIVITY 2-2 ANSWERS   *Step 2: The classes are* Member, Item, Loan, Fine, *and* Librarian. *Step 3: The attributes associated with the* Loan *class are* MemberNumber, ItemNumber, *and* ReturnDate.

Creating a Class Diagram Using UML Modeler

To create a class diagram using UML Modeler, follow these steps (you can also create it by hand):

1. Start UML Modeler, and choose File ➤ Open. Then select the UMLAct2_1 project and click OK.

2. You should be presented with the use case diagram developed in Activity 2-1. In the main explorer window located in the upper-left corner of the screen, select the UMLAct2_1 node. Double-click the UMLAct2_1 class diagram node in the Properties Editor. The main window will display an editor for creating the class diagram (see Figure 2-17).

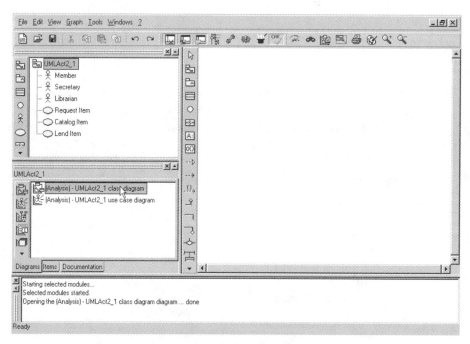

Figure 2-17. Creating a class diagram in UML Modeler

3. Along the left side of the editor window are shapes used in creating class diagrams. Click the Create a Class button (see Figure 2-18). Draw the Class shape on the design surface.

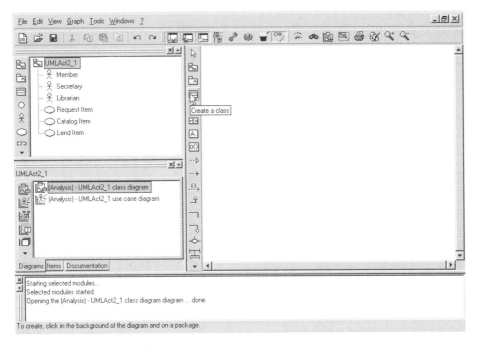

Figure 2-18. Adding a Class shape

4. Right-click the Class shape on the design surface and choose Modify. You will be presented with a Class dialog box.

NOTE   *To get this to work, first deselect the class by clicking on the design surface.*

5. Next, change the name of the Class shape to **Member**. Under the Notes tab, enter the following description: **Used to encapsulate and process member data info.** After entering the description, click OK. Click OK again to close the Class dialog box.

6. Repeat the procedures in step 4 to add the following classes to the diagram:

- **Loan**: Encapsulates and manages the details of an item currently on loan

- **Item**: Encapsulates and manages data associated with items that are available for loan

- **Book**: A specialization of an Item

- **Movie**: A specialization of an Item

7. From the Shapes toolbox, click and drag an Association Link shape onto the design surface. Attach end 1 to Member and end 2 to Loan. Right-click the Association Link shape and click Modify. You are presented with a Binary Association dialog box. In the association's Properties tab, change the In the Association or the Aggregation box to Makes A. Change the Quantity drop-down list of the end pointing to the Member class to 1 and change the end pointing to the Loan class to 0..4. This indicates that a Member class may be associated with up to four instances of a Loan class (see Figure 2-19). Click OK to close the Binary Association dialog box.

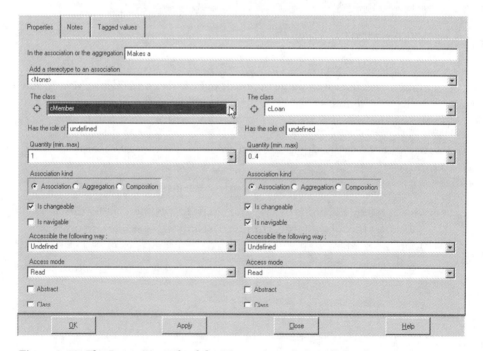

Figure 2-19. The Properties tab of the Binary Association dialog box

8. Repeat step 7 to create a "contains a" Association Link shape between the Loan class and the Item class. This should be a one-to-one association.

9. From the Shapes toolbox, choose the Generalization Relationship shape and draw a Generalization Relationship shape on the design surface. Attach the tail (end 1) of the Generalization arrow to the Book class and attach the head (end 2) of the arrow to the Item class. This indicates inheritance and shows that a Book class is a specialization of the Item class.

10. Repeat step 9 to show the relationship between the Movie class and the Item class.

11. Along the left side of the class diagram editor window, click the Attribute button. In the class diagram, click the Member class to add an attribute. Right-click the attribute and select Modify.

NOTE   *To get this to work, first deselect the class by clicking on the design surface.*

12. Next, change the name to **MemberNumber**, change the Class drop-down list to Integer, and click OK.

13. Repeat step 12 to add a FirstName string type, LastName string type, and Email string type attribute to the Member class.

14. Your completed diagram should be similar to the one shown in Figure 2-20. Save the file (File ➤ Save).

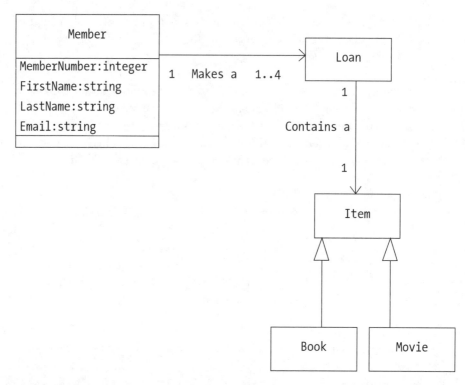

Figure 2-20. Completed use case diagram

Summary

In this chapter you did the following:

- Discussed the goals of the object-oriented design process

- Explored UML

- Became familiar with some of the design documents and diagrams produced using UML

- Looked at how a Software Requirement Specification defines the scope of the system

- Revealed how use case diagrams define the system boundaries and identify the external entities that will use the system

- Saw how a class diagram models the structure of the classes that will be developed to implement the system

- Discussed how the class diagram represents the various class associations

In this chapter you looked at how you model the class structure of your applications. This includes identifying the necessary classes, identifying the attributes of these classes, and establishing the structural relationships required among the classes. In the next chapter you will continue your study of object-oriented design. In particular, you will look at modeling how the objects in your applications will collaborate to carry out the functionality of the application.

Designing
OOP Solutions:
Modeling the
Object Interaction

THE PREVIOUS CHAPTER focused on modeling the static (organizational) aspects of an object-oriented programming solution. It introduced and discussed the methodologies of the Unified Modeling Language. You also looked at the purpose and structure of use case diagrams and class diagrams. This chapter continues the discussion of Unified Modeling Language modeling techniques and focuses on modeling the dynamic (behavioral) aspects of an object-oriented programming solution. The focus in this chapter is on how the objects in the system must interact with each other and what activities must occur to implement the solution.

After reading this chapter you should be familiar with the following:

- The purpose of scenarios and how they extend the use case models

- How sequence diagrams model the time-dependent interaction of the objects in the system

- How collaboration diagrams model the contextual interaction of the objects in the system

- The importance of graphical user interface design and how it fits into the object-oriented design process

Understanding Scenarios

Scenarios help determine the dynamic interactions that will take place between the objects (class instances) of the system. A scenario is a textual description of the internal processing needed to implement the functionality documented by a use case. Remember that a use case describes the functionality of the system from the viewpoint of the system's external users. A scenario takes the use case and opens it up. In other words, its purpose is to describe the steps that must be carried out internally by the objects making up the system.

Figure 3-1 shows the Process Movie Rental use case for a video rental application.

The following text describes the use case:

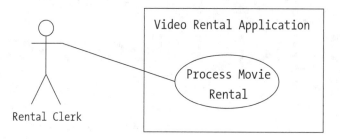

Figure 3-1. Process Movie Rental use case

Preconditions: The customer makes a request to rent a movie from the rental clerk. The customer has a membership in the video club and supplies the rental clerk with their membership card and personal identification number (PIN). The customer's membership is verified. The customer information is displayed and the customer's account is verified to be in good standing.

Description: The movie is confirmed to be in stock. Rental information is recorded, and the customer is informed of the due date.

Postconditions: None.

The following scenario describes the internal processing of the Process Movie Rental use case:

1. The movie is verified to be in stock.

2. The number of available copies in stock is decremented.

3. The due date is determined.

4. The rental information is recorded including the movie title, copy number, current date, and due date.

5. The customer is informed of the rental information.

This scenario describes the best possible execution of the use case. Because exceptions can occur, a single use case can spawn multiple scenarios. For example, another scenario created for the Process Movie Rental use case could describe what happens when a movie is not in stock.

After you map out the various scenarios for a use case, you can create interaction diagrams to determine which classes of objects will be involved in carrying out the functionality of the scenarios. The interaction diagrams also reveal what operations will be required of these classes of objects. Interaction diagrams come in two flavors: sequence diagrams and collaboration diagrams.

Introducing Sequence Diagrams

A *sequence diagram* models how the classes of objects interact with each other (or collaborate) over time as the system runs. The sequence diagram is a visual, two-dimensional model of the interaction taking place and is based on a scenario. Figure 3-2 shows a generic sequence diagram.

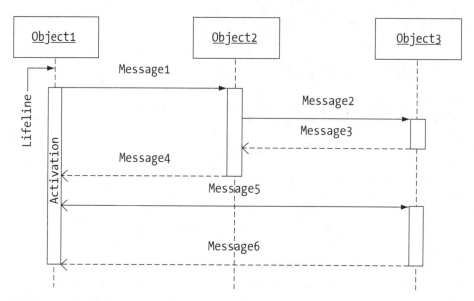

Figure 3-2. Generic sequence diagram

As Figure 3-2 demonstrates, the flow of messages from object to object is represented horizontally. The time flow of the interactions taking place is depicted vertically starting from the top and progressing downward. Objects are next to each other, and a dashed line extends from each of them downward. This dashed line represents the *lifeline* of the object. Rectangles on the lifeline represent *activations* of the object. The height of the rectangle represents the duration of the object's activation.

In object-oriented programming (OOP), objects interact by passing messages to each other. An arrow starting at the initiating object and ending at the receiving object depicts the interaction. A dashed arrow drawn back to the initiating object represents a return message. The messages depicted in the sequence diagram will form the basis of the methods of the classes of the system. Figure 3-3 shows a sample sequence diagram for the Process Movie Rental scenario.

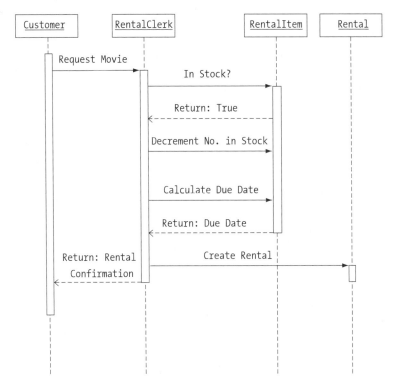

Figure 3-3. Process Movie Rental sequence diagram

As you analyze the sequence diagram, you gain an understanding of the classes of objects that will be involved in carrying out the program processing and what methods you will have to create and attach to those classes. You should also model the classes and methods depicted in the sequence diagram in the class diagram. These design documents must be continually cross-referenced and revised when needed.

The sequence diagram in Figure 3-3 reveals that there will be four objects involved in carrying out the Process Movie Rental scenario. The Customer object is an instance of the Customer class and is responsible for encapsulating and maintaining the information pertaining to a customer. The RentalClerk object is an instance of the RentalClerk class and is responsible for managing the processing involved in renting a movie. The RentalItem object is an instance of the RentalItem class and is responsible for encapsulating and maintaining the information pertaining to a video available for rent. The Rental object is an instance of the Rental class and is responsible for encapsulating and maintaining the information pertaining to a video currently being rented.

Message Types

By analyzing the sequence diagram you can determine what messages must be passed between the objects involved in the processing. In OOP, messages are passed *synchronously* or *asynchronously*. When messages are passed synchronously, the sending object suspends processing and waits for a response before continuing. A line drawn with a solid arrowhead in the sequence diagram represents synchronous messaging. When an object sends an asynchronous message, the object continues processing and is not expecting an immediate response from the receiving object. A line drawn with a half arrowhead in the sequence diagram represents asynchronous messaging. An object may also send a message to transfer control to another object. This is referred to as a *simple* or *flat* message and is depicted by an open arrowhead in the sequence diagram. A dashed arrow usually depicts a response message. Figure 3-4 demonstrates these different types of messages.

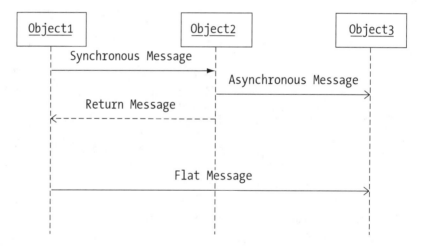

Figure 3-4. Diagramming various message types

By studying the sequence diagram for the Process Movie Rental scenario shown in Figure 3-3, it reveals the types of messages that must occur. For example, the RentalClerk object initiates a synchronous message with the RentalItem object requesting information on whether a copy of the movie is in stock. The RentalItem object then sends a response back to the RentalClerk object indicating a copy is in stock.

Recursive Messages

In OOP it is not uncommon for an object to have an operation that invokes another object instance of itself. This is referred to as *recursion*. A message arrow that loops back toward the calling object represents recursion in the sequence diagram. The end of the arrow points to a smaller activation rectangle, representing a second object activation drawn on top of the original activation rectangle (see Figure 3-5). For example, an Account object calculates compound interest for overdue payments. To calculate the interest over several compound periods, it needs to invoke itself several times.

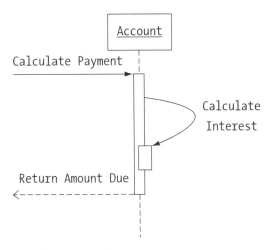

Figure 3-5. Diagramming a recursive message

Message Iteration

Sometimes a message call is repeated until a condition is met. For example, when totaling rental charges, an Add method is called repeatedly until all rentals charged to the customer have been added to the total. In programming terminology this is an *iteration*. A rectangle drawn around the iterating messages represents an iteration in a sequence diagram. The binding condition of the iteration is depicted in the upper-left corner of the rectangle. Figure 3-6 shows an example of an iteration depicted in a sequence diagram.

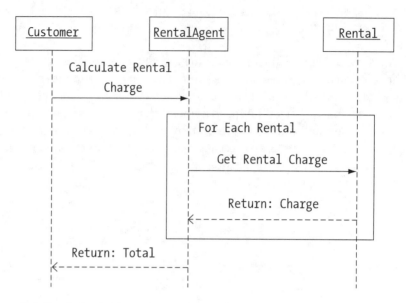

Figure 3-6. Depicting an iterative message

Message Constraints

Message calls between objects may have a conditional constraint attached to them. For example, the status of a customer has to be in good standing order for them to rent a movie. You place the condition of the constraint within brackets ([]) in the sequence. The message will only be sent if the condition evaluates to true (see Figure 3-7).

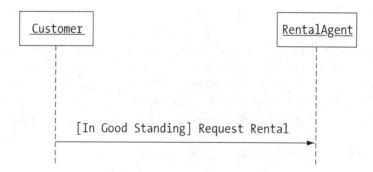

Figure 3-7. Identifying conditional constraints

Message Branching

When conditional constraints are tied to message calling, you often run into
a branching situation where, depending on the condition, different messages
may be invoked. Figure 3-8 represents a conditional constraint when requesting
a movie rental. If the status of the rental item is in stock, a message is sent to the
Rental object to create a rental. If the status of the rental item is out of stock, then
a message is sent to the Reservation object to create a reservation.

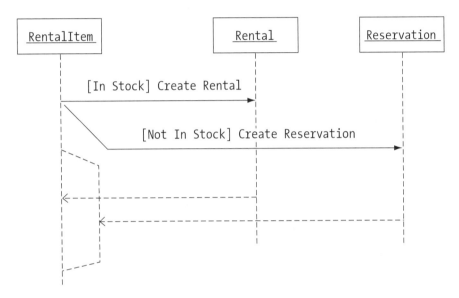

Figure 3-8. Branching messages in a sequence diagram

To avoid confusion, when you diagram the return from a branching call, you
split the lifeline of the calling object. You then draw one return message on each
line. This avoids the confusion that would occur if they both returned to the same
lifeline. This could be erroneously interpreted as both returns occurring one after
the other in sequence.

When branching occurs in a sequence diagram, the diagram is actually modeling different scenarios of the same use case. Including different scenarios in the
same sequence diagram can become confusing. It is often a much better idea to
model each scenario with its own separate sequence diagram.

ACTIVITY 3-1. CREATING A SEQUENCE DIAGRAM

After completing this activity you should be familiar with the following:

- Producing a sequence diagram to model object interaction

- Using UML Modeler to create a sequence diagram

- Adding methods to the class diagram

Examining the Scenario

The following scenario was created for a use case in the user group library application introduced in Activity 2-1. It describes the processing involved when a member borrows an item from the library:

> *When a member makes a request to borrow an item, the librarian checks the member's records to make sure no outstanding fines exist. Once the member passes these checks, the item is checked to see if it is available. Once the item availability has been confirmed, a loan is created recording the item number, member number, check out date, and return date.*

By examining the noun phrases in the scenario, you can identify which objects will be involved in carrying out the processing. The objects identified should also have a corresponding class depicted in the class diagram that has been previously been created. From the scenario depicted, you can identify five objects: Member, Librarian, Item, Loan, and LoanHistory.

Once the objects have been identified and cross-referenced with the class diagram, the next step is to identify the messaging that must occur between these objects to carry out the task. You can look at the verb phrases in the scenario to help identify these messages. For example, the phase *request to borrow item* indicates a message interaction between the Member object and the Librarian object. The other interactions depicted in the scenario are as follows:

- The Librarian object checks the lending history of the member with the LoanHistory object.

- The Librarian object checks the availability of the item through the Item object.

- The Librarian object updates the availability of the item through the Item object.

- The Librarian creates a Loan object containing loan information.

- The Librarian returns loan information to the Member object.

Creating a Sequence Diagram Using UML Modeler

Follow these steps to create a sequence diagram using UML Modeler:

1. Start UML Modeler. Choose File ➤ New. Change the project name to **UMLAct3_1** and click OK.

2. Locate the Properties Editor located along the left side of the screen. On the left side of the Properties Editor, click the Create a Sequence Diagram button (see Figure 3-9).

3. You will be presented with a design surface in the main editor window. Along the left side of the window are shapes used in creating sequence diagrams. Click the Create an Instance button (see Figure 3-10). Draw the Instance shape (object) on the design surface. Change the name of the object to **Member**.

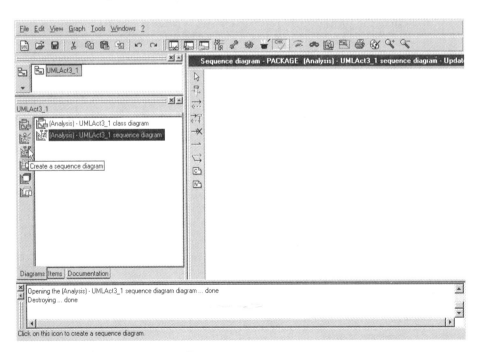

Figure 3-9. Adding a sequence diagram

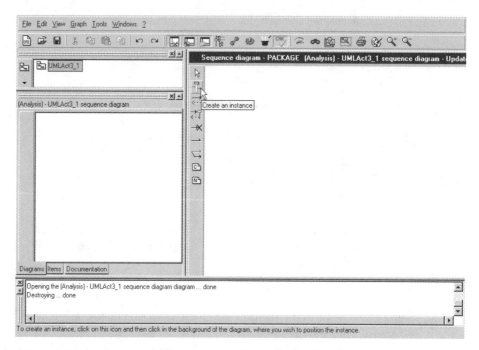

Figure 3-10. Adding an object instance to the sequence diagram

4. Repeat the procedures in step 3 to add Librarian, LoanHistory, Item, and
   Loan objects to the diagram. You should lay them out left to right across
   the page (see Figure 3-11).

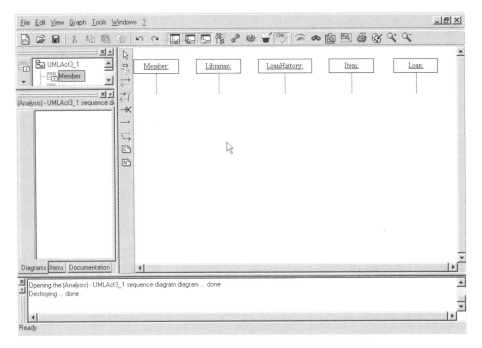

Figure 3-11. Object layout in the sequence diagram

5. From the Shapes toolbox, click the Create a Sequence Message button. Draw a Message shape between the Member object and the Librarian object. Attach the tail (end 1) of the arrow to the Member object's lifeline and the head of the arrow (end 2) to the Librarian object's lifeline. Click the message arrow to select it. It will turn blue. Next, right-click the message arrow and choose Modify. Change the name of the message to **request item**. Right-click the return arrow (the dashed line) and choose Modify. Change the name to **return loan info**.

6. Repeat step 5 to create a message from the Librarian object to the LoanHistory object. Attach the tail (end 1) of the arrow to the Librarian object's lifeline after the "request item" message but before the "return loan info" message. Attach the head of the arrow (end 2) to the LoanHistory object's lifeline. Name the calling message (the solid line) **check history**. Name the return message (the dashed line) **return history info** (see Figure 3-12).

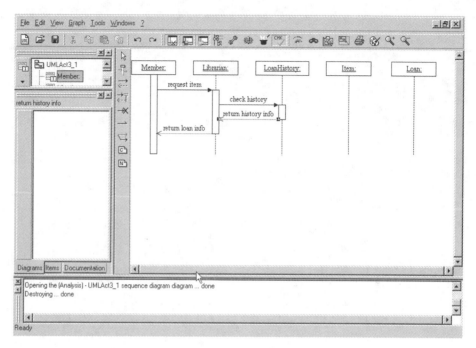

Figure 3-12. Message layout in the sequence diagram

7. Repeat step 5 again to create a message from the `Librarian` object to the `Item` object. Attach the tail (end 1) of the arrow to the `Librarian` object's lifeline after the "return history info" message but before the "return loan info" message. Attach the head of the arrow (end 2) to the `Item` object's lifeline. Name the calling message **check availability**. Name the return message **return availability info**.

8. Repeat step 5 once more to create a message from the `Librarian` object to the `Item` object. Attach the tail (end 1) of the arrow to the Librarian object's lifeline after the "return availability info" message but before the "return loan info" message. Attach the head of the arrow (end 2) to the `Item` object's lifeline. Name the calling message **update status**. Name the return message **return update confirmation**.

9. From the Shapes toolbox, click the Create a Message button. Draw a Message shape between the `Librarian` object and the `Loan` object. Attach the tail (end 1) of the arrow to the `Librarian` object's lifeline after the "return update confirmation" message but before the "return loan info" message. Attach the head of the arrow (end 2) to the `Loan` object's lifeline. Change the name of the message to **create loan object**.

10. Your completed diagram should be similar to the one shown in Figure 3-13. Save the file.

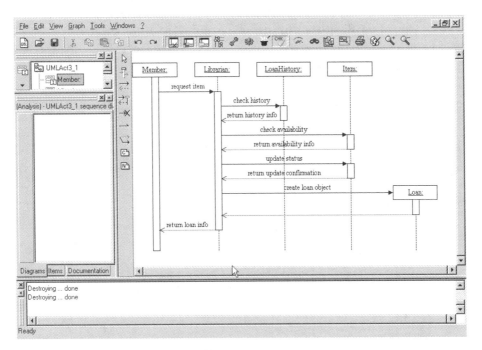

Figure 3-13. Completed sequence diagram

Adding Methods to the Class Diagram

After you have developed the sequence diagram, you begin to gain an understanding of the methods that must be included in the various classes of the application. You achieve the message interaction depicted in the sequence diagram by a method call from the initiating object (client) to the receiving object (server). The method being called is defined in the class that the server object is instantiated as. For example, the "request item" message in the sequence diagram indicates that the Librarian class needs a method that processes this message call.

Follow these steps to add the methods:

1. In the main explorer window located in the upper-left corner of the screen, select the UMLAct3_1 node. Double-click the UMLAct3_1 class diagram node in the Properties Editor. The main window will display an editor for creating the class diagram.

2. Draw a class shape on the designer surface and rename it **Librarian**.

3. Along the left side of the class diagram editor window, click the Create Operation button. In the class diagram, click the Member class to add an operation. Right-click the operation and select Modify. You will be presented with the Operation dialog box, shown in Figure 3-14. Change the name to **RequestLoanItem**.

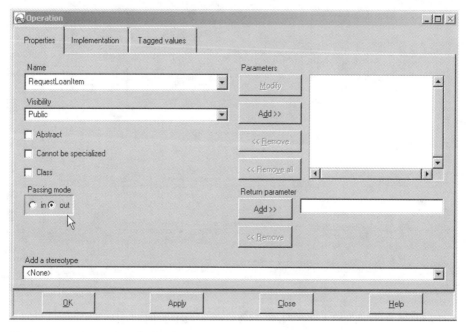

Figure 3-14. Operation dialog box

4. The parameters represent information passed in when the method is called. Add a parameter by clicking the Add button located in the Parameters section of the Operation dialog box. You will be presented with the Parameter dialog box shown in Figure 3-15. Change the name of the parameter to **ItemNumber** and under the Class drop-down list, choose Integer. Click OK to close the Parameter dialog box.

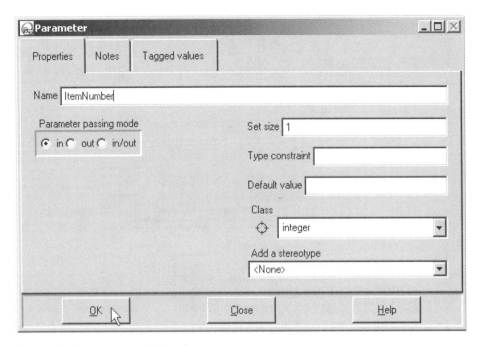

Figure 3-15. Parameter dialog box

5. The return parameter represents information passed back to the client object. Add a return parameter by clicking the Add button located in the Return Parameter section of the Operation dialog box. You will be presented with the Return Parameter dialog box shown in Figure 3-16. Under the Class drop-down list, choose Integer, which will represent the loan number that will be returned to the Member object. Click OK to close the Return Parameter dialog box. Click OK to close the Operation dialog box.

6. Repeat steps 2 through 5 to add an Item class with a CheckAvailability method that receives an integer representing the item number and returns a Boolean indicating if the item is in stock.

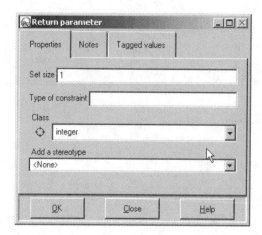

Figure 3-16. Return Parameter dialog box

7. In the main explorer window, expand the Item node and expand the CheckAvailability node. Information about the operation and parameters is displayed (see Figure 3-17).

8. Save the project and exit UML Modeler.

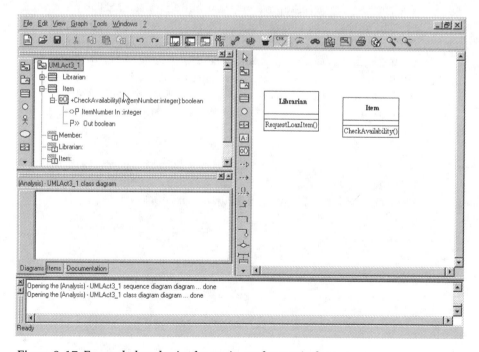

Figure 3-17. Expanded nodes in the main explorer window

Although sequence diagrams are useful at revealing the object interaction necessary to implement the functionality of the system, they are not the only UML diagram used for this purpose. A second type of activity diagram, the collaboration diagram, is also helpful when modeling object interaction.

Using Collaboration Diagrams

Although *collaboration diagrams* convey essentially the same information as the sequential diagrams, they are laid out slightly differently. In the collaboration diagram, the time-sequencing order of interaction is de-emphasized, and the context and organization of the interacting objects are emphasized. Rectangles represent objects, and association lines similar to those seen in the class diagram connect them. You draw arrows next to the association lines from the initiating object to the receiving object to represent the messages being paced between the objects. Just as in the sequence diagrams, the shape of the arrowhead indicates whether the message is synchronous or asynchronous. Because there is no timeline in the diagram, numbers represent the sequence of the messaging. Figure 3-18 shows a generic example of a collaboration diagram. *Collaberation diagram*

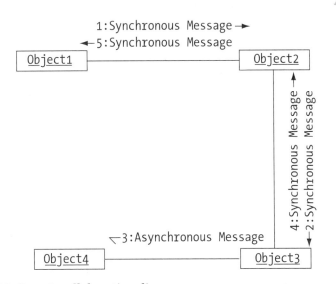

Figure 3-18. Generic collaboration diagram

Like the sequence diagrams, the collaboration diagrams are created from the use case scenarios. The sequence diagrams and the corresponding collaboration diagrams should be cross-checked with one and other for consistency. Figure 3-19 shows a collaboration diagram for the Process Movie Rental scenario developed earlier.

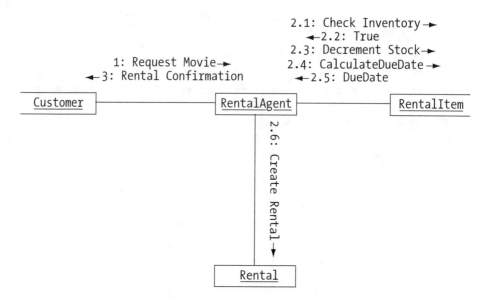

Figure 3-19. Process Movie Rental collaboration diagram

Indicating Message Order

The numbering of the messages in Figure 3-19 represents the use of *nesting*. Messages grouped together to accomplish a task use a nested numbering system. This makes it easier to revise the set of procedures grouped together without affecting the numbering of the rest of the messages. For example, you need to add a message call that checks to make sure the rental item has not been reserved. You could easily revise Figure 3-19 to include this message call; you would only have to alter the nested numbering of message 2.

Iteration, Constraints, and Branching

Some of the advanced features you modeled with the sequence diagrams were iteration, conditional constraints, and branching. Figure 3-6 demonstrated how you depict an iteration in a sequence diagram. Figure 3-20 demonstrates how this same iteration would be depicted with a collaboration diagram.

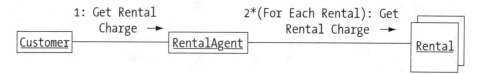

Figure 3-20. Iterations in collaboration diagrams

The asterisk after the message number indicates it will be sent multiple times. You place the binding condition of the iteration in parentheses following the asterisk. The stacking of the object rectangles indicates that multiple object instances occur in the iteration.

Figure 3-21 shows part of a collaboration diagram that depicts conditional constraints and branching. This diagram is equivalent to the sequence diagram shown in Figure 3-8. Notice that the conditional constraints appear in brackets and the branches have the same sequence numbers.

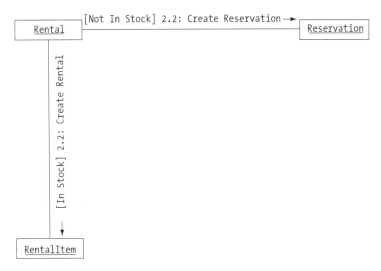

Figure 3-21. Conditional constraints in collaboration diagrams

Although the interaction diagrams are valuable for modeling the interaction among the different objects involved in carrying out the functionality of the system, a third type of diagram often further documents the dynamic interactions of the system. Instead of focusing on the objects involved in the system processing, an *activity diagram* focuses on the different activities that have to occur during the processing.

Understanding Activity Diagrams

An activity diagram illustrates the flow of activities that need to occur during an operation or process. You can construct the activity diagram to view the workflow at various levels of focus. A high, system-level focus would represent each use case as an activity and would diagram the workflow among the different use cases. A mid-level focus would diagram the workflow occurring within a particular use case. A low-level focus would diagram the workflow that occurs within a particular operation of one of the classes of the system.

The activity diagram consists of the starting point of the process represented by a solid circle and transition arrows representing the flow or transition from one activity to the next. Rounded rectangles represent the activities, and a bull's eye circle represents the ending point of the process. For example, Figure 3-22 shows a generic activity diagram that represents a process that starts with activity A proceeds to activity B and concludes.

Figure 3-22. Generic activity diagram

Decision Points and Guard Conditions

Often one activity will conditionally follow another. For example, in order to rent a video, a PIN number verifies membership. An activity diagram represents conditionality by a *decision point* (represented by a diamond) with the *guard condition* (the condition that has to be met to proceed) in brackets next to the flow line (see Figure 3-23).

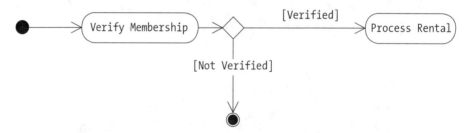

Figure 3-23. Indicating decision points and guard conditions

Parallel Processing

In some cases, two or more activities can run in parallel instead of sequentially. A solid bold line drawn perpendicularly to the transition arrow represents the splitting of the paths. After the split, a second solid bold line represents the merge. Figure 3-24 shows an activity diagram for the processing of a movie return. The order in which the increment inventory and the remove rental activities occur does not matter. The parallel paths in the diagram represent this parallel processing.

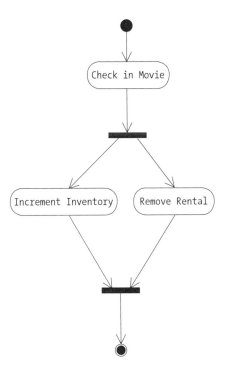

Figure 3-24. Parallel processing depicted in an activity diagram

Activity Ownership

The activity diagram's purpose is to model the control flow from activity to activity as the program processes. The diagrams shown thus far do not indicate which objects have responsibility for these activities. To signify object ownership of the activities, you segment the activity diagram into a series of vertical columns called *swim lanes*. The object role at the top of the swim lane is responsible for the activities in that lane. Figure 3-25 shows an activity diagram with swim lanes included for processing a movie rental.

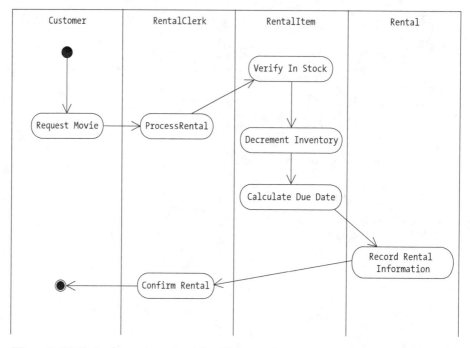

Figure 3-25. Swim lanes in an activity diagram

ACTIVITY 3-2. CREATING AN ACTIVITY DIAGRAM

After completing this activity you should be familiar with the following:

- Using an activity diagram to model control flow as the program completes an activity

- Using UML Modeler to create an activity class diagram

Identifying Objects and Activities

Follow these steps to identify the objects and activities:

1. Examine the following scenario developed for a use case from the user group library application:

After viewing the list of available loan items, members request an item to check out on loan. The librarian enters the member number and retrieves information about outstanding loans and any unpaid fines. If the member has fewer than four outstanding loans and does not have any outstanding fines, the loan is processed. The librarian retrieves information on the loan item to determine if it is currently on loan. If the item is available, it is checked out to the member.

— member
Librarian
loan
loanHistory
loan Item

2. By identifying the nouns and noun phrases in the use case scenario, you can get an idea of what objects will perform the tasks in carrying out the activities. Remember these objects are instances of the classes identified in the class diagram. The following objects will be involved in carrying out the activities: Member, Librarian, LoanHistory, Item, and Loan.

3. The verb phrases help identify the activities carried out by the objects. These activities should correspond to the methods of the classes in the system. Match the following activities to the appropriate objects:

   - Request movie

   - Process rental

   - Check availability

   - Check member's loan status

   - Update item status

   - Calculate due date

   - Record rental info

   - Confirm rental

ACTIVITY 3-2 ANSWERS   Member: *Request movie.* Librarian: *Process rental, Confirm rental.* LoanHistory: *Check member's loan status.* Item: *Check availability, Update item status.* Loan: *Calculate due date, Record rental info.*

Creating an Activity Diagram Using UML Modeler

Follow these steps to create an activity diagram:

1. Start UML Modeler. Choose File ➢ Open. Choose the UMLAct3_1 project and click OK.

2. You should be presented with the use case and sequence diagrams developed in Activity 3-1. In the main explorer window located in the upper-left corner of the screen, select the UMLAct3_1 node. On the toolbar located at the left of the main explorer window, click the Associate an Activity Graph button. This will add an ActivityGraph node to the main explorer window (see Figure 3-26).

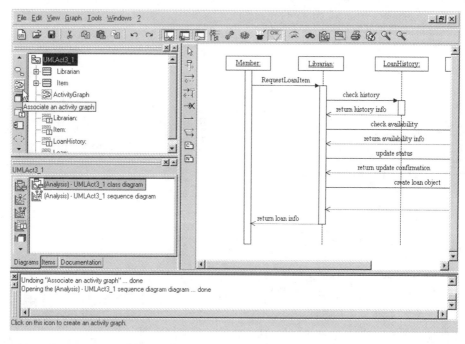

Figure 3-26. Adding an activity graph

3. Click the `ActivityGraph` node in the main explorer window. The Properties Editor (located below the main explorer window) will display a Create an Activity Diagram button in its toolbar on the left side of the window. Click this button to add an activity diagram to the project. You will see an activity diagram designer in the main editor window. The toolbar located at the left of the designer window contains shapes used in creating activity diagrams (see Figure 3-27).

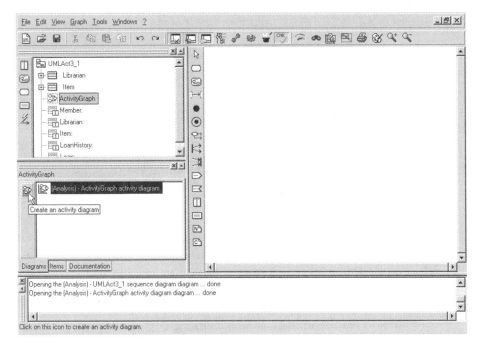

Figure 3-27. Activity diagram designer

4. Click the Create a Partition button in the designer toolbar and add a partition to the diagram. Change the name of the partition to **Member**.

5. Repeat the procedures in step 4 to add partitions for the `Librarian`, `LoanHistory`, `Item`, and `Loan` objects.

6. From the Shapes toolbar, click the Initial State shape and add it to the `Member` partition. Below the Initial State in the `Member` partition, add an Action State shape. Rename the Action State to **Request Item**. Add a transition shape (arrow) from the Initial State to the Request Item action state. Your diagram should be similar to Figure 3-28.

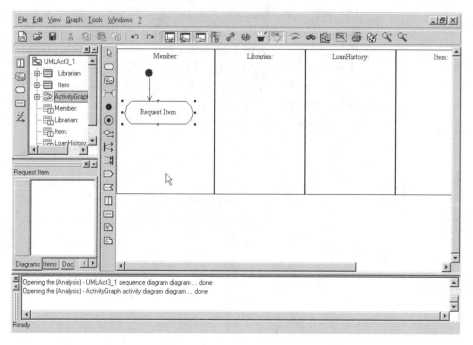

Figure 3-28. Creating the activity diagram

7. Under the Librarian partition, add a Process Loan action state and a Transition shape from the Request Item action to the Process Loan action state.

8. Under the LoanHistory partition, add a Check Member Status action state and a Transition shape from the Process Loan action to the Check Member Status action state.

9. From the Shapes toolbar, click the Conditional Branch shape and add it to the LoanHistory partition below the Check Member Status action state. Add a Transition from the Check Member Status action state to the Conditional Branch. From the Conditional Branch, add a Transition to a Deny Loan action state under the Librarian partition. Right-click the Transition shape and choose Modify. Enter a guard condition of **fail**. Also add a transition to a Check Item Status action state under the Item partition with a guard condition of **pass**. Your diagram should be similar to Figure 3-29.

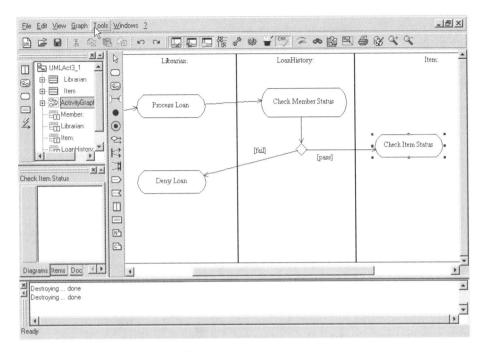

Figure 3-29. A branching condition

10. Repeat step 9 to create a Conditional Branch from the Check Item Status action. If the item is in stock, add a Transition to an Update Item Status action state under the Item partition. If the item is out of stock, add a Transition to the Deny Loan action state under the Librarian partition.

11. From the Update Item Status action state, add a Transition shape to a Record Loan Info action state under the Loan partition.

12. From the Record Loan Info action state, add a Transition shape to a Confirm Loan action state under the Librarian partition.

13. From the Shapes toolbar, click the Final State shape and add it to the bottom of the Member partition. Add a Transition shape from Deny Loan to the final Action state. Add another Transition shape from the Confirm Loan action state to the final action state.

14. Your completed diagram should be similar to the one shown in Figure 3-30. Save the project and exit UML Modeler.

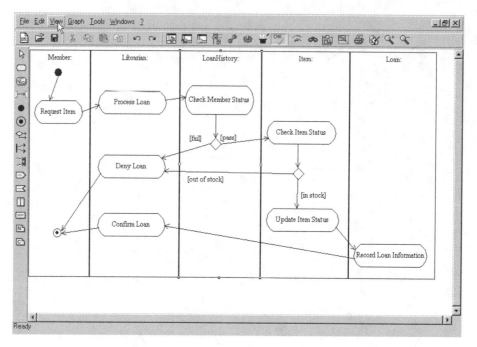

Figure 3-30. Completed activity diagram

Thus far, the discussions of object-oriented analysis and design have focused on modeling the functional design and the internal processing of the application. Successful modern software applications rely on a rich set of graphical user interfaces (GUIs) to expose this functionality to the users of the application. Although an in-depth discussion of GUI design is beyond the scope of this book, it is worthwhile to discuss the importance of good GUI design and look at some modeling techniques you can incorporate into the GUI design process.

Exploring GUI Design

In modern software systems, one of the most important aspects of an application is how well it interacts with the users. Gone are the days when users would interact with the application by typing cryptic commands at the DOS prompt. Modern operating systems employ GUIs, which are, for the most part, intuitive to use. Users have also grown used to the polished interfaces of the commercial office-productivity applications. Users have come to expect the same ease of use and intuitiveness built into applications developed in-house.

The design of the user interface should not be done haphazardly, but it should be planned in conjunction with the business logic design. The success of most applications is judged by the response of the users toward the application. If users are not comfortable when interacting with the application and the application does not improve the productivity of the user, it is doomed to failure. To the user, the application is the interface. It does not matter how pristine and clever the business logic code may be, if the user interface is poorly designed and implemented, the application will not be acceptable to the users. It is often hard for developers to remember that it is the user who drives the software development.

Although the Unified Modeling Language (UML) was not specifically designed for GUI design, many software architects and programmers have incorporated some of the UML diagrams to help when modeling the user interface of the application.

GUI Activity Diagrams

The first step in developing a user interface design is to perform a task analysis to discover how users will need to interact with the system. The task analysis is based on the use cases and scenarios that have been modeled previously. You can then develop activity diagrams to model how the interaction between the user and the system will take place. Figure 3-31 shows an activity diagram modeling the activities the user goes through to record rental information.

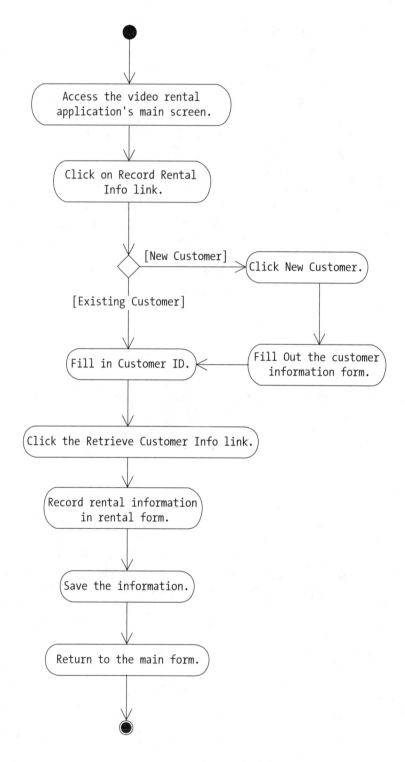

Figure 3-31. GUI modeling with an activity diagram

Interface Prototyping

After you have identified and prioritized the necessary tasks, you can develop a prototype sketch of the various screens that will make up the user interface. Figure 3-32 shows a prototype sketch of the Customer Info Screen.

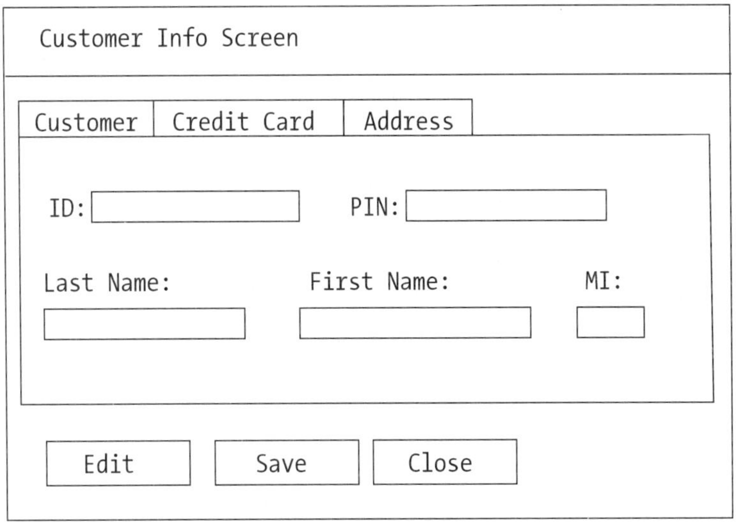

Figure 3-32. GUI prototype sketch

Interface Flow Diagrams

Once you have prototyped the various screens, you can use interface flow diagrams to model the relationships and flow patterns among the screens that make up the user interface. Figure 3-33 shows a partial interface flow diagram for the video rental application.

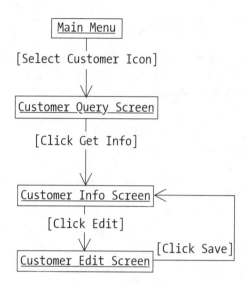

Figure 3-33. Interface flow diagramming

GUI Class Diagrams

In many OOP languages, the forms and the controls (textboxes, buttons, and so on) that make up the interfaces are objects based on system classes. You can use class diagrams to model the forms and the objects they contain. Figure 3-34 shows the aggregation between the Customer Info Screen and its composite controls.

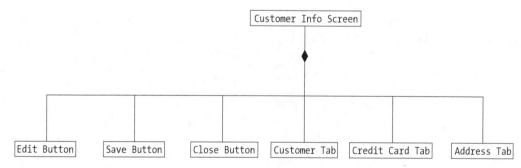

Figure 3-34. A GUI class diagram

Application Prototyping

Once you have roughed out the screen layout and the design of the user interface, you can develop a simple prototype. The prototype should contain skeleton code that simulates the functionality of the system. At this point there should not be a great effort put into integrating the user interface front end with the business functionality of the application. The idea is to let the users interact with a working prototype to obtain feedback of the design and have the users suggest any design changes and improvements needed in the application's UI. The processes of refining and testing of the user interface will be iterative and will most likely continue through several cycles. Once the user interface design and the internal functional design of the application have been completed and prototyped, the next step in the application development cycle is to start coding the application.

Summary

In this chapter you became familiar with the following:

- The purpose of scenarios and how they extend the use cases models

- How sequence diagrams model the time dependent interaction of the objects in the system

- How collaboration diagrams model the contextual interaction of the objects in the system

- The importance of graphical user interface design and how it fits into the object-oriented design process

The goal of the past two chapters was to introduce you to some of the common modeling diagrams and concepts involved in software design and UML. You have not yet looked at how you would go about developing the various diagrams and models from scratch. In Chapter 4, "Designing OOP Solutions: A Case Study," you will take the concepts developed thus far and try to implement them by designing a solution for a sample case study.

CHAPTER 4

Designing
OOP Solutions:
A Case Study

DESIGNING SOLUTIONS FOR AN APPLICATION is not an easy endeavor. Becoming an accomplished designer takes time and a conscious effort, which explains why many developers avoid it like the plague. You can study all the theories and know all the buzzwords, but the only way to truly develop your modeling skills is to roll up your sleeves, get your hands dirty, and start modeling. In this chapter you will go through the process of modeling an office-supply ordering system. Although this is not a terribly complex application, it will serve to help solidify the modeling concepts covered in the previous two chapters. By analyzing the case study, you will also gain a better understanding of how a model is developed and how the pieces fit together.

Developing an Office-Supply Ordering System

There are several steps to developing an office-supply ordering system, from creating a System Requirement Specification (SRS) to designing the user interface model. Before you start developing the ordering system, you need some background information about the project.

Getting the Case Study Background

Your company currently has no standard way for departments to order office supplies. Each department separately implements its own ordering process. As a result, it is next to impossible to track company-wide spending on supplies, which impacts the ability to forecast budgeting and identify abuses. Another problem with the current system is it does not allow for a single contact person who could negotiate better deals with the various vendors.

As a result, you have been asked to help develop a company-wide Office-Supply Ordering (OSO) application. After interviewing the various clients of the proposed system, you develop the SRS shown in the next section. Remember from Chapter 2, "Designing OOP Solutions: Identifying the Class Structure," that the SRS scopes the system requirements, defines the system boundaries, and identifies the users of the system.

Creating the System Requirement Specification

You have identified the following system users:

- **Purchaser**: Employee who has the right to initiate a request for supplies

- **Department Manager**: Tracks and approves supply requests from department purchasers

- **Supply Vendor Processing Application**: Receives XML order files generated by the system

- **Purchase Manager**: Updates supply catalog, tracks supply requests, and checks in delivered items

You have identified the following system requirements:

- Users must log in to the system by supplying a username and password.

- Purchasers will view a list of supplies that are available to be ordered.

- Purchasers will be able to filter the list of supplies by category.

- Purchasers can request multiple supplies in a single purchase request.

- A department manager can request general supplies for the department.

- Department managers must approve or deny supply requests for their department at the end of each week.

- If department managers deny a request, they must supply a short explanation outlining the reason for the denial.

- Department managers must track spending within their departments and ensure there are sufficient funds for approved supply requests.

- A purchase manager maintains the supply catalog and ensures it is accurate and up-to-date.

- A purchase manager checks in the supplies when they are received and organizes the supplies for distribution.

- Supply requests that have been requested but not approved are marked with a status of pending.

- Supply requests that have been approved are marked with a status of approved and an order is generated.

- Once an order is generated, an XML document containing the order details is placed in an order queue. Once the order has been placed in the queue, it is marked with a status of placed.

- A separate Supply Vendor Processing Application (SVP) will retrieve the order XML files from the queue, parse the documents, and distribute the line items to the appropriate vendor queues. The vendor will retrieve the order XML documents from the queue.

- When all the items of an order are checked in, the order is marked with a status of fulfilled and the purchaser is informed that the order is ready for pick up.

Developing the Use Cases

After generating the SRS and getting the appropriate system users to sign off on it, the next step is to develop the use cases, which will define how the system will function from the user perspective. The first step in developing the use cases is to define the actors. Remember from Chapter 2, "Designing OOP Solutions: Identifying the Class Structure," the actors represent the external entities (human or other systems) that will interact with the system. From the SRS, you can identify the following actors that will interact with the system:

- Purchaser

- Department Manager

- Purchase Manager

- Supply Vendor Processing Application

Now that you have identified the actors, the next step is to identify the various use cases with which the actors will be involved. By examining the requirement statements made in the SRS, you can identify the various use cases. For example, the statement *Users must log in to the system by supplying a username and password* indicates the need for a Login use case. Table 4-1 identifies the use cases for the OSO application.

Table 4-1. Use Cases of the OSO Application

NAME	ACTOR(S)	DESCRIPTION
Login	Purchaser, Department Manager, Purchase Manager	Users see a login screen. They then enter their username and password. They either click Log In or Cancel. After login, they see a screen containing product information.
View Supply Catalog	Purchasers, Department Manager, Purchaser Manager	Users see a catalog table that contains a list of supplies. The table contains information such as the supply name, category, description, and cost. Users can filter supplies by category.
Purchase Request	Purchaser, Department Manager	Purchasers select items in the table and click a button to add them to their cart. A separate table shows the items in their cart, the number of each item requested and the cost, as well as the total cost of the request.
Department Purchase Request	Department Manager	Department managers select items in the table and click a button to add them to their cart. A separate table shows the items in their cart, the number of each item requested and the cost, as well as the total cost of the request.
Request Review	Department Manager	Managers see a screen that lists all pending supply requests for members of their department. They review the requests and mark them as approved or denied. If they deny the request, they enter a brief explanation.
Track Spending	Department Manager	Managers see a screen that lists the monthly spending of department members as well as the running total of the department.
Maintain Catalog	Purchase Manager	The Purchase Manager has the ability to update product information, add products, or mark products as discontinued. The administrator can also update category information, add categories, or mark categories as discontinued.

(Continued)

Table 4-1. Use Cases of the OSO Application (Continued)

NAME	ACTOR(S)	DESCRIPTION
Item Check In	Purchase Manager	The Purchase Manager sees a screen for entering the order number. The Purchase Manager then sees the line items listed for the order. The items that have been received are marked. When all the items for an order are received, it is marked as fulfilled.
Order Placement	Supply Vendor Processing Application	The Supply Vendor Processing Application checks the queue for outgoing order XML files. Files are retrieved, parsed, and sent to the appropriate vendor queue.

Diagramming the Use Cases

Now that you have identified the various use cases and actors, you are ready to construct a visual design of the use cases using a UML modeling program. Figure 4-1 shows a preliminary use case model developed with Objecteering's UML Modeler, which was introduced in Chapter 2, "Designing OOP Solutions: Identifying the Class Structure."

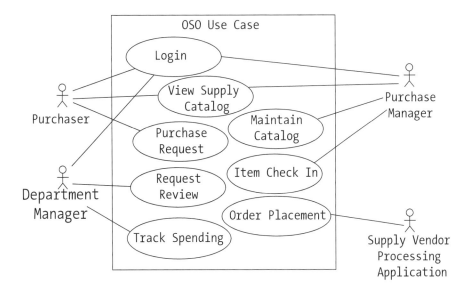

Figure 4-1. Preliminary OSO use case diagram

Once you have diagrammed the use cases, you now look for any relationships that may exist between the use cases. Two relationships that may exist are the "includes" relationship and the "extends" relationship. Remember from the discussions in Chapter 2, "Designing OOP Solutions: Identifying the Class Structure," that when a use case includes another use case, the use case being included needs to run as a precondition. For example, the Login use case of the OSO application needs to be included in the View Supply Catalog use case. The reason you make Login a separate use case is that the Login use case can be reused by one or more other use cases. In the OSO application, the Login use case will also be included with the Track Spending use case. Figure 4-2 depicts this inclusion relationship.

NOTE *In some modeling tools, the inclusion relationship may be indicated in the use case diagram by the "uses" keyword.*

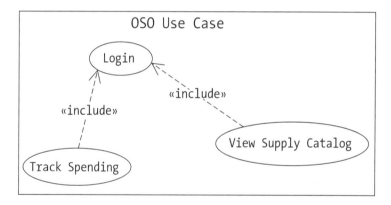

Figure 4-2. Inclusion of the Login use case

The "extends" relationship exists between two use cases when—depending on a condition—a use case will extend the behavior of the initial use case. In the OSO application, when a manager is making a purchase request, she can indicate that she will be requesting a purchase for the department. In this case, the Department Purchase Request use case becomes an extension of the Purchase Request use case. Figure 4-3 diagrams this extension.

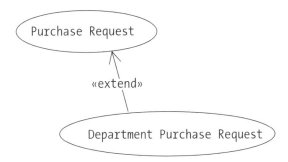

Figure 4-3. Extending the Purchase Request use case

After analyzing the system requirements and use cases, you can make the system development more manageable by breaking up the application and developing it in phases. In phase one, you can develop the purchase request portion of the application. Employees and department managers will use this part of the application to make purchase requests. Figure 4-4 shows the use case diagram for this phase.

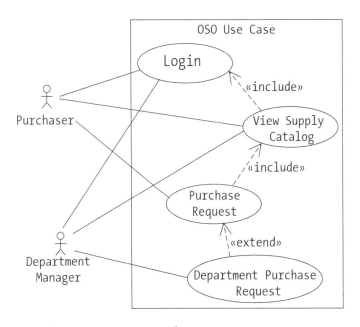

Figure 4-4. Purchase Request use case diagrams

Modeling the Class Structure of the OSO Application

After you have identified the various use cases, you now can start identifying the classes the system needs to include to carry out the functionality described in the use cases. To identify the classes, you drill down into each use case and define a series of steps needed to carry it out. It is also helpful to identify the noun phrases in the use case descriptions. The noun phrases are often good indicators of the classes that will be needed.

For example, the following steps describe the View Supply Catalog use case:

1. User has logged in and been assigned a user status level. (This is the precondition.)

2. Users are presented with a catalog table that contains a list of supplies. The table contains information such as the supply name, category, description, and cost.

3. Users can filter supplies by category.

4. Users are given the choice of logging out or making a purchase request. (This is the postcondition.)

From this description you can identify a class that will be responsible for retrieving product information from the database and filtering the products being displayed. The name of this class will be the `ProductCatalog` class.

Examining the noun phrases in the use case descriptions dealing with making purchase requests reveals the candidate classes for the OSO application (see Table 4-2).

Table 4-2. OSO Candidate Classes Used to Make Purchase Requests

USE CASE	CANDIDATE CLASSES
Login	User, username, password, success, failure
View Supply Catalog	User, catalog table, supplies, information, supply name, category, description, cost
Purchase Request	Purchaser, items, cart, number, item requested, cost, total cost
Department Purchase Request	Department manager, items, cart, number, item requested, cost, total cost, department purchase request

Now that you have identified the candidate classes, you must eliminate the classes that indicate redundancy. For example, a reference to items and line items would represent the same abstraction. You can also eliminate classes that represent attributes and not objects. Username, password, and cost are examples of noun phrases that represent attributes. Some classes are vague or generalizations of other classes. User is actually a generalization of purchaser and manager. Classes may also actually refer to the same object abstraction but indicate a different state of the object. For example, the supply request and order represent the same abstraction before and after approval. You should also filter out classes that represent implementation constructs such as list and table. For example, a cart is really a collection of order items for a particular order.

Using these elimination criteria, you can whittle down the class list to the following candidate classes:

- Employee

- Manager

- Order

- OrderItem

- ProductCatalog

- Product

You can also include classes that represent the actors that will interact with the system. These are special classes called *actor classes* and are included in the class diagram to model the interface between the system and the actor. For example, you could designate a Purchaser actor class that represents the graphical user interface (GUI) that a Purchaser (Employee or Manager) would interact with to make a purchase request. Because these classes are not actually part of the system, the internal implementations of these classes are encapsulated and they are treated as black boxes to the system.

You can now start formulating the class diagram for the purchase request portion of the OSO application. Figure 4-5 shows the preliminary class diagram for the OSO application.

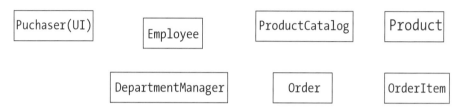

Figure 4-5. Preliminary OSO class diagram

Adding Attributes to the Classes

The next stage in the development of the class model is to identify the level of abstraction the classes must implement. You must determine what state information is relevant to the OSO application. This required state information will in turn be implemented through the attributes of the class. Analyzing the system requirements for the Employee class reveals the need for a login name, password, department, and whether they are a manager. You also need an identifier such as an employee ID to uniquely identify various employees. An interview with managers revealed the need to include the first and last names of the employee so that they can track spending by name. Table 4-3 summarizes the attributes that will be included in the OSO classes.

Table 4-3. OSO Class Attributes

CLASS	ATTRIBUTE	TYPE
Employee	EmployeeID	Integer
	LoginName	String
	Password	String
	Department	String
	FirstName	String
	LastName	String
Manager	EmployeeID	Integer
	LoginName	String
	Password	String
	Department	String
	FirstName	String
	LastName	String
Order	OrderNumber	Long
	OrderDate	Date
	Status	String
OrderItem	ProductNumber	String
	Quantity	Short
	UnitPrice	Decimal
Product	ProductNumber	String
	ProductName	String
	Description	String
	UnitPrice	Decimal
	VendorCode	String
ProductCatalog	None	

Figure 4-6 shows the OSO class diagram with the class attributes. I have left out the attributes for the DepartmentManager class. The DepartmentManager will probably inherit the attributes listed for the Employee class.

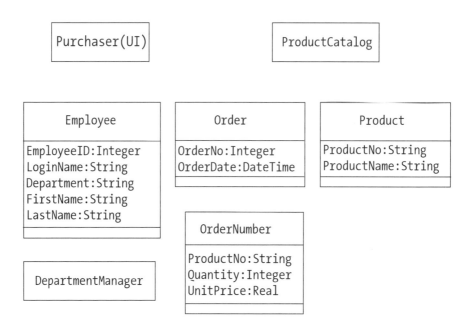

Figure 4-6. OSO Purchase Request component class diagram with attributes added

Identifying Class Associations

The next stage in the development process is to model the class associations that will exist in the OSO application. If you study the use cases and SRS, then you can gain an understanding of what types of associations you need to incorporate into the class structural design.

> **NOTE** *You may find that you need to further refine the SRS to expose these relationships.*

For example, an employee will be associated with an order. By examining the multiplicity of the association, you discover that an employee can have multiple orders, but an order can only be associated with one employee. Figure 4-7 models this association.

Figure 4-7. Depicting the association between the Employee *class and the* Order *class*

If you look at the class attributes you will notice that the `Employee` class and the manager class have the same attributes. This makes sense because a manager is also an employee. For the purpose of this application, a manager represents an employee with specialized behavior. This specialization is represented by an inheritance relationship. Figure 4-8 shows how this inheritance is represented in the class diagram.

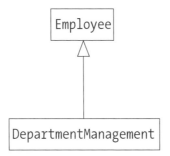

Figure 4-8. The `DepartmentManager` *class inheriting from the* `Employee` *class*

The following statements sum up the associations in the OSO class structure:

- An `Order` is an aggregation of `OrderItems`.

- An `Employee` can have multiple `Orders`.

- An `Order` is associated with one `Employee`.

- The `ProductCatalog` is associated with multiple `Products`.

- A `Product` is associated with the `ProductCatalog`.

- An `OrderItem` is associated with one `Product`.

- A `Product` may be associated with multiple `OrderItems`.

- A `DepartmentManager` is an `Employee` with specialized behavior.

Figure 4-9 shows these various associations.

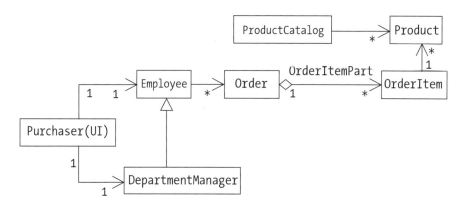

Figure 4-9. The OSO Purchase Request component class diagram with associations added

> **NOTE** *The class attributes have been excluded for greater clarity.*

Modeling the Class Behaviors of the OSO Application

Now that you have sketched out the preliminary structure of the classes, you are ready to model how these classes will interact and collaborate. The first step in this process is to drill down into the use case descriptions and create a more detailed scenario of how the use case will be carried out. The following scenario describes one possible sequence for carrying out the Login use case.

1. The user is presented with a login dialog box.

2. The user enters a login name and a password.

3. The user submits the information.

4. The name and password are checked and verified.

5. The user is presented with a supply request screen.

Although this scenario depicts the most common processing involved with the Login use case, other scenarios may be needed to describe anticipated alternate outcomes. The following scenario describes an alternate processing of the Login use case:

1. The user is presented with a login dialog box.

2. The user enters a login name and a password.

3. The user submits the information.

4. The name and password are checked but cannot be verified.

5. The user is informed of the incorrect login information.

6. The user is presented with a login dialog box again.

7. The user either tries again or cancels the login request.

At this point it may help to create a visual representation of the scenarios outlined for the use case. Remember from Chapter 3, "Designing OOP Solutions: Modeling the Object Interaction," that activity diagrams are often used to visualize use case processing. Figure 4-10 shows an activity diagram constructed for the Login use case scenarios.

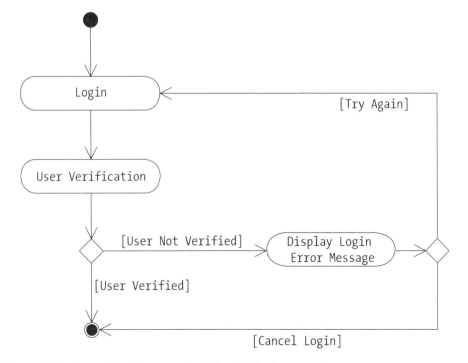

Figure 4-10. An activity diagram depicting the login scenarios

After analyzing the process involved in the use case scenarios, you can now turn your attention to assigning the necessary behaviors to the classes of the system. To help identify the class behaviors and interactions that need to occur an interaction diagram is constructed. As discussed in Chapter 3, "Designing OOP Solutions: Modeling the Object Interaction," interaction diagrams can take the form of either a sequence diagram or a collaboration diagram. Sequence diagrams focus on the order of the object interactions taking place, and collaboration diagrams focus on the links occurring between the objects. Figure 4-11 shows a sequence diagram for the Login use case scenarios. The Purchaser(UI) class calls the Login method that has been assigned to the Employee class. The message returns information that will indicate whether the login has been verified.

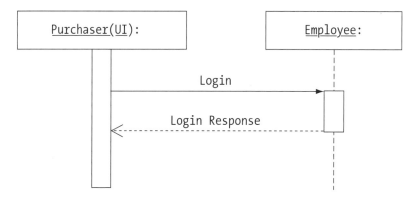

Figure 4-11. A sequence diagram depicting the login process

The next use case we will analyze is the View Supply Catalog use case. The following scenario describes the use case:

1. User logged in and has been verified.

2. User views a catalog table that contains information on supply name, category, description, and price.

3. User chooses to filter the table by category, selects a category, and refreshes the table.

From this scenario you can identify a method of the ProductCatalog class that needs to be developed that will return a listing of product categories. The Purchaser class will invoke this method. Another method the ProductCatalog class needs is one that will return a product list filtered by category. The sequence diagram displayed in Figure 4-12 shows the interaction that occurs between the Purchaser(UI) class and the ProductCatalog class.

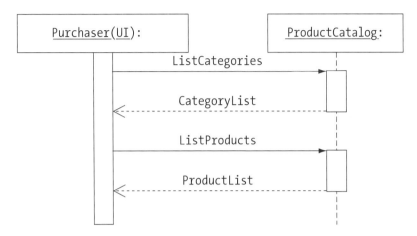

Figure 4-12. Sequence diagram for the View Supply Catalog scenario

The following scenario was developed for the Purchase Request:

1. A purchaser has logged in and has been verified as an employee.

2. The purchaser selects items from the product catalog and adds them to the order request (shopping cart), indicating the number of each item requested.

3. After completing the item selections for the order, the purchaser submits the order.

4. Order request information is updated and an order ID is generated and returned to the purchaser.

From the scenario you can identify an AddItem method of the Order class that needs to be created. This method will accept a product ID and a quantity and then return the subtotal of the order. The Order class will in turn need to call a method of the OrderItem class, which will create an instance of an order item. A SubmitOrder method of the Order class will also be needed that will submit the request and the return order ID of the generated order. Figure 4-13 shows the associated sequence diagram for this scenario.

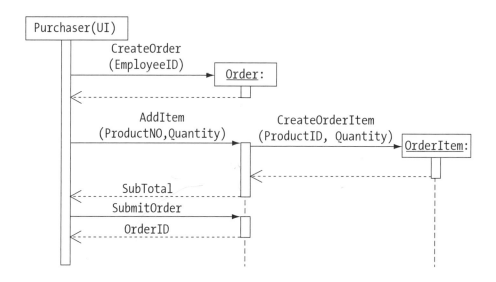

Figure 4-13. Purchase Request sequence diagram

Some other scenarios that need to be included are deleting an item from the shopping cart, changing the quantity of an item in the cart, and canceling the order process. You will also need to include similar scenarios and create similar methods for the Department Purchase Request use case. After analyzing the scenarios and interactions that need to take place, a class diagram was developed for the Purchase Request portion of the application (see Figure 4-14).

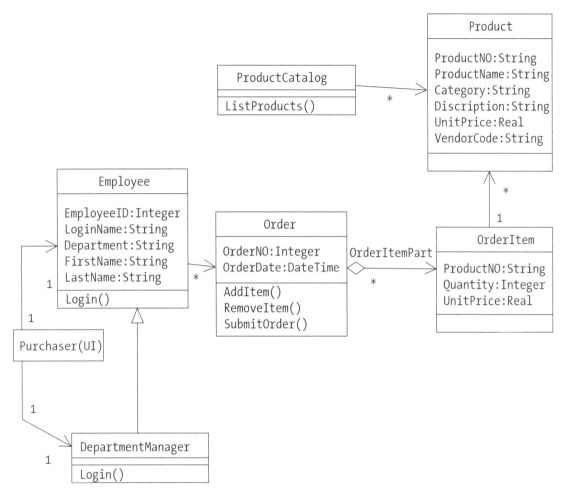

Figure 4-14. OSO Purchase Request class diagram

Developing the User Interface Model Design

At this point in the application design process, you do not want to commit to a particular GUI implementation (in other words, a technology-specific one). It is helpful, however, to model some of the common elements and functionality required of a GUI for the application. This will help you create a prototype user interface that can be used to verify the business logical design that has been developed. The users will be able to interact with the prototype and provide feedback and verification of the logical design.

The first prototype screen that needs to be implemented is the login screen. You can construct an activity diagram to help define the activities the user needs to perform when logging into the system (see Figure 4-15).

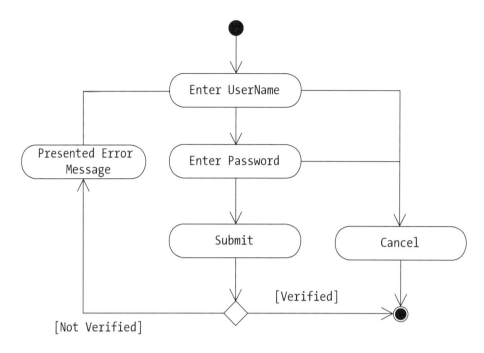

Figure 4-15. User login activity diagram

Analyzing the activity diagram reveals that you can implement the login screen as a fairly generic interface. This screen should allow the user to enter a username and password. It should include a way to indicate that the user is logging on as either an employee or a manager. The final requirement is to include a way for the user to abort the login process. Figure 4-16 shows a prototype sketch of the login screen.

```
OSO Login:
─────────────────────────────────────────────

           Name: [              ]       [  OK  ]
       Password: [              ]       [Cancel]

```

Figure 4-16. Login screen prototype

The next screen you need to consider is the product catalog screen. Figure 4-17 depicts the activity diagram for viewing and filtering the products.

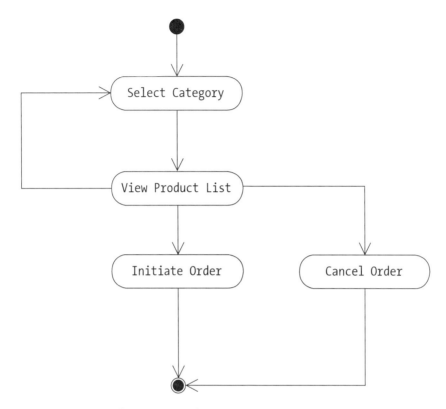

Figure 4-17. View products activity diagram

The activity diagram reveals that the screen needs to show a table or list of products and product information. Users must be able to filter the products by category, which can be initiated by selecting a category from a category list. The user also needs to be able to initiate an order request or exit the application. Figure 4-18 shows a prototype screen that can be used to view the products.

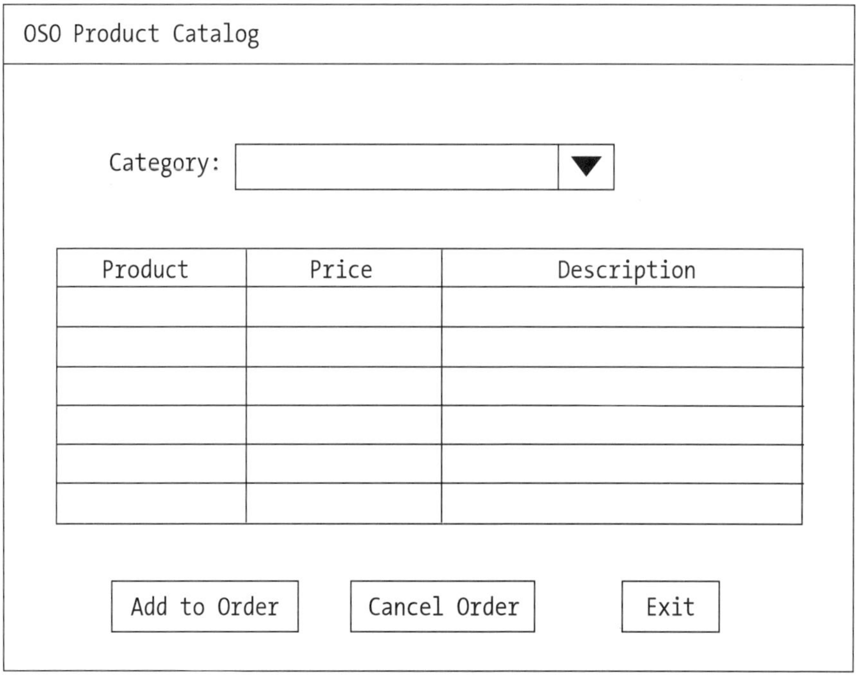

```
┌─────────────────────────────────────────────────────────────────┐
│ OSO Product Catalog                                               │
├─────────────────────────────────────────────────────────────────┤
│                                                                   │
│                                                                   │
│        Category:  ┌──────────────────────────┬───┐               │
│                   │                          │ ▼ │               │
│                   └──────────────────────────┴───┘               │
│                                                                   │
│        ┌───────────────┬───────────────┬───────────────────────┐ │
│        │    Product    │     Price     │     Description        │ │
│        ├───────────────┼───────────────┼───────────────────────┤ │
│        │               │               │                        │ │
│        ├───────────────┼───────────────┼───────────────────────┤ │
│        │               │               │                        │ │
│        ├───────────────┼───────────────┼───────────────────────┤ │
│        │               │               │                        │ │
│        ├───────────────┼───────────────┼───────────────────────┤ │
│        │               │               │                        │ │
│        ├───────────────┼───────────────┼───────────────────────┤ │
│        │               │               │                        │ │
│        └───────────────┴───────────────┴───────────────────────┘ │
│                                                                   │
│                                                                   │
│      ┌───────────────┐  ┌──────────────┐     ┌────────┐          │
│      │ Add to Order  │  │ Cancel Order │     │  Exit  │          │
│      └───────────────┘  └──────────────┘     └────────┘          │
│                                                                   │
└─────────────────────────────────────────────────────────────────┘
```

Figure 4-18. View products screen prototype

The final screen that needs to be prototyped for this part of the application is the shopping cart interface. This will facilitate the adding and removing items from an order request. It also needs to allow the user to submit the order or abort an order request. Figure 4-19 is a prototype sketch of the order request screen.

Figure 4-19. Order request screen prototype

Avoiding Some Common OOP Design Pitfalls

Now that you have come to the end of the preliminary design for this phase of the OSO application implementation, let's review some of the common traps that you should avoid:

Confusing Modeling with Documenting: The main value in modeling is not the diagrams produced but rather the process one goes through to produce the diagrams.

Not Involving the Users in the Process: It is worth emphasizing that users are the consumers of your product. They are the ones who define the business processes and functional requirements of the system.

Trying to Model the Whole Solution at One Time: When developing complex systems, break up the system design and development into manageable components. Plan to produce the software in phases. This will provide for faster modeling, developing, testing and release cycles.

Striving to Create a Perfect Model: No model will be perfect from the start. Successful modelers understand that the modeling process is iterative and models are continuously updated and revised throughout the application development cycle.

Thinking There Is Only One True Modeling Methodology: Just as there are many different equally viable OOP languages, there are many equally valid modeling methodologies for developing software. Choose the one that works best for you and the project at hand.

Reinventing the Wheel: Look for patterns and reusability. If you analyze many of the business processes that applications attempt to solve, a consistent set of modeling patterns emerge. Create a repository where you can leverage these existing patterns from project to project and from programmer to programmer.

Letting the Data Model Drive the Business Logic Model: It is generally a bad idea to develop the data model (database structure) first and then build the business logical design on top of it. The solution designer should first ask what business problem needs to be solved and then build a data model to solve the problem.

Confusing the Problem Domain Model with the Implementation Model: You should develop two distinct but complementary models when designing applications. A domain model design describes the scope of the project and the processing involved in implementing the business solutions. This includes what objects will be involved, their properties and behaviors, and how they interact and relate to each other. The domain model should be implementation agnostic. You should be able to use the same domain model as a basis for several different architecturally specific implementations. In other words, you should be able to take the same domain model and implement it using a Visual Basic rich-client, two-tier architecture or a C# (or Java for that matter) n-tier distributed Web application.

Summary

Now that you have analyzed the domain model of the OSO application, you are ready to transform the design into an actual implementation. The next section of this book will introduce you to the Visual Basic .NET language. You will look at the .NET Framework and discuss how Visual Basic applications are built on top of the framework. You will be introduced to working in the Visual Studio Integrated Development Environment. You will become familiar with the syntax of the Visual Basic .NET language. The next section will also demonstrate the process of implementing OOP constructs such as class structures, object instantiation, inheritance, and polymorphism in the Visual Basic .NET language. You will revisit this case study in Chapter 9, "OSO Application Revisited: Implementing the Business Logic," at which time you will look at transforming the application design into actual implementation code.

Part Two

Object-Oriented Programming with Visual Basic .NET

CHAPTER 5

Introducing VB .NET

To EFFECTIVELY PROGRAM in Visual Basic you need to understand the underlying supporting mechanisms that enable it to function. The transition between Visual Basic 6.0 and the current .NET version has been quite dramatic. For several years there has been an evolution in business application programming. The transition included an application development shift from a two-tier, tightly coupled model into a multitiered, loosely coupled model often involving data transfer over the Internet or a corporate intranet. In an effort to allow programmers to be more productive and deal with the complexities of this type of model, Microsoft developed the .NET Framework.

After reading this chapter you should be familiar with the following:

- The .NET Framework

- Features of the Common Language Runtime

- How the Just-In-Time compiler works

- The .NET Framework Class Library

- Namespaces and assemblies

- The features of the Visual Studio Integrated Development Environment

Goals of the .NET Framework

The .NET Framework is a collection of fundamental classes designed to provide the common services needed to run applications. Microsoft designed the framework with certain goals in mind. What were these goals and how does the .NET Framework achieve them? The following sections answer these questions.

Support of Industry Standards

Microsoft wanted the framework to be based on industry standards and practices. As a result, the framework relies heavily on such industry standards as Extensible Markup Language (XML) and Simple Object Access Protocol (SOAP). Microsoft has also submitted a Common Language Infrastructure (CLI) Working Document to the European Computer Manufacturers Association (ECMA), which oversees many of the common standards in the computer industry. The CLI is a set of specifications needed to create compilers that conform to the .NET Framework. Third-party vendors can use these specifications to create .NET-compliant language compilers—for example, Interactive Software Engineering (ISE) has created a .NET compiler for Eifle. Third-party vendors can also create a Common Language Runtime (CLR) that will allow .NET-compliant languages to run on different platforms. For example, a CLR could be developed that gives Visual Basic (VB) applications the ability to run on the Linux platform.

Extensibility

To create a highly productive environment in which to program, Microsoft realized the framework had to be extensible. As a result, Microsoft has exposed the framework class hierarchy to developers. Through inheritance and inter-faces, you can easily access and extend the functionality of these classes. For example, you could create a button control class that not only inherits its base functionality from the button class exposed by the .NET Framework but that also extends the base functionality in a unique way required by your application.

Microsoft has also made it a lot easier to work with the underlying operating system. By repackaging and implementing the Windows operating system Application Programming Interface (API) functions in a class-based hierarchy, Microsoft has made it more intuitive and easier for object-oriented programmers to work with the functionality exposed by the underlying operating system.

Unified Programming Models

Another important goal Microsoft incorporated into the framework was cross-language independence and integration. To achieve this goal, all languages that support the Common Language Specification (CLS) compile into the same intermediate language, support the same set of basic data types, and expose the same set of code accessibility methods. As a result, not only can classes developed in the different CLS-compliant languages communicate seamlessly with one another, you can implement OOP constructs across languages. For example, you could develop a class written in VB that inherits from a class written using C#.

Microsoft has developed five languages that support the .NET Framework. Along with VB, the languages are C#, managed C++, JScript, and J#. In addition to these languages, many third-party vendors have developed versions of other popular languages designed to run under the .NET Framework, such as Perl and SmallTalk.

Easier Deployment

Microsoft needed a way to simplify application deployment. Before the development of the framework, when components were deployed, component information had to be recorded in the system registry. Many of these components, especially system components, were used by several different client applications. When a client application makes a call to the component, the registry is searched to determine the metadata needed to work with the component. If a newer version of the component is deployed, it replaces the registry information of the old component. Often the new components were incompatible with the old version and caused existing clients to fail. You have probably experienced this problem installing a service pack that ends up causing more problems than it fixes!

The .NET Framework combats this problem by storing the metadata for working with the component in a *manifest*, which is packaged with the assembly containing the component code. By default an assembly is marked as private and placed in the same directory as the client assembly. This ensures that the component assembly is not inadvertently replaced or modified and also allows for a simpler *xcopy* deployment because there is no need to work with the registry. If a component needs to be shared, then its assembly has to be deployed to a special directory referred to as the Global Assembly Cache (GAC). The manifest of the assembly contains versioning information and newer versions of the component can be deployed side by side with the older versions in the GAC. By default client assemblies continue to request and use the assemblies they were intended to. Older client assemblies will no longer fail when newer versions of the component are installed.

Improved Memory Management

A common problem of programs developed for the Windows platform has been memory management. Often these programs have caused memory leaks. This occurs when the program allocates memory from the operating system but fails to release it after it is done working with it. This problem is compounded when the program is intended to run for a long time, such as a service that runs in the background. To combat this problem, the .NET Framework uses nondeterministic finalization. Instead of relying on the applications to deallocate the unused memory, the framework uses a garbage collection object. The garbage collector periodically scans for unused memory blocks and returns them back to the operating system.

Improved Security Model

Implementing security in today's highly distributed Internet-based applications is an extremely important issue. In the past, security has focused on the user of the application. Security identities were checked when users logged into an application and their identities were passed along as the application made calls to remote servers and databases. This type of security model has proven to be inefficient and complicated to implement for today's enterprise-level, loosely coupled systems. In an effort to make security easier to implement and more robust, the .NET Framework uses the concept of code identity and code access. When an assembly is created, it is given a unique identity. When a server assembly is created you can grant access permissions and rights. When a client assembly calls a server assembly the runtime will check the permissions and rights of the client and grant or deny access to the server code accordingly. Because each assembly has an identity we can also restrict access of the assembly through the operating system. If a user downloads a component from the Web, for example, they can restrict its ability to read and write files on their system.

Components of the .NET Framework

Now that you have seen some of the major goals of the .NET Framework, let's take a look at the components that make up the framework.

Common Language Runtime

The fundamental component of the .NET Framework is the Common Language Runtime (CLR). This manages the code being executed and provides for a layer of extraction between the code and the operating system. Built into the CLR are mechanisms for the following:

- Loading code into memory and preparing it for execution

- Converting the code from the intermediate language (IL) to native code

- Managing code execution

- Managing code and user level security

- Automated deallocation and release of memory

- Debugging and tracing code execution

- Providing structured exception handling

Framework Base Class Library

Built on top of the CLR is the .NET Framework base class library. Included in this class library are reference types and value types that encapsulate access to the system functionality. *Types* are data structures. A reference type is a complex type—for example, classes and interfaces. A value type is simple type—for example, integer or Boolean. Programmers use these base classes and interfaces as the foundation on which they build applications, components, and controls. Some of the functionality included in the base class library are types that encapsulate data structures, perform basic input/output operations, invoke security management and manage network communication . . . just to name a few.

Data and XML Classes

Built on top of the base classes are classes that support data management. This set of classes is often referred to as ADO.NET. Using the ADO.NET object model, programmers can access and manage data stored in a variety of data storage structures through managed providers. Microsoft has written and tuned the ADO.NET classes and object model to work efficiently in a loosely coupled, disconnected, multitiered environment. Under the hood ADO.NET works with data in an XML-structured format. Using this type of structure instead of a binary format makes it much easier to pass data using Hypertext Transfer Protocol (HTTP) and sharing data between disparate systems. Another advantage of ADO.NET is that it not only exposes the data from the database, but also the metadata associated with the data. Data is exposed as a sort of mini-relational database. This makes it efficient to get the data and work with it while disconnected from the data source until synchronization needs to takes place.

Microsoft has provided support for several data providers. Data stored in Microsoft SQL Server 7.0 and later can be accessed through the SQL data provider. An OLEDB manage provider is also included as a generic provider for systems currently exposed through an OLEDB provider, such as DB2 and Oracle. Because the OLEDB data provider does not interface directly with the database engine but rather talks to the OLEDB Provider, which then talks to the database engine, using the OLEDB data provider is less efficient and robust then using a native provider. Because of the extensibility of the .NET Framework and Microsoft's commitment to open-based standards, it is anticipated that many third-party developers and data storage vendors will begin supplying native data providers for other data stores.

ADO.NET is heavily dependent upon XML to store, manipulate, and pass data and metadata. Rich support is provided by ADO.NET to manipulate, search, and transform XML data. As a matter of fact, programmers using ADO.NET can work with any data storage device on any platform that can expose its data in a standard XML format. You can also read in an XML data structure, expose it as a relational data structure for clients to work with and manipulate, and then convert it back to an XML format for data storage or transport.

Web Forms and Services

The .NET Framework exposes a base set of classes that can be used on a Web server to create user interfaces and services exposed to Web-enabled clients. These classes are collectively referred to as ASP.NET. Using ASP.NET you can develop one user interface that can dynamically respond to the type of client device making the request. At runtime the .NET Framework takes care of discovering the type of client making the request (browser type and version) and exposing an appropriate interface. The creation of Graphical User Interfaces (GUI) for Web applications running on a Windows client has become more robust because the .NET Framework exposes much of the API functionality that previously had been only exposed to traditional Windows Forms-based C++ and VB applications. Another improvement in Web application development using the .NET Framework is that server-side code can be written in any .NET-compliant language. Prior to .NET, server-side code had to be written in a scripting language such as VBScript or JScript.

Incorporated into ASP.NET are base class and interface support for creating Web-based services. Microsoft's vision is that Web Services will provide functionality similar to the components developed using previous versions of VC++ and VB. Because these components were based on binary standards, it was not easy to communicate with the components through firewalls and across the Internet. The proprietary nature of the components also limited the types of clients that could effectively use and interact with the components. Microsoft has addressed these limitations by exposing Web Services through Internet standards such as XML and SOAP. The current version of Web Services components can easily interact and expose their services to any client that is XML enabled and can communicate via HTTP.

Windows Forms

Understanding that not all applications built with the .NET Framework will be Web applications, Microsoft has exposed a rich set of classes for building Windows GUI applications. Microsoft has wrapped functionality previously exposed through cryptic API calls into the object-oriented class structure of the .NET Framework. In the past, developing Windows GUIs in VC++ was dramatically different then developing them in VB. Although developing GUIs in VB was easy and could be accomplished very quickly, VB developers were isolated and not fully exposed to the underlying features of the Windows API. Because Windows GUI development has been incorporated into the .NET Framework set of base classes, Windows GUI development has become consistent across the various .NET-enabled programming languages. Microsoft has also exposed advanced Windows GUI functionality equally among the .NET-compliant languages.

Understanding Assemblies and Manifests

.NET applications are organized and packaged into *assemblies.* All code executed by the .NET runtime must be contained in an assembly. The assembly contains the code, resources, and a manifest (metadata about the assembly) needed to run the application. Assemblies can be organized into a single file, where all this information is incorporated into a single DLL or EXE file, or multiple files where the information is incorporated into separate DLL files, graphics files, and a manifest file. One of the main functions of an assembly is to form a boundary for types, references, and security. Another important function of the assembly is to form a unit for deployment.

One of the most crucial portions of an assembly is the manifest; in fact, every assembly must contain a manifest. The purpose of the manifest is to describe the assembly. It contains such things as the identity of the assembly, a description of the classes and other data types the assembly exposes to clients, any other assemblies it needs to reference, and security details needed to run the assembly. By default when an assembly is created it is marked as private. A copy of the assembly must be placed in the same directory or a bin subdirectory of any client assembly that uses it. If the assembly must be shared between multiple client assemblies, it is placed in the GAC, a special Windows folder. To convert a private assembly into a shared assembly, a utility program must be run to create encryption keys and the assembly must be signed with the keys. After signing the assembly, another utility must be used to add the shared assembly into the GAC. By mandating such stringent requirements for creating and exposing shared assemblies, Microsoft is trying to ensure that naming collisions and malicious tampering of shared assemblies will not occur.

Referencing Assemblies and Namespaces

To organize and make the .NET Framework more manageable, Microsoft has organized the .NET Framework into a hierarchical structure. This hierarchical structure is organized into what are referred to as *namespaces*. By organizing the framework into namespaces, any naming collisions that may occur are greatly reduced. Organizing related functionality of the framework into namespaces has also greatly enhances its usability for developers. For example, if you want to build a window's GUI, it is a pretty good bet the functionality you need exists in the System.Windows.Forms namespace.

All of the .NET Framework classes reside in the System namespace. The System namespace is further subdivided by functionality. The functionality required to work with a database is contained in the System.Data namespace. Some namespaces run several levels deep; for example, the functionality used to connect to a SQL Server database is contained in the System.Data.SqlClient namespace. To gain access to the classes in the framework, you have to reference the assembly that contains the namespace in your code. An assembly may be organized into a single namespace or multiple namespaces. Several assemblies may also be organized into the same namespace. Once the assembly has been referenced, you can access classes in the assembly by providing its fully qualified name. For example, if you want to add a menu item to a form you would create an instance of the System.Windows.Forms.MenuItem class, like so:

```
Private WithEvents MenuItem as System.Windows.Forms.MenuItem
```

Fortunately in Visual Basic you can use the imports statement so that you do not have to continually reference the fully qualified name in the code:

```
Imports System.Windows.Forms
Private WithEvents MenuItem as MenuItem
```

Compiling and Executing Managed Code

When .NET code is compiled, it is converted into a .NET Portable Executable (PE) file. The compiler translates the source code into Microsoft intermediate language (MSIL) format. MSIL is CPU-independent code, which means it has to be further converted into native code before executing. Along with the MSIL code, the PE file contains the metadata information contained within the manifest. The incorporation of the metadata in the PE file makes the code *self-describing*. There is no need for additional type library or Interface Definition Language (IDL) files. Because the source code for the various .NET-compliant languages are compiled into the same MSIL and metadata format based upon a common type system, the .NET platform supports language integration. This is a step beyond Microsoft's COM components where, for example, client code written in VB could instantiate and use the methods of a component written in C++. With .NET language integration you can, for example, write a .NET class in VB that inherits from a class written in C# and then overrides some of its methods.

Before the MSIL code in the PE file is executed, a .NET Framework Just-In-Time (JIT) compiler converts it into CPU-specific native code. To improve efficiency, the JIT compiler does not convert all the MSIL code into native code at the same time. MSIL code is converted on an as-needed basis. When a method is executed, the compiler checks to see if the code has already been converted and placed in cache. If it has, the compiled version is used; otherwise the MSIL code is converted and stored in the cache for future calls. Because JIT compilers are written to target different CPU- and OS-specific platforms, developers are freed from having to rewrite their applications to target various platforms. It is conceivable that the programs you write for running on a Windows 2000 server platform will also run on a Unix server. All that is needed is for someone to write a JIT compiler for the Unix architecture.

Using the Visual Studio Integrated Development Environment

It is interesting to note that you can write VB .NET code using a simple text editor and compile it with a command-line compiler. You will find, however, that programming enterprise-level applications using a text editor can be frustrating and not very efficient. Most programmers who code for a living find the use of an Integrated Development Environment (IDE) invaluable in terms of ease of use and increased productivity. Microsoft has developed an exceptional IDE in Visual Studio (VS). Integrated into Visual Studio are many features that make programming for the .NET Framework more intuitive, easier, and productive. VS includes the following:

- Editor features such as auto syntax check, autocomplete, and color highlighting

- One IDE for all .NET languages

- Extensive debugging support including the ability to set breakpoints, step through code, and view and modify variables

- Integrated help documentation

- Drag-and-drop GUI development

- XML and HTML editing

- Automated deployment tools that integrate with Windows Installer

- The ability to view and manage servers from within the IDE

- A fully customizable and extensible interface

The following activity will introduce you to some of the many features available in the VS IDE. Do not get caught up on the coding details but rather concentrate on getting used to working within the VS IDE. As you progress through this book many of the concepts introduced will become more concrete.

ACTIVITY 5-1. TOURING VISUAL STUDIO .NET

In this activity you will become familiar with the following:

- Creating a .NET project and setting project properties

- Using the various editor windows in the VS IDE

- Using the auto syntax check and autocompletion features of the VS IDE

- Compiling assemblies with the VS IDE

Customizing the IDE

To customize the IDE, follow these steps:

1. Launch Visual Studio by clicking Start ➤ Programs ➤ Microsoft Visual Studio .NET and then clicking Microsoft Visual Studio .NET.

2. After VS launches you will be presented with the Start Page. The Start Page contains several tabs on the left side of the window. You should currently be on the Get Started tab. This page has a button for creating new projects and opening existing projects.

> **TIP** *If this is the first time you have launched VS, the My Profile tab will be active. Select the Get Started tab.*

3. Click the What's New tab. The links and information contained on this page are downloaded from Microsoft's developer Web site and contain up-to-date information on resources available for Visual Studio. Take some time to investigate the information and the various links exposed to you on the Start Page.

4. Click the My Profile tab located on the left side of the Start Page.

5. You should see a page that allows you to create a user profile, which controls how the IDE is laid out. Investigate the different settings and how they change the window layout. When you are done investigating the various profiles, select the custom profile with the default keyboard scheme and the Visual Basic 6.0 window layout.

> **TIP** *As you become more comfortable working in the IDE, try experimenting with the different layouts.*

6. Click the Get Started tab located on the left side of the Start Page. On the Tools menu, choose Options. You should be presented with the Options dialog box, which allows you to further customize many aspects of the IDE (see Figure 5-1).

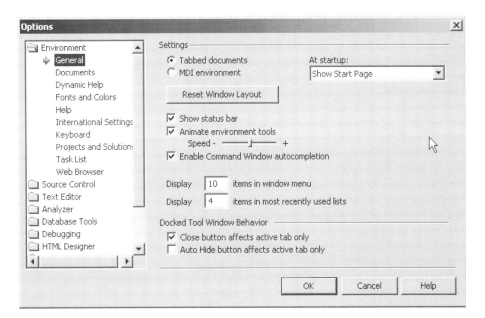

Figure 5-1. Options dialog box

7. Click the Environment folder to expand it. Select Projects and Solutions under the Environment tab. You are presented with options to change the default location of projects and how changes are saved when you build and run a solution. Investigate some of the other customizable options available. Close the Options window when you are done.

Creating a New Project

To create a new project, follow these steps:

1. On the Start Page, under the Get Started tab, click the New Project button.

> **TIP** *You can also use the File menu and select New ➤ Project.*

2. You will be presented with the New Project window. The New Project window allows you to create various projects using built-in templates. There are templates for creating Visual Basic projects, Visual C# projects, Deployment projects, as well as many others (see Figure 5-2).

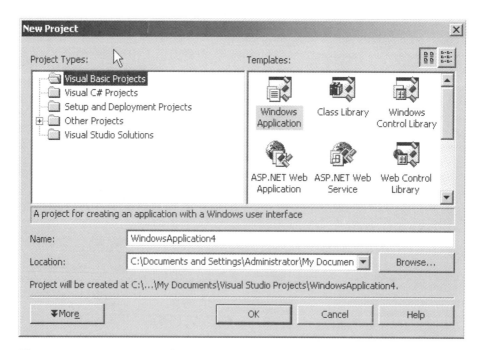

Figure 5-2. New Project window

3. Click the Visual Basic Projects folder. Observe the various VB project templates. There are templates for creating Windows applications, Web applications, class libraries, as well as many others.

4. Click the Windows Application template. Change the name of the application to **DemoChapter5** and click the OK button.

5. When the project opens you will be presented with a form designer for a default form (named Form1) that has been added to the project. To the right of this window you should see the Solution Explorer.

Investigating the Solution Explorer and Class View

To use the Solution Explorer and Class View, follow these steps:

1. The Solution Explorer displays the projects and files that are part of the current solution (see Figure 5-3). By default when you create a project, a solution file is created with the same name as the project. The solution files contain some global information, project linking information, and customization settings such as a task list and debugging information. A solution may contain more than one related project.

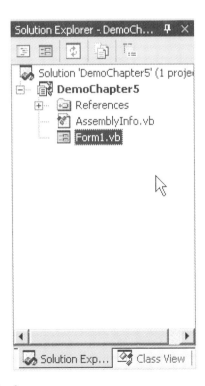

Figure 5-3. Solution Explorer

2. Under the solution node is the project node. The project node organizes the various files and settings related to a project. The project file organizes this information in an XML document, which contains references to the class files that are part of the project, any external references needed by the project, and compilation options that have been set.

3. Under the project node is a References node. If you expand this node you will see a list of the default references that have been included for this type of project. Because this is a Windows application project type, a reference to the System.Windows.Forms namespace has been included by default.

4. Another node visible under the project node is a file called AssemblyInfo.vb. This file contains metadata information that will be compiled as part of the assembly manifest. Double-click this file in the Solution Explorer and review some of the metadata attributes contained in this file.

5. The final item listed under the project node is the class file for the Form1 class. This file has a .vb extension to indicate it is written in VB code. By default the name of the file has been set to the same name as the form. Double-click the file in the Solution Explorer, and the form is shown in Design View. Click the View Code button in the toolbar at the top of the Solution Explorer, and the code editor for the Form1 class will open.

6. By right-clicking the items listed in the Solution Explorer, you gain access to context menus that allow you to perform standard actions on the item selected, such as adding files, deleting files, and viewing property pages. Right-click the DemoChapter5 project in the Solution Explorer and add a class file named **DemoClass1**. The file is added to the Solution Explorer, and it opens in the code editor.

7. Right-click the DemoChapter5 project in the Solution Explorer and choose Properties. The project Property Pages window is displayed (see Figure 5-4). Expand the Common Properties folder and choose General. Notice that, by default, the assembly name and root namespace are set to the name of the project. Form1 has also been designated as the startup object. Close the Property Pages window.

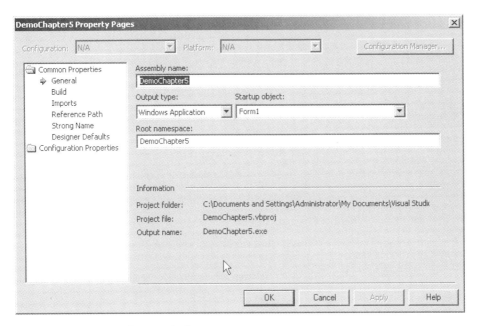

Figure 5-4. Property Pages window

8. At the bottom of the Solution Explorer are two tabs for switching between the Solution Explorer and the Class View. Click the Class View tab. The Class View organizes the project files in terms of the namespace hierarchy. Currently there is only one namespace defined in the project, DemoChapter5, which was created by default when you created the project.

9. Listed under the namespaces are the classes that belong to the namespace. Currently there are two classes, DemoClass1 and Form1. Double-clicking the class node in the Class View will bring up its associated code editor.

10. Under the class node is a listing of the class's methods and properties as well as nodes for base classes inherited by the class and any interfaces implemented by the class. If you expand the bases and interfaces node listed under the Form1 node, you will notice that it inherits from the System.Windows.Forms.Form base class (see Figure 5-5). You can further expand this node to show the methods, properties, and events inherited from this base class.

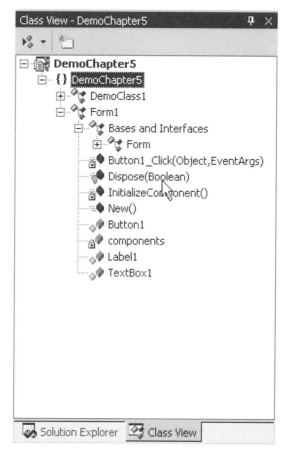

Figure 5-5. Expanded nodes in the Class View

11. Double-click the DemoClass1 node in the Class View to bring up its code editor. Wrap the class definition code in a namespace declaration as shown:

```
Namespace MyDemoNamespace
    Public Class DemoClass1
    End Class
End Namespace
```

12. Notice the updated hierarchy in the Class View. DemoClass1 now belongs to the MyDemoNamespace, which belongs to the DemoChapter5 namespace. The fully qualified name of DemoChapter5 is now DemoChapter5.MyDemoNamespace.DemoClass1.

13. Add the following code to the `DemoClass1` definition:

```
Namespace MyDemoNamespace
    Public Class DemoClass1
        Inherits System.Collections.CaseInsensitiveComparer
    End Class
End Namespace
```

As you add the code, notice the auto selection drop-down list provided (see Figure 5-6). Pressing the Tab key will select the current item on the list.

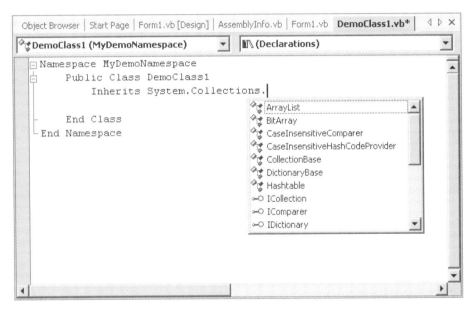

Figure 5-6. Code selection drop-down list

14. A `Bases and Interfaces` node has been added beneath the `DemoClass1` node in the Class View. Expand this node and you will see the base `CaseInsensitiveComparer` class node. Expand this node, and you will see the methods and properties of the `CaseInsensitiveComparer` class.

15. Right-click the `Compare` method node under the `CaseInsensitiveComparer` class node in the Class View and choose Browse Definition. The Object Browser window is opened as a tab in the main window and information on the `Compare` method is displayed. Notice it takes two object arguments, compares them, and returns an integer value based on the result.

> **TIP** *You can also initiate this step by double-clicking the Compare method node in the Class View.*

16. The Object Browser enables you to explore the object hierarchies and to view information about items and methods within the hierarchy (see Figure 5-7). Take some time to explore the Object Browser; when you are finished, close the Object Browser.

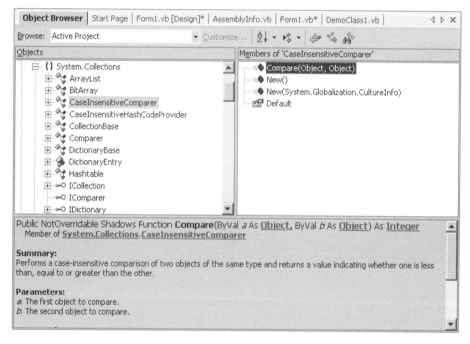

Figure 5-7. Object Browser

Exploring the Toolbox and Properties Window

To explore the Toolbox and Properties Editor, follow these steps:

1. In the main window, select the Form1.vb [Design] tab. Locate the Toolbox tab to the left of the main editing window. Hover the cursor over the tab and it should expand. In the upper-right corner of the Toolbox, you should see the Auto Hide icon. Click the icon to turn off the auto hide feature (see Figure 5-8).

> **TIP** *The Auto Hide icon looks like a thumbtack.*

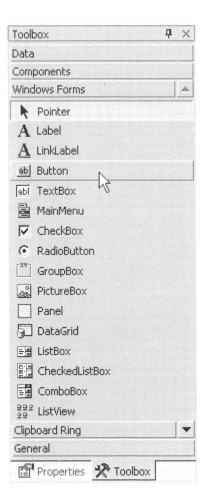

Figure 5-8. Toolbox

2. Under the Windows Forms tab of the Toolbox are controls that you can drag and drop onto your form to build the GUI. There are also other tabs that contain nongraphical components that help make some common programming tasks easier to create and manage. For example, the Data tab contains controls for accessing and managing data stores. You can use the Clipboard Ring tab to access recently copied code.

3. Under the Windows Forms tab, select the Label control. Move the cursor over the form; it should change to a crosshairs pointer. Draw a label on the form by clicking, dragging, and then releasing the mouse. In a similar fashion draw a TextBox control and a Button control on the form. Figure 5-9 shows how the form should look.

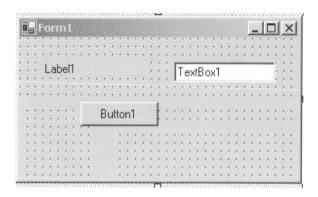

Figure 5-9. Sample form layout

4. Turn the auto hide feature of the Toolbox back on by clicking the thumb-tack icon in the upper-right corner of the Toolbox window.

5. Locate the Properties tab to the right of the main editing window. Hover the cursor over the tab, and it should expand. Turn off the auto hide feature of the window.

TIP *If you cannot locate the Properties tab, you can select it under the View menu.*

6. The Properties window displays the properties of the currently selected object in the Design View. You can also edit many of the object's properties through this window.

7. In the Form1 Design window, click Label1. The Label1 control should be selected in the drop-down list at the top of the Properties window (see Figure 5-10). Locate the Text property and change it to **Enter your password:**.

TIP *You may have to resize the label on the form to see all the text.*

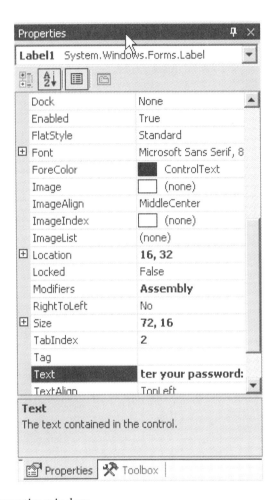

Figure 5-10. Properties window

8. Clear the Text property of TextBox1 and set its PasswordChar to *. Change the Text property of Button1 to **OK**.

9. Save the project by choosing Save All under the File menu.

Building and Executing the Assembly

To build and execute the assembly, follow these steps:

1. In the Solution Explorer, click Form1. At the top of the Solution Explorer, click the View Code toolbar button. The code editor for Form1 will be displayed in the main editing window.

2. The code editor includes a section of collapsed code that was added by the Windows Form Designer when you were dropping controls on the form and setting properties. You can expand and view this code by clicking the plus sign to the left of the code region. After expanding the region and examining some of the code, collapse the region by clicking the minus sign.

3. In the left drop-down list at the top of the code editor, select the Button1 control. In the right drop-down list, select the click event. A method that handles the button-click event is added to the code editor.

4. Add the following code to the method. This code will display a message box containing the password entered in TextBox1:

   ```
   MesgBox("Your password is " & TextBox1.Text)
   ```

5. You should see a blue squiggly line appear under the word MesgBox. The auto syntax check features indicates that MesgBox is not a recognized word. Delete the *e* in MesgBox and move the cursor to the next line of code. The blue squiggly line should disappear.

6. Under the Build menu, choose Build Solution. The Output window shows the progress of compiling the assembly (see Figure 5-11). Once the assembly has been compiled, it is ready for execution.

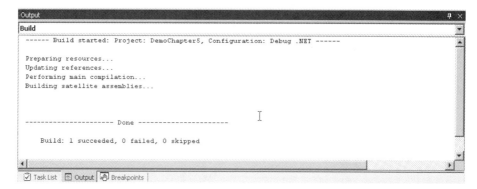

Figure 5-11. Progress of build displayed in the Output window

7. Under the Debug menu, choose Start. This runs the assembly in debug mode. Once the form loads, enter a password and click the OK button. You should see a message box containing the password. Close the message box and the form.

8. Under the File menu choose Save All and exit Visual Studio by selecting Exit under the File menu.

ACTIVITY 5-2. USING THE DEBUGGING FEATURES OF VISUAL STUDIO .NET

In this activity you will become familiar with the following:

- Setting breakpoints and stepping through the code

- Using the various debugging windows in the VS IDE

- Locating and fixing build errors using the Task List window

Stepping Through Code

To step through your code, follow these steps:

1. Start Visual Studio. Select File ➢ Open ➢ Project.

2. Navigate to the `Activity5_2Starter` folder, click the `Act5_2.sln` file, and then click Open.

3. When the project opens, it will contain a form and a class file. You will use these files to test some of the debugging features available in VS .NET.

4. In the Solution Explorer, right-click Form1 and select View Code. Locate the `btnLoadList_Click` method. This code instantiates an instance of the `List` class, calls the `ListNumbers` method, and then fills the ListBox with a list of numbers returned from the method.

5. To set a breakpoint, place the curser on the declaration line of the `btnLoadList_Click` method, right-click and choose Insert Breakpoint. A red dot will appear in the left margin indicating a breakpoint has been set (see Figure 5-12).

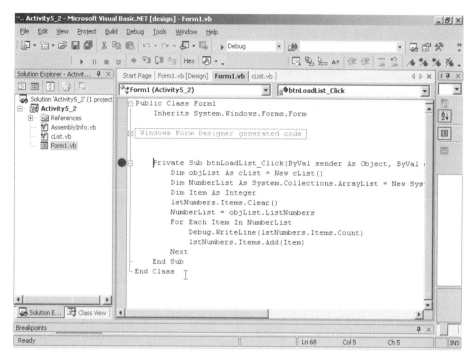

Figure 5-12. Setting a breakpoint in the code editor

6. On the Debug menu, choose Start. When the form appears, click the Load List button. Program execution will pause at the breakpoint. A yellow arrow indicates the next line of code that will be executed.

7. Under the View menu, choose Toolbars and click the Debug toolbar. (A check next to the toolbar name indicates it is visible.) To step through the code one line at a time, select the Step Into button on the Debug toolbar (see Figure 5-13). Continue stepping through the code until you get to the ListNumbers function in the List class.

TIP *You can also find the Step Into feature under the Debug menu.*

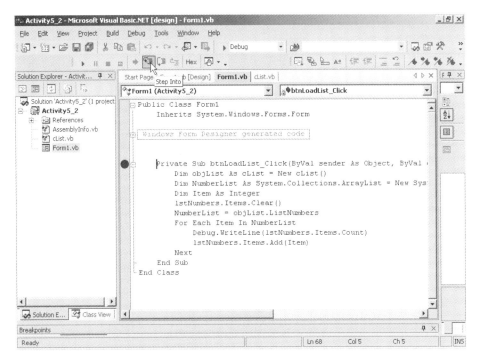

Figure 5-13. Using the Debug toolbar

8. Step through the code until the for-next loop has looped a couple of times. At this point you are probably satisfied this code is working and want to step out of this method. On the Debug toolbar, click the Step Out button. You should return to the btnLoadList_Click method of Form1.

9. Continue stepping through the code until the for-next loop has looped a couple of times. At this point you may want to return to runtime mode; to do this, click the Continue button on the Debug toolbar.

10. When the form appears, click the Load List button to enter break mode again. Step through the code until you get to the line that calls the ListNumbers method of the objList object:

```
NumberList = objList.ListNumbers
```

11. On the Debug toolbar, choose the Step Over button. This will execute the method and reenter break mode after execution returns to the calling code. After stepping over the method, continue stepping through the code for several lines and then choose Stop on the Debug toolbar. Click the red dot in the left margin to remove the breakpoint.

Setting Conditional Breakpoints

To set conditional breakpoints, follow these steps:

1. In the Solution Explorer, right-click List and select View Code. Locate the ListNumbers method. Set a breakpoint on the following line of code:

```
NumberList.Add(i)
```

2. Open the Breakpoints window by selecting Windows ➤ Breakpoints under the Debug menu. You can also press the Ctrl+Alt+B keys. You should see the breakpoint you just set listed.

3. Right-click the breakpoint in the Breakpoints window and select Properties. You will see the Breakpoint Properties dialog box (see Figure 5-14).

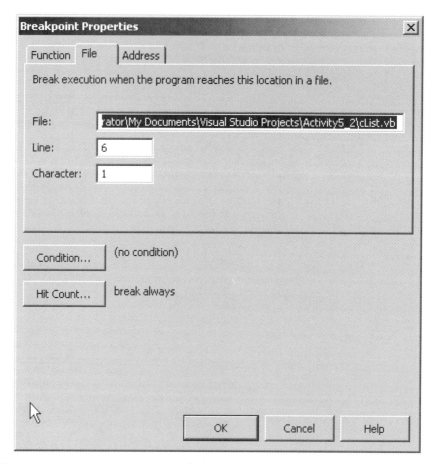

Figure 5-14. Breakpoint Properties dialog box

4. On the File tab of the Breakpoint Properties dialog box, click the Condition button. You will be presented with Breakpoint Condition dialog box. Enter **i** = **3** into the condition expression and click the OK button (see Figure 5-15). Click the OK button to close the Breakpoint Properties page.

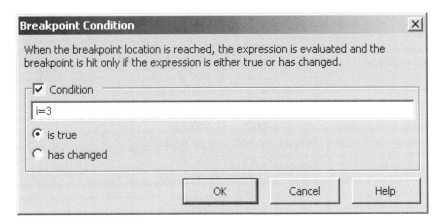

Figure 5-15. Breakpoint Condition dialog box

5. On the Debug menu, choose Start. When the form appears, click the Load List button. Program execution will pause, and you will see a yellow arrow indicating the next line that will be executed.

6. On the Debug menu, choose Windows and click the Locals window. The Locals window is displayed at the bottom of the screen (see Figure 5-16). The value of i is displayed in the Locals window. Verify that it is 3. Step through the code using the Debug toolbar and watch the value of i change in the Locals window. Click the Stop Debugging button in the Debug toolbar.

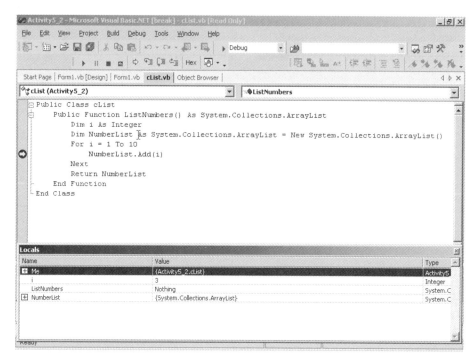

Figure 5-16. Locals window

7. Locate the Output window at the bottom of your screen and click the Breakpoints tab. Right-click the breakpoint in the Breakpoints window and select Properties. Click the Condition button, clear the current condition by deleting the condition text, and click the OK button. Click the Hit Count button, set it to break when the hit count equals 4, and click OK. Close the Breakpoint Properties page.

8. On the Debug menu, choose Start. When the form appears, click the Load List button. Program execution will pause. A yellow arrow is visible indicating the next line of code that will execute.

9. Right-click the NumberList statement and select Add Watch. A Watch window will be displayed with NumberList in it. Notice that NumberList is a System.Collections.ArrayList type. Expand the plus sign next to NumberList. Click the plus sign next to the _Items entry. Verify that the array contains three items (see Figure 5-17). Step through the code and watch the array fill with items. Click the Stop Debugging button in the Debugger toolbar.

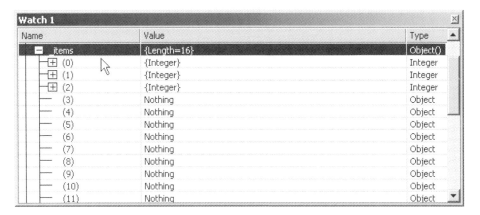

Figure 5-17. The Watch window

10. To find out more about the System.Collections.ArrayList type, high-light the code statement in the code editor and press the F1 key. A Help window is displayed with information about the type.

Locating and Fixing Build Errors

To locate and fix build errors, follow these steps:

1. In the Solution Explorer, right-click Form1 and select View Code. Locate the btnLoadList_Click method. Locate the following line of code and comment it out by placing a single quote in front of it:

```
Dim Item As Integer
```

2. On the Build menu, choose Build Solution. The Task List window will appear at the bottom of the screen indicating two build errors (see Figure 5-18).

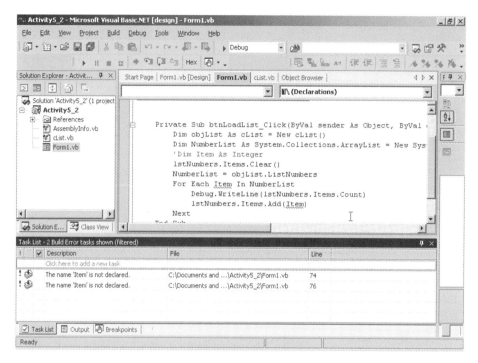

Figure 5-18. Locating build errors with the Task List window

3. Double-click the line containing the build error in the Task List window. The corresponding code will become visible in the code editor.

4. Uncomment the line you commented in step 1 by deleting the single quote. On the Build menu, choose Build Solution. This time the Output window is displayed at the bottom of the screen indicating no build errors.

5. Save the project and exit Visual Studio.

Summary

In this chapter you looked at the following:

- The main components that make up the .NET Framework

- Some of the features of the Common Language Runtime

- How .NET code compiles and executes

- The .NET Framework class library

- How code is organized into namespaces and assemblies

- The features of the Visual Studio integrated development environment

This chapter introduced you to the fundamentals of the .NET Framework. You reviewed some of the underlying goals of the .NET Framework. You also looked at how the .NET Framework is structured and how code is compiled and executed by the CLR. These concepts are relevant and consistent across all .NET-compliant programming languages. The next chapter is the first in a series of three that looks at how the OOP concepts—such as class structure, inheritance, and polymorphism—are implemented in Visual Basic .NET code.

CHAPTER 6

Creating Classes

IN THE PREVIOUS CHAPTER you looked at how the .NET Framework was developed and how programs execute under the framework. The chapter introduced you to the Visual Studio Integrated Development Environment, and you gained some familiarity with working in it. You are now ready to start coding! This chapter is the first of three that will introduce you to how classes are created and used in Visual Basic. This chapter covers the basics of creating and using classes. You will create classes, add attributes and methods, and instantiate object instances of the classes in client code.

After reading this chapter you should be familiar with the following:

- How objects used in object-oriented programming are dependent upon class definition files

- The important role encapsulation plays in object-oriented programming

- How to define the properties and methods of a class

- The purpose of class constructors

- Using instances of classes in client code

- The process of overloading class constructors and methods

- Creating and testing class definition files with Visual Studio

Introducing Objects and Classes

In Object-Oriented Programming (OOP), you use objects in your programs to encapsulate the data associated with the entities with which the program is working. For example, a human resources application would need to work with employees. Employees have attributes associated with them that need to be tracked. You may be interested in such things as their names, addresses, departments, and so on. Although you would track the same attributes for all employees, each employee would have unique values for these attributes. In the human resources application, an `Employee` object would obtain and modify the attributes associated with an employee. In OOP, the attributes of an object are referred to as *properties*.

Along with the properties of the employees, the human resource application also needs an established set of *behaviors* exposed by the `Employee` object. For example, one behavior of an employee the human resources department would be interested in is the ability to request time off. In OOP, objects expose behaviors through *methods*. The `Employee` object would contain a `RequestTimeOff` method that would encapsulate the implementation code.

The properties and methods of the objects used in OOP are defined through *classes*. A class is a blueprint that defines the attributes and behaviors of the objects that are created as instances of the class. If you have completed the proper analysis and design of the application, you should be able to refer to the Unified Modeling Language (UML) design documentation to determine what classes need to be constructed and the properties and methods these classes will contain. The UML class diagram contains the initial information you need to construct the classes of the system.

To demonstrate the construction of a class using Visual Basic (VB), you will create a simple `Employee` class. The `Employee` class will have properties and methods that encapsulate and work with employee data as part of a fictitious human resources application.

Defining Classes

Let's walk through the source code needed to create a class definition. The first line of code defines the code block as a class definition using the keyword class followed by the name of the class. The keyword `Public` is an access modifier that makes this class available to all client code. The class definition block ends with the `End Class` statement. For example:

```
Public Class Employee
......
End Class
```

Creating Class Properties

After defining the starting and ending point of the class code block, the next step is to define the instance variables contained in the class. These variables will hold the data that an instance of your class will manipulate. The `Private` keyword ensures that these instance variables can only be manipulated by the code inside the class.

NOTE *For more information on scoping, see Appendix A, "Fundamental Programming Concepts."*

For example:

```
Private _empID As Integer
Private _loginName As String
Private _password As String
Private _department As String
Private _fullName As String
```

When a user of the class (*client code*) needs to query or set the value of these instance variables, public properties are exposed to them. Inside the property block of code there is a Set block and a Get block. The Get block returns the value of the private instance variable to the user of the class. This code provides a readable property. The Set block provides a write-enabled property; it passes a value sent in by the client code to the corresponding private instance variable. For example:

```
Public Property FullName()
        Get
            Return _fullName
        End Get
        Set(ByVal Value)
            _fullName = Value
        End Set
End Property
```

Newcomers to OOP often ask why you need to go through so much work to get and set properties—couldn't you just create public instance variables that the user could read and write to directly? The answer lies in one of the fundamental tenants of OOP: *data encapsulation*. Data encapsulation means that the client code does not have direct access to the data. When working with the data, the client code must use clearly defined properties and methods accessed through an instance of the class. Some of the benefits of encapsulating the data in this way are the following:

- Preventing unauthorized access to the data

- Ensuring data integrity through error checking

- Creating read-only or write-only properties

- Isolating users of the class from changes in the implementation code

For example, you could check to make sure the password is at least six characters long:

```
Public Property Password() As String
       Get
             Return _password
       End Get
       Set(ByVal Value As String)
           if Len(Value) >= 6 then
               _password = Value
           Else
               Throw New Exception("Password must be at least 6 characters.")
           end if
       End Set
    End Property
```

Restricting Property Access

By using the ReadOnly keyword and eliminating the Set block inside the Property block, you create a read-only property. The following code shows how to make the EmployeeID property read-only:

```
Public ReadOnly Property EmployeeID() As Integer
       Get
             Return _empID
       End Get
End Property
```

Conversely, if you use the WriteOnly keyword and eliminate the Get block, you create a write-only property. The following code shows a password property that has been made a write-only property:

```
Public WriteOnly Property Password() As String
       Set(ByVal Value As String)
           _password = Value
       End Set
End Property
```

Creating Class Methods

Class methods define the behaviors of the class. Class methods take the form of either a function or a subprocedure. Remember that a function returns a value back to the calling code, and a sub procedure does not. A behavior you could define for the Employee class is a method that would verify employee logins:

```
Public Sub Login(ByVal loginName As String, ByVal password As String)
        'Data normally retrieved from database. Hard coded for demo only.
        If loginName = "Smith" And _password = "js" Then
            _empID = 1
            Department = "IS"
            FullName = "Jerry Smith"
        ElseIf loginName = "Jones" And password = "mj" Then
            _empID = 2
            Department = "HR"
            FullName = "Mary Jones"
        Else
            Throw New Exception("Login incorrect.")
        End If
End Sub
```

When client code calls the Login method of the class, the login name and password are checked. If they match a current employee, the instance of the class is populated with attributes of the employee. If the login name and password do not match a current employee, an exception is passed back to the client code.

> **NOTE** *For more information on exceptions, see Appendix B, "Error Handling in VB .NET."*

When an employee needs to be added to the database, a method of the Employee class called AddEmployee is defined that returns the newly assigned employee ID to the client. The method also populates the object instance of the Employee class with the attributes of the newly added employee. For example:

```
Public Function AddEmployee(ByVal loginName As String, _
    ByVal password As String, ByVal department As String, _
    ByVal fullName As String) As Integer
        'Data normally saved to database.
        _empID = 3
        LoginName = loginName
```

```
            Password = password
            Department = department
            FullName = fullName
            Return EmployeeID
End Function
```

The following activity introduces you to developing and using classes in the Visual Studio development environment.

In this activity you will become familiar with the following:

- Creating a VB class definition file using Visual Studio

- Creating and using an instance of the class from VB client code

Creating the Employee *Class*

To create the Employee class, follow these steps:

1. Start Visual Studio. On the File menu, choose Open ➤ Project.

2. Navigate to the Activity6_1Starter folder, click the Act6_1.sln file, and click Open.

3. When the project opens it will contain a login form. You will use this form later to test the Employee class you create.

4. On the Project menu, choose Add Class.

5. In the Add New Item dialog box, rename the class file to **Employee.vb** and click Open.

6. Visual Studio adds the Employee.vb file to the project and adds the following class definition code to the file:

```
Public Class Employee
End Class
```

7. Add code to create the following private instance variables to the class definition file:

```
Private _empID As Integer
Private _loginName As String
Private _password As String
Private _securityLevel As Integer
```

8. Next, add the following public properties to access the private instance variables defined in step 7:

```
Public ReadOnly Property EmployeeID() As Integer
    Get
        Return _empID
    End Get
End Property
Public Property LoginName() As String
    Get
        Return _loginName
    End Get
    Set(ByVal Value As String)
        _loginName = Value
    End Set
End Property
Public Property Password() As String
    Get
        Return _password
    End Get
    Set(ByVal Value As String)
        _password = Value
    End Set
End Property
Public ReadOnly Property SecurityLevel() As Integer
    Get
        Return _securityLevel
    End Get
End Property
```

9. Add the following Login method to the class definition:

```
Public Sub Login(ByVal loginName As String, ByVal password As String)
            LoginName = loginName
            Password = password
```

```
'Data normally retrieved from database. Hard coded for demo only
If loginName = "Smith" And password = "js" Then
    _empID = 1
    _securityLevel = 2
ElseIf loginName = "Jones" And password = "mj" Then
    _empID = 2
    _securityLevel = 4
Else
    Throw New Exception("Login incorrect.")
End If
End Sub
```

10. On the Build menu, choose Build Solution and make sure there are no build errors in the Task List window. If there are, fix them and rebuild.

Testing the Employee Class

To test the Employee class, follow these steps:

1. Open frmLogin in the code editor and locate the btnLogin click event code.

> **TIP** *Double-clicking the Login button in the form designer will also bring up the event code in the code editor.*

2. Declare and instantiate a variable of type Employee called oEmployee:

```
Dim oEmployee As Employee = New Employee()
```

3. Call the Login method of the oEmployee object, passing in the values of the login name and the password from the textboxes on the form:

```
oEmployee.Login(txtName.Text, txtPassword.Text)
```

4. Show a message box stating the user's security level retrieved by reading the SecurityLevel property of the oEmployee object:

```
MsgBox("You have security clearance level " & _
oEmployee.SecurityLevel.ToString)
```

5. On the File menu, choose Save All.

6. On the Build menu, choose Build Solution and make sure there are no build errors in the Task List window. If there are, fix them and rebuild.

7. On the Debug menu, choose Start to run the project. Test the login form by entering a login name of **Smith** and a password of **js**. You should get a message indicating a security level of 2. Try entering your name and a password of **pass**; you should get a message indicating the login failed.

8. After testing the login procedure, close the form, which in turn will stop the debugger.

Using Constructors

In OOP you use *constructors* to perform any processing that needs to occur when an object instance of the class becomes instantiated. For example, you could initialize properties of the object instance or establish a database connection. When an object instance of a class is instantiated by client code, a constructor method called New is executed. The following constructor is used in the Employee class to initialize the properties of an object instance of the Employee class. An employee ID is passed in to the constructor to retrieve the values from data storage:

```
Public Sub New(ByVal empID As Integer)
        _empID = empID

        'retrieval of data is hardcoded for testing purposes only
        If _empID = 1 Then
            LoginName = "Smith"
            Password = "js"
            Department = "IS"
            FullName = "Jerry Smith"
        ElseIf _empID = 2 Then
            LoginName = "Jones"
            Password = "mj"
            Department = "HR"
            FullName = "Mary Jones"
        Else
            Throw New Exception("Invalid EmployeeID")
        End If
End Sub
```

Using Destructors

Microsoft has incorporated automatic memory into the Common Language Runtime (CLR) in the form of a system Garbage Collector (GC) class. When an object is created in code, the CLR allocates the memory from the *managed heap*. The managed heap is a portion of the system's memory reserved for the CLR. Periodically the GC checks the managed heap for objects that are no longer referenced, and it releases the memory. Although using an automated GC process has many advantages for .NET developers, it has a downside; programmers do not know when an object will be garbage collected.

> **NOTE** *This is referred to as* nondeterministic finalization.

When the GC cleans up an object, the GC executes a destructor method (in .NET languages this is the `Finalize` method) for the object. Because of the time delay between when an object is no longer referenced and when it gets garbage collected, relying on a destructor to clean up system resources such as database connections can cause significant performance problems. You could force the collection of an object, thereby forcing the execution of the `Finalize` method, by calling the `Collect` method of the GC system class. However, this also causes significant processing overhead and a degradation of system performance.

To get around these problems, Microsoft recommends that if you need to run cleanup code when a client no longer needs an object, then create a custom method that the client code will call when it no longer needs the object reference. The following code implements a custom `Dispose` method that cleans up resources. A call to the `Dispose` method is also added to the `Finalize` method of the class so that if the client forgets to call the `Dispose` method, it will be called when an object instance is garbage collected:

```
Public Sub Dispose()
    'Clean up code goes here.
End Sub
Protected Overrides Sub Finalize()
    Dispose()
End Sub
```

> **NOTE** *Error checking should be included so that an error is not triggered when the* Dispose *method is called a second time.*

> **TIP**   *Implementing a custom* `Dispose` *method is not trivial. I suggest you thoroughly review the .NET Framework documentation before attempting it.*

Overloading Methods

The ability to overload methods is a useful feature of OOP languages. You overload methods in a class by defining multiple methods that have the same name but contain different signatures. A *method signature* is a combination of the name of the method and its parameter type list. If you change the parameter type list, you create different method signatures. Parameter type lists can differ by containing a different number of parameters or different parameter types. The compiler will determine which method to execute by examining the parameter type list passed in by the client. It is important to note that changing how a parameter is passed (in other words, from byVal to byRef) does not change the method signature. Altering the return type of the method will also not create a unique method signature.

> **NOTE**   *For a more detailed discussion of method signatures and passing arguments, refer to Appendix A, "Fundamental Programming Concepts."*

Suppose you want to provide two methods of the Employee class that will allow you to add an employee to the database. The first method assigns a username and password to the employee when they are added. The second method adds the employee information but defers the assignment of username and password until later. You can easily accomplish this by overloading the AddEmployee method of the Employee class (as shown in Listing 6-1).

Listing 6-1. Overloading the AddEmployee *Method*

```
Public Function AddEmployee(ByVal loginName As String, _
    ByVal password As String, ByVal department As String, _
    ByVal fullName As String) As Integer
    'Data normally saved to database.
    _empID = 3
    LoginName = loginName
    Password = password
    Department = department
    FullName = fullName
    Return EmployeeID
```

```
End Function
Public Function AddEmployee(ByVal department As String, _
    ByVal fullName As String) As Integer
    'Data normally saved to database.
    _empID = 3
    LoginName = ""
    Password = ""
    Department = department
    FullName = fullName
    Return EmployeeID
End Function
```

Because the parameter type list of the first method (string, string) differs from the parameter type list of the second method (string, string, string, string), the compiler can determine which method to invoke.

A common technique in OOP is to overload the constructor of the class. For example, when an instance of the Employee class is created, one constructor could be used for new employees and another could be used for current employees by passing in the employee ID when the class instance is instantiated by the client (shown in Listing 6-2).

Listing 6-2. Overloading the Constructor

```
Public Sub New()
        _empID = -1
 End Sub
 Public Sub New(ByVal empID As Integer)
    _empID = empID
        'retrieval of data is hardcoded for testing purposes only.
        If empID = 1 Then
            LoginName = "Smith"
            Password = "js"
            Department = "IS"
            FullName = "Jerry Smith"
        ElseIf empID = 2 Then
            LoginName = "Jones"
            Password = "mj"
            Department = "HR"
            FullName = "Mary Jones"
        Else
            Throw New Exception("Invalid EmployeeID")
        End If
 End Sub
```

When client code instantiates an instance of the class, the compiler will examine the arguments passed and determine which constructor to use.

The following activity introduces you to overloading constructors and methods using the Visual Studio development environment.

ACTIVITY 6-2. OVERLOADING METHODS AND CONSTRUCTORS

In this activity you will become familiar with the following:

- Creating and overloading the class constructor method

- Using overloaded constructors of a class from client code

- Overloading a method of a class

- Using overloaded methods of a class from client code

Creating and Overloading Class Constructors

To create and overload class constructors, follow these steps:

1. Start Visual Studio, and select File ➢ Open Project.

2. Navigate to the `Activity6_2Starter` folder, click the `Act6_2.sln` file, and then click Open.

3. When the project opens, it will contain a frmEmployeeInfo form that you will use to test the `Employee` class. The project also contains the `Employee.vb` file that contains the `Employee` class definition code.

4. Open the code window for the `Employee.vb` file and examine the code. The class contains several properties pertaining to employees that need to be maintained.

5. Add the following private method to the class that simulates the generation of a new employee ID:

```
Private Function GetNextID() As Integer
     'simulates the retrival of next
     'available id from data base.
     Return 100
End Function
```

6. Locate the default class constructor Sub New() and add code that calls the GetNextID method and assigns the return value to the private instance variable _empID:

```
Public Sub New()
      intEmpID = GetNextID()
End Sub
```

7. Overload the default constructor method by adding a second Sub New method with an integer parameter of empID:

```
Public Sub New(ByVal empID As Integer)
       'Constructor for existing employee
End Sub
```

8. Add the following code that simulates extracting the employee data from a database and assigns the data to the instance properties of the class:

```
'Simulates retrieval from database
If empID = 1 Then
    _empID = empID
    LoginName = "smith"
    Password = "js"
    SSN = 123456789
    Department = "IS"
ElseIf empID = 2 Then
    _empID = empID
    LoginName = "jones"
    Password = "mj"
    SSN = 987654321
    Department = "HR"
Else
    Throw New Exception("Invalid Employee ID")
End If
```

9. On the Build menu, choose Build Solution and make sure there are no build errors in the Task List window. If there are, fix them and rebuild.

Testing the Employee Class Constructors

To test the Employee class constructors, follow these steps:

1. Open the frmEmployeeInfo code in the code editor and locate the btnNewEmp click event code.

2. Declare and instantiate a variable of type Employee called oEmployee:

   ```
   Dim oEmployee As Employee = New Employee()
   ```

3. Show a message to the user that a new employee ID has been generated and employee information can be updated to the database:

   ```
   MsgBox("A new employee id has been generated of " & _
   oEmployee.EmployeeID & "." & vbCrLf & _
   "Fill in the values for the " & _
   "new employee and press update.")
   ```

4. Update the EmployeeID textbox with the employee ID and disable the EmployeeID textbox:

   ```
   txtEmpID.Text = oEmployee.EmployeeID.ToString
   txtEmpID.Enabled = False
   clear the remaining text boxes.
   txtLoginName.Text = ""
   txtPassword.Text = ""
   txtSSN.Text = ""
   txtDepartment.Text = ""
   ```

5. On the Build menu, choose Build Solution and make sure there are no build errors in the Task List window. If there are, fix them and rebuild.

6. Locate the btnExistingEmp click event code.

7. Declare and instantiate a variable of type Employee called oEmployee. Retrieve the employee ID from the txtEmpID textbox and pass it as an argument in the constructor:

   ```
   Dim oEmployee As Employee = New Employee(CInt(txtEmpID.Text))
   ```

8. Show a message to the user that information for the employee has been retrieved and employee information can be changed and updated to the database:

```
MsgBox("Information for Employee ID " & _
oEmployee.EmployeeID & "." & vbCrLf & _
"Make any necessary changes for the " & _
"employee and press update.")
```

9. Update the EmployeeID textbox with the employee ID and disable the EmployeeID textbox:

```
txtEmpID.Text = oEmployee.EmployeeID.ToString
txtEmpID.Enabled = False
```

10. Fill in the remaining textboxes with the values of the Employee object's properties:

```
txtLoginName.Text = oEmployee.LoginName
txtPassword.Text = oEmployee.Password
txtSSN.Text = oEmployee.SSN.ToString
txtDepartment.Text = oEmployee.Department
```

11. On the Build menu, choose Build Solution and make sure there are no build errors in the Task List window. If there are, fix them and rebuild.

12. On the Debug menu, choose Start to run the project and test the code.

13. When the employeeInfo form is displayed, click the New Employee button.

14. Click the Reset button.

15. Enter a value of 1 for the employee ID and click the Get Existing Employee button.

16. After testing the constructors, close the form, which will in turn stop the debugger.

Overloading a Class Method

To overload a class method, follow these steps:

1. Open the `Employee.vb` code in the code editor.

2. Add the following `Update` method to the class definition file. This method simulates the updating of the employee security information to a database:

```
Public Function Update(ByVal loginName As String, _
    ByVal password As String) As String
    LoginName = loginName
    Password = password
    Return "Security Info Updated."
End Function
```

3. Add a second `Update` method that will simulate the updating of the employee human resources data to a database:

```
Public Function Update(ByVal SSNumber As Integer, _
    ByVal department As String) As String
    SSN = SSNumber
    Department = department
    Return "HR Info Updated."
End Function
```

4. On the Build menu, choose Build Solution and make sure there are no build errors in the Task List window. If there are, fix them and rebuild.

Testing the Overloaded `Update` Method

To test the overloaded `Update` method, follow these steps:

1. Open the frmEmployeeInfo code in the code editor and locate the btnUpdateSI click event code.

2. Declare and instantiate a variable of type `Employee` called oEmployee. Retrieve the employee ID from the txtEmpID textbox and pass it as an argument in the constructor:

```
Dim oEmployee As Employee = New Employee(CInt(txtEmpID.Text))
```

3. Call the Update method, passing the values of the login name and password from the textboxes. Show the method return message to the user in a message box:

```
MsgBox(oEmployee.Update(txtLoginName.Text, txtPassword.Text))
```

4. Update the login name and password textboxes with the property values of the Employee object:

```
txtLoginName.Text = oEmployee.LoginName
txtPassword.Text = oEmployee.Password
```

5. Add similar code to the btnUpdateHR click event procedure to simulate updating the human resources information:

```
Dim oEmployee As Employee = New Employee(CInt(txtEmpID.Text))
MsgBox(oEmployee.Update(CInt(txtSSN.Text), txtDepartment.Text))
txtSSN.Text = oEmployee.SSN.ToString
txtDepartment.Text = oEmployee.Department
```

6. On the Build menu, choose Build Solution and make sure there are no build errors in the Task List window. If there are, fix them and rebuild.

7. On the Debug menu, choose Start to run the project and test the code.

8. Enter a value of 1 for the employee ID and click the Get Existing Employee button.

9. Change the values for the security information and click the Update button.

10. Change the values for the human resources information and click the Update button.

11. After testing the Update method, close the form, which will in turn stop the debugger.

Summary

In this chapter you looked at the following:

- How objects used in OOP are dependent upon class definition files

- The important role encapsulation plays in OOP

- How to define the properties and methods of a class

- The purpose of class constructors

- Using instances of classes in client code

- The process of overloading class constructors and methods

- Creating and testing class definition files with Visual Studio

This chapter gave you a firm foundation in creating and using classes in VB code. Now that you are comfortable constructing and using classes, you are ready to look at implementing some of the more advanced features of OOP. In the next chapter you will concentrate on how inheritance and polymorphism are implemented in VB code. As an object-oriented programmer, it is important for you to become familiar with these concepts and learn how to implement them in your programs.

CHAPTER 7

Creating Class Hierarchies

IN THE PREVIOUS CHAPTER you looked at how to create classes, add attributes and methods, and instantiate object instances of the classes in client code. This chapter introduces you to *inheritance*. Inheritance is one of the most powerful and fundamental features of any object-oriented programming language. Using inheritance, you create base classes that encapsulate common functionality. Other classes can be derived from these base classes. The derived classes inherit the properties and methods of the base classes and extend the functionality as needed.

Another fundamental object-oriented programming feature introduced in this chapter is *polymorphism*. Polymorphism allows a base class to define methods that will be implemented by any derived classes. The base class defines the message signature that derived classes must adhere to, but the implementation code of the method is left up to the derived class. The power of polymorphism is the fact that clients know they can implement methods of classes of the base type in the same fashion. Even though the internal processing of the method may be different, the client knows the inputs and outputs of the methods will be the same.

After reading this chapter you should be familiar with the following:

- Creating base classes

- Creating derived classes

- Using base and derived classes in client code

- How access modifiers are used to control inheritance

- Overriding base class methods

- Implementing interfaces

- Implementing polymorphism through inheritance

- Implementing polymorphism through interfaces

Understanding Inheritance

One of the most powerful features of any Object-Oriented Programming (OOP) language is inheritance. Inheritance is the ability to create a base class with properties and methods that can be used in classes derived from the base class. The purpose of inheritance is to create a base class that encapsulates properties and methods needed in multiple derived classes of the same type. For example, you could create a base class Account. A GetBalance method is defined in the Account class. You can then create two separate classes, a SavingsAccount and a CheckingAccount class. Because the SavingsAccount and the CheckingAccount class use the same logic to retrieve balance information, they would inherit the GetBalance method from the base class Account. This enables you to create one common code base that is easier to maintain and manage. The derived classes are not limited to the properties and methods of the base class, however. The derived classes would define methods and properties that must be made unique to them. For example, when withdrawing money from a checking account, the business rules require that a minimum balance be maintained. A minimum balance is not required when withdrawing money from a savings account. In this case, each of the derived classes would contain its own unique definition of a Withdraw method.

To create a derived class in Visual Basic code, you use the Inherits keyword along with the name of the base class when defining the derived class. Listing 7-1 demonstrates the creation of a CheckingAccount class derived from an Account base class.

Listing 7-1. Creating CheckingAccount

```
Public Class Account
     Private m_lngAccountNumber As Long
Public Property AccountNumber() As Long
        Get
             Return m_lngAccountNumber
        End Get
        Set(ByVal Value As Long)
            m_lngAccountNumber = Value
        End Set
     End Property
     Public Function GetBalance() As Double
         'Code to retrieve account balance from db.
     End Function
End Class

Public Class CheckingAccount
    Inherits Account
```

```
        Private m_dblMinBalance As Double
        Public Sub Withdraw(ByVal Amount As Double)
              'Code to withdraw from account.
        End Sub
End Class
```

The following code could be implemented by a client creating an object instance of CheckingAccount. Notice to the client there is no distinction made between the call to the GetBalance method and the call to the Withdraw method. In this case, the client has no knowledge of the Account class; instead, both methods appear to have been defined by CheckingAccount.

```
Dim oCheckAccount As CheckingAccount = New CheckingAccount()
oCheckAccount.AccountNumber = 1000
oCheckAccount.GetBalance()
oCheckAccount.Withdraw(500)
```

Using MustInherit

At this point a client can access the GetBalance method through an instance of the derived CheckingAccount class or directly through an instance of the base Account class. Sometimes you may want to have a base class that cannot be instantiated by client code. Access to the methods and properties of the class must be through a derived class. In this case, you would construct the base class using the MustInherit modifier. The following code shows the Account class definition with the MustInherit key word added:

```
Public MustInherit Class Account
```

This makes the Account class an *abstract* class. An abstract class is a class that defines the interfaces of the methods and properties that will be inherited by the derived classes. Because an abstract class does not contain any implementation code, only the interface definitions, it cannot be instantiated directly. For clients to gain access to the GetBalance method, they must instantiate an instance of the derived CheckingAccount class.

Using NotInheritable

By default all classes can be inherited. When creating classes that can be inherited, you must take care that they are not modified in such a way that derived classes no longer function in the intended way. If you are not careful, you can create complex inheritance chains that are hard to manage and debug. For example, you create a derived CheckingAccount class based on the Account class. Another programmer can come along and create a derived class based on the CheckingAccount and use it in ways you never intended. (This could easily occur in large programming teams with poor communication and design.) Using the NotInheritable modifier you can create classes that you know will not be derived from. This type of class is often referred to as a *sealed* or *final* class. By making a class not inheritable, you avoid the complexity and overhead associated with altering the code of base classes. The following code demonstrates the use of the NotInheritable modifier when constructing a class definition:

```
Public NotInheritable Class CheckingAccount
```

Using Access Modifiers in Base Classes

When setting up class hierarchies using inheritance it is important you manage how the properties and methods of your classes are accessed. Two access modifiers you have looked at this far are Public and Private. If a method or property of the base class is exposed as Public, it is accessible by both the derived class and any client of the derived class. If you expose the property or method of the base class as Private, then it is not accessible directly by the derived class or the client. There are times when you may want to expose a property or method of the base class to a derived class but not to a client of the derived class. In this case you would use the Protected access modifier. The following code demonstrates the use of the Protected access modifier:

```
Protected Function GetBalance() As Double
            'Code to retrieve account balance from db.
End Function
```

By defining the GetBalance method as protected it becomes accessible to the derived class CheckingAccount but not to the client code accessing an instance of the CheckingAccount class.

ACTIVITY 7-1. CREATING AND USING BASE AND DERIVED CLASSES WITH VISUAL STUDIO

In this activity you will become familiar with the following:

- Creating a base class and derived classes

- Using access modifiers in the base class

- Creating an abstract base class

Creating the Account Class

To create the Account class, follow these steps:

1. Start Visual Studio. On the File menu, choose Open ➤ Project.

2. Navigate to the Activity7_1Starter folder, click on the Act7_1.sln file, and then click Open.

3. When the project opens, it will contain a teller form. You will use this form later to test the classes you will create.

4. On the Project menu, choose Add Class.

5. In the Add New Item dialog box, rename the class file to **Account.vb** and click Open.

6. The Account.vb file is added to the project, and the Account class definition code is added to the file.

7. Add code to create the following Protected instance variable to the class definition file:

```
Protected m_intAccountNumber As Integer
```

8. Add the following GetBalance method to the class definition:

```
Public Function GetBalance(ByVal AccountNumber As Integer) As Double
        m_intAccountNumber = AccountNumber
        'Data normally retrieved from database. Hard coded for demo only
        If m_intAccountNumber = 1 Then
                Return 1000
        ElseIf m_intAccountNumber = 2 Then
                Return 2000
        Else
                Throw New Exception("Account number incorrect.")
        End If
End Function
```

9. After the Account class, add the following code to create the CheckingAccount and SavingsAccount derived classes:

```
Public Class CheckingAccount
        Inherits Account
End Class
Public Class SavingsAccount
        Inherits Account
End Class
```

10. On the Build menu, choose Build Solution and make sure there are no build errors in the Task List window. If there are, fix them and rebuild.

Testing the Classes

To test the classes, follow these steps:

1. Open the frmTeller in the code editor and locate the btnGetBalance click event code.

2. Inside the event procedure, prior to the Try block, declare and instantiate a variable of type CheckingAccount called oCheckingAccount, a variable of type SavingsAccount called oSavingsAccount, and a variable of type Account called oAccount:

```
Dim oCheckingAccount As CheckingAccount = New CheckingAccount()
Dim oSavingsAccount As SavingsAccount = New SavingsAccount()
Dim oAccount As Account = New Account()
```

3. Depending on which radio button is selected, call the `GetBalance` method of the appropriate object and pass the account number value from the account number textbox. Show the return value in the balance textbox. Place the following code in the `Try` block prior to the `Catch` statement:

```
If rdbChecking.Checked Then
    txtBalance.Text = oCheckingAccount.GetBalance _
        (CInt(txtAccountNumber.Text)).ToString
ElseIf rdbSavings.Checked Then
    txtBalance.Text = oSavingsAccount.GetBalance _
        (CInt(txtAccountNumber.Text)).ToString
ElseIf rdbGeneral.Checked Then
    txtBalance.Text = oAccount.GetBalance _
        (CInt(txtAccountNumber.Text)).ToString
End If
```

4. On the Build menu, choose Build Solution and make sure there are no build errors in the Task List window. If there are, fix them and rebuild.

5. On the Debug menu, choose Start to run the project. Enter an account number of **1** and click the `GetBalance` button for the `CheckingAccount` type. You should get a balance of 1,000. Test the other account types you should get the same result.

6. After testing, close the form, which in turn will stop the debugger.

Creating a Protected Method

At this point, the `GetBalance` method of the base class is public, which means that it can be accessed by client code of the derived classes. You will alter this so that the `GetBalance` method can only be accessed by the code of the derived classes and not by clients of the derived classes. To alter the `GetBalance` method, follow these steps:

1. Locate the `GetBalance` method of the `Account` class.

2. Change the access modifier of the `GetBalance` method from `Public` to `Protected`.

3. Switch to the frmTeller code editor and locate the `btnGetBalance` click event code.

4. Hover the cursor over the call to the GetBalance method of the oCheckingAccount object. You will see a warning stating that it is a protected function and not accessible in this context.

5. Comment out the code between the Try and the Catch statements.

6. Switch to the Account.vb code editor.

7. Add code to create the following private instance variable to the SavingsAccount class definition file:

```
Private m_dblBalance As Double
```

8. Add the following Withdraw method to the SavingsAccount class. This function calls the protected method of the Account base class:

```
Public Function Withdraw(ByVal AccountNumber As Integer, _
    ByVal Amount As Double) As Double
    m_dblBalance = GetBalance(AccountNumber)
    If m_dblBalance >= Amount Then
        m_dblBalance -= Amount
        Return m_dblBalance
    Else
        Throw New Exception("Not enough funds.")
    End If
End Function
```

9. On the Build menu, choose Build Solution and make sure there are no build errors in the Task List window. If there are, fix them and rebuild.

Testing the Withdraw Method

To test the Withdraw method, follow these steps:

1. Open the frmTeller in the code editor and locate the btnWithdraw click event code.

2. Inside the event procedure, prior to the Try block, declare and instantiate a variable of type SavingsAccount called oSavingsAccount:

```
Dim oSavingsAccount As SavingsAccount = New SavingsAccount()
```

3. Call the `Withdraw` method of the `oSavingsAccount`. Pass the account number value from the account number textbox and the withdraw amount from the amount textbox. Show the return value in the balance text box. Place the following code in the `Try` block prior to the `Catch` statement:

```
txtBalance.Text = oSavingsAccount.withdraw _
    (CInt(txtAccountNumber.Text), CDbl(txtAmount.Text)).ToString
```

4. On the Build menu, choose Build Solution and make sure there are no build errors in the Task List window. If there are, fix them and rebuild.

5. On the Debug menu, choose Start to run the project and test the `Withdraw` method of the `SavingsAccount` class.

6. Enter an account number of **1** and a withdraw amount of **200**. You should get a resulting balance of 800.

7. Enter an account number of **1** and a withdraw amount of 2,000. You should get an insufficient funds message.

8. After testing the `Withdraw` method, close the form, which in turn will stop the debugger.

Creating an Abstract Class

At this point the `Account` base class is public, which means that it can be instantiated by client code of the derived classes. You will alter this so that the `Account` base class can only be accessed by the code of the derived classes and cannot be instantiated and accessed by clients of the derived classes. To create the abstract class, follow these steps:

1. Locate the `Account` class definition in the `Account.vb` code.

2. Add the `MustInherit` keyword to the class definition code.

```
Public MustInherit Class Account
```

3. On the Build menu, choose Build Solution. You should receive a build error in the Task List window. Find the line of code causing the error:

```
Dim oAccount As Account = New Account()
```

4. Comment out the line of code, and on the Build menu, choose Build Solution. It should now build with no errors.

5. Save and close the project.

Overriding Methods of the Base Class

When a derived class inherits a method from the base class, it inherits the implementation of the method defined in the base class. As the designer of the base class you may want to allow a derived class its own unique implementation of the method. This is known as *overriding* the base class method. By default the derived class cannot override the implementation code of the base class. To allow overriding of a method of the base class, you include the keyword Overridable in the method definition. In the derived class, you define a method with the same method signature and indicate it is overriding a base class method with the Overrides key word. The following code demonstrates the creation of an Overridable deposit method in the Account base class:

```
Public Overridable Sub Deposit(ByVal Amount As Double)
    'Base class implementation code.
End Sub
```

To override the deposit method in the derived CheckingAccount class, you would use the following code:

```
Public Overrides Sub Deposit(ByVal dblAmount As Double)
    'Derived class implementation code.
End Sub
```

One caveat to watch out for is when a derived class inherits from the base class and a second derived class inherits from the first derived class. When a method overrides a method in the base class, it becomes overridable by default. To limit an overriding method from being overridden further up the inheritance chain, you must include the NotOverridable keyword in front of the Overrides keyword in the method definition of the derived class. The following code in the CheckingAccount class would prevent the overriding of the Deposit method if the CheckingAccount was derived from:

```
Public NotOverridable Overrides Sub Deposit(ByVal Amount As Double)
    'Derived class implementation code.
End Sub
```

When you indicate that a base class method is overridable, derived classes have the option of overriding the method or using the implementation provided by the base class. There may be some cases where you want to use a base class method as a template for the derived classes. The base class has no implementation code but is used to define the method signatures used in the derived classes. Remember, this type of class is referred to as an *abstract* base class. You define the class with the `MustInherit` keyword and then define the method with the `MustOverride` key word. The following code is used to create an abstract `Account` base class:

```
Public MustInherit Class Account
    'Other code here . . .
    Public MustOverride Sub Deposit(ByVal Amount As Double)
End Class
```

Notice that because there is no implementation code defined in the base class for the deposit method, the `End Sub` statement is omitted.

Using `MyBase`, `MyClass`, *or* `Me`?

A situation may arise in which you are calling an overridable method in the base class from another method of the base class, and the derived class overrides the method of the base class. When a call is made to the base class method from an instance of the derived class, the base class will call the overridden method of the derived class. Listing 7-2 shows an example of this situation. A `CheckingAccount` base class contains an overridable `GetMinBalance` method. The `InterestBearingCheckingAccount` class, inheriting from the `CheckingAccount` class, overrides the `GetMinBalance` method.

Listing 7-2. Overriding the `GetMinBalance` *Method*
```
Public Class CheckingAccount
    Private m_dblBalance As Double = 2000
    Public ReadOnly Property Balance()
        Get
            Return m_dblBalance
        End Get
    End Property
    Public Overridable Function GetMinBalance() As Double
        'This function is overidden in a derived class.
        'Base class functionality implemented here.
        Return 200
    End Function
```

```
        Public Overridable Sub Withdraw(ByVal Amount As Double)
            Dim dblMinBalance As Double = GetMinBalance()
            If dblMinBalance < (Balance - Amount) Then
                m_dblBalance -= Amount
            Else
                Throw New Exception("Minimum balance error.")
            End If
        End Sub
End Class
Public Class InterestBearingCheckingAccount
    Inherits CheckingAccount
    Public Overrides Function GetMinBalance() As Double
        'This function is overidden.
        'Derived class functionality implemented here.
        Return 1000
    End Function
End Class
```

A client instantiates an object instance of the InterestBearingCheckingAccount class and calls the Withdraw method. In this case the overridden GetMinimumBalance of the InterestBearingCheckingAccount is executed and a minimum balance of 1,000 is used:

```
Private oInterestBearingChecking As InterestBearingCheckingAccount = _
        New IntrestBearingCheckingAccount()
oInterestBearingChecking.Withdraw(500)
```

When the call was made to the Withdraw method, you could have prefaced it with the Me qualifier:

```
Dim dblMinBalance As Double = Me.GetMinBalance()
```

Because the Me qualifier is the default qualifier if none is used, the code would execute the same way as previously demonstrated. The most derived class implementation (that has been instantiated) of the method is executed. In other words, if a client instantiates an instance of the InterestBearingCheckingAccount class, as was demonstrated previously, the base class's call to the GetMinimumBalance is made to the derived class's implementation. On the other hand, if a client instantiates an instance of the CheckingAccount class, the base class's call to the GetMinimumBalance is made to its own implementation.

Using MyClass

There may be times when you want to make sure the base class will call its own method implementation even though the client is using an object instance of the derived class. In this situation, the MyClass qualifier prefaces the call to the over-ridden base class method. In Listing 7-3, a call is made to a method that determines the account's average balance for the month. Depending on the result, the CalculateInterest method of the base class will either call its own implementation of the GetInterestRate method or the derived class's implementation.

Listing 7-3. Determining the Account's Average Monthly Balance

```
Public Class CheckingAccount
    Public Function GetAverageBalance() As Double
        Dim dblAverageBalance as Double
        'Determine average monthly balance
        Return dblAverageBalance
    End Function
    Public Overridable Function GetInterestRate() As Single
        Dim sngInterestRate as Single
        'Retrieve current rate
        Return sngInterestRate
    End Function
    Public Sub CalculateInterest(ByVal Amount As Double)
        Dim sngInterestRate as Single
          If GetAverageBalance() < 1000 then
                'Call the base class method
                sngInterestRate = MyBase.GetInterestRate()
            Else
                'Call the derived class method
                sngInterestRate = Me.GetInterestRate()
        End If
            'code continues....
    End Sub
End Class
```

Be careful not to confuse the MyClass qualifier with the Me qualifier. The Me qualifier is the default qualifier if none is used. When the Me qualifier is used, the most derived class implementation of the method is executed. This is different from the MyClass qualifier, which will use the current class's implementation.

Using MyBase

In some cases you may want to develop a derived class method that still uses the implementation code in the base class but also augments it with its own implementation code. In this case you would create an overriding method in the derived class and call the code in the base class using the MyBase qualifier. The following code demonstrates the use of the MyBase qualifier:

```
Public Overrides Sub Deposit(ByVal Amount As Double)
    'Derived class implementation code.
    'Call to base clase implementation.
    MyBase.Deposit(Amount)
End Sub
```

This technique is particularly useful if the base class has overloaded constructors that you need to call. In this case you would call the overloaded constructor from the derived class's constructor using the MyBase qualifier. One important point to remember is that a call to the base class constructor must be the first executable code statement in the derived class's constructor. The following code shows the process of calling the base class's constructor from a derived class's constructor:

```
Public Sub New()
    'call to base constructor.
    MyBase.new()
    'derived class constructor code.
    m_minBalance = 100
End Sub
```

ACTIVITY 7-2. OVERRIDING BASE CLASSES

In this activity you will become familiar with the following:

- Overriding methods of a base class

- Using the MyBase and the MyClass qualifiers in base and derived classes

Overriding the Account *Class*

To override the Account class, follow these steps:

1. Start Visual Studio. On the File menu, choose Open ➢ Project.

2. Navigate to the Activity7_2Starter folder, click the Act7_2.sln file, and then click Open.

3. When the project opens, it will contain a teller form. You will use this form later to test the classes you will create.

4. The project also contains a BankClasses.vb file. This file contains code for the Account base class and the derived classes SavingsAccount and Checking account.

5. Examine the Withdraw method defined in the base class Account. This function checks to see whether there are sufficient funds in the account and, if there are, updates the balance. You will override this function in the CheckingAccount class to ensure that a minimum balanced is maintained.

6. Change the Withdraw method definition in the Account class to indicate it is overridable:

    ```
    Public Overridable Function Withdraw(ByVal intAccountNumber As Integer, _
        ByVal dblAmount As Double) As Double
    ```

7. Add the following GetMinimumBalance method to the CheckingAccount class definition:

    ```
    Public Function GetMinimumBalance() As Double
        Return 200
    End Function
    ```

8. Add the following overriding Withdraw method to the CheckingAccount class definition. This method adds a check to see that the minimum balance is maintained after a withdrawal:

    ```
    Public Overrides Function Withdraw(ByVal Amount As Double) As Double
        If m_dblBalance >= Amount + GetMinimumBalance() Then
            m_dblBalance -= Amount
            Return m_dblBalance
    ```

```
        Else
              Throw New Exception("Not enough funds.")
        End If
    End Function
```

9. On the Build menu, choose Build Solution and make sure there are no build errors in the Task List window. If there are, fix them and rebuild.

Testing the Withdraw Methods

To test the Withdraw methods, follow these steps:

1. Open the frmTeller in the code editor and locate the btnWithdraw click event code.

2. Depending on which radio button is selected, call the Withdraw method of the appropriate object and pass the value of the txtAmount textbox. Show the return value in the txtBalance textbox:

```
If rdbChecking.Checked Then
    txtBalance.Text =
oCheckingAccount.Withdraw(CDbl(txtAmount.Text)).ToString
ElseIf rdbSavings.Checked Then
    txtBalance.Text =
oSavingsAccount.Withdraw(CDbl(txtAmount.Text)).ToString
End If
```

3. On the Build menu, choose Build Solution and make sure there are no build errors in the Task List window. If there are, fix them and rebuild.

4. On the Debug menu, choose Start to run the project.

5. Enter an account number of **1**, choose the Checking option button, and click the Get Balance button. You should get a balance of 1,000.

6. Enter a withdrawal amount of **200** and click the withdraw button. You should get a resulting balance of 800.

7. Enter a withdraw amount of **700** and click the Withdraw button. You should get an insufficient funds message because the resulting balance would be less than the 200 minimum balance.

8. Enter an account number of **1**, choose the Savings option button and click the Get Balance button. You should get a balance of 1,000.

9. Enter a withdraw amount of **600** and click the Withdraw button. You should get a resulting balance of 400.

10. Enter a withdraw amount of **400** and click the Withdraw button. You should get a resulting balance of 0 because there is no minimum balance for the savings account that uses the Account base class's Withdraw method.

11. After testing, close the form, which in turn will stop the debugger.

Using the MyBase Qualifier

At this point the Withdraw method of the CheckingAccount class overrides the Account class's Withdraw method. None of the code in the base class's method is executed. You will now alter the code so that when the CheckingAccount class's code is executed, it also executes the base class's Withdraw method. Follow these steps:

1. Locate the Withdraw method of the Account class.

2. Change the implementation code so that it decrements the balance by the amount passed to it:

```
Public Overridable Function Withdraw _
    (ByVal Amount As Double) As Double
    m_dblBalance -= Amount
    Return m_dblBalance
End Function
```

3. Change the Withdraw method of the CheckingAccount class so that after it checks for sufficient funds it calls the Withdraw method of the Account base class:

```
Public Overrides Function Withdraw(ByVal Amount As Double) As Double
    If m_dblBalance >= Amount + GetMinimumBalance() Then
        Return MyBase.Withdraw(Amount)
    Else
        Throw New Exception("Not enough funds.")
    End If
End Function
```

4. Add a `Withdraw` method to the `SavingsAccount` class that is similar to the `Withdraw` method of the `CheckingAccount` class but does not check for a minimum balance:

```
Public Overrides Function Withdraw(ByVal Amount As Double) As Double
    If m_dblBalance >= Amount Then
        Return MyBase.Withdraw(Amount)
    Else
        Throw New Exception("Not enough funds.")
    End If
End Function
```

5. On the Build menu, choose Build Solution and make sure there are no build errors in the Task List window. If there are, fix them and rebuild.

Testing the `Withdraw` Method

To test the `Withdraw` method, follow these steps:

1. On the Debug menu, choose Start to run the project.

2. Enter an account number of **1**, choose the Checking option button and click the Get Balance button. You should get a balance of 1,000.

3. Enter a withdraw amount of **600** and click the Withdraw button. You should get a resulting balance of 400.

4. Enter a withdraw amount of **300** and click the Withdraw button. You should get an insufficient funds message because the resulting balance would be less than the 200 minimum.

5. Enter an account number of **1**, choose the Savings option button and click the Get Balance function. You should get a balance of 1,000.

6. Enter a withdraw amount of **600** and click the Withdraw button. You should get a resulting balance of 400.

7. Enter a withdraw amount of **300** and click the Withdraw button. You should get a resulting balance of 100 because there is no minimum balance for the savings account that uses the `Account` base class's `Withdraw` method.

8. After testing, close the form, which in turn will stop the debugger.

Using the MyClass *Qualifier*

To demonstrate the use of the MyClass qualifier, you will create an InterestCheckingAccount that represents an interest earning checking account that will derive from the CheckingAccount. To create the InterestCheckingAccount, follow these steps:

1. Alter the GetMinimumBalance method of the CheckingAccount class so that it is overridable.

2. Add the following code to create the InterestCheckingAccount:

```
Public Class InterestCheckingAccount
      Inherits CheckingAccount
      Public Overrides Function GetMinimumBalance() As Double
            Return 400
      End Function
End Class
```

3. Replace the existing code in the Withdraw method with following code. This code makes a call to the GetMinimumBalance method of the derived InterestCheckingAccount and the GetMinimumBalance method of the base CheckingAccount class and uses the larger in the calculation:

```
Dim dblMinimumBalance As Double
If GetMinimumBalance() >= MyClass.GetMinimumBalance Then
    dblMinimumBalance = GetMinimumBalance()
Else
    dblMinimumBalance = MyClass.GetMinimumBalance
End If

If m_dblBalance >= Amount + dblMinimumBalance Then
        Return MyBase.Withdraw(Amount)
Else
    Throw New Exception("Not enough funds.")
End If
```

4. On the Build menu, choose Build Solution and make sure there are no build errors in the Task List window. If there are, fix them and rebuild.

Testing the GetMinimumBalance *Methods*

To test the GetMinimumBalance methods, follow these steps:

1. Open the frmTeller in the code editor and locate and uncomment the following line of code located near the top of the file:

```
Private oInterestCheckingAccount As _
InterestCheckingAccount = New InterestCheckingAccount()
```

2. Locate the btnBalance click event and uncomment the following ElseIf block of code. This will call the GetBalance method for the oInterestCheckingAccount object:

```
ElseIf rdbInterestChecking.Checked Then
    oInterestCheckingAccount.AccountNumber = CInt(txtAccountNumber.Text)
    txtBalance.Text = oInterestCheckingAccount.GetBalance().ToString
```

3. Change the If block in the btnWithdraw event to call the Withdraw method of the oInterestCheckingAccount object if the InterestChecking radio button is selected:

```
If rdbChecking.Checked Then
    txtBalance.Text = oInterestCheckingAccount.Withdraw _
        (CDbl(txtAmount.Text)).ToString
ElseIf rdbInterestChecking.Checked Then
    txtBalance.Text = oInterestCheckingAccount.Withdraw _
        (CDbl(txtAmount.Text)).ToString
ElseIf rdbInterestChecking.Checked Then
    txtBalance.Text = oInterestCheckingAccount.Withdraw _
        (CDbl(txtAmount.Text)).ToString
End If
```

4. On the Build menu, choose Build Solution and make sure there are no build errors in the Task List window. If there are, fix them and rebuild.

5. On the Debug menu, choose Start to run the application.

6. Enter an account number of **1**, choose the Interest Checking option button and click the Get Balance button. You should get a balance of 1,000.

7. Enter a withdraw amount of **400** and click the Withdraw button. You should get a resulting balance of 600.

8. Enter a withdraw amount of **300** and click the Withdraw button. You should get an insufficient funds message because the resulting balance would be less than the 400 minimum set in the `InterestCheckingAccount`.

9. Close the form, which in turn will stop the debugger.

10. Change the return value of the `InterestCheckingAccount` class's `getMinimumBalance` method to 100.

11. On the Build menu, choose Build Solution and make sure there are no build errors in the Task List window. If there are, fix them and rebuild.

12. On the Debug menu, choose Start to run the application.

13. Enter an account number of **1**, choose the Interest Checking option button and click the Get Balance button. You should get a balance of 1,000.

14. Enter a withdraw amount of **500** and click the Withdraw button. You should get a resulting balance of 500.

15. Enter a withdraw amount of **200** and click the Withdraw button. You should get a balance of 300, which is more than the minimum of 200 set by the `CheckingAccount` class's `GetMinimumBalance` method.

16. Enter a withdraw amount of **150** and click the Withdraw button. You should get an insufficient funds message because the resulting balance would be less than the 200 minimum set in the `CheckingAccount`. Remember, the code you added to the `CheckingAccount` class's `Withdraw` method calls both the `CheckingAccount` class's `GetMinimumBalance` method and the `InterestCheckingAccount` class's `GetMininmumBalance` method and uses the greater value:

```
If GetMinimumBalance() >= MyClass.GetMinimumBalance Then
    dblMinimumBalance = GetMinimumBalance()
Else
    dblMinimumBalance = MyClass.GetMinimumBalance
End If
```

17. Close the form, which in turn will stop the debugger. Exit Visual Studio

Overloading Methods of the Base Class

Methods inherited by the derived class can be overloaded. You overload
a method by using the key word `Overloads` when defining the method. The
method signature of the overloaded class must use the same name as the overloaded method, but the parameter lists must differ. This is the same as when you
overload methods of the same class except that the `Overloads` keyword is
optional and usually omitted. The following code demonstrates the overloading
of a derived method:

```
Public Class Account
    Public Sub Withdraw(ByVal Amount As Double)
        'implementation code
    End Sub
End Class
Public Class CheckingAccount
    Inherits Account
    Public Overloads Sub Withdraw(ByVal Amount As Double, _
        ByVal MinimumBalance As Double)
        'Implementation code
    End Sub
End Class
```

Using Shadowing

When a derived class inherits a method from the base class, it may shadow the
method instead of overriding the method. If a method is defined in the derived
class with the same method signature as the method of the base class, then it
effectively hides the method of the base class. In this situation, not only is the
method of the base class hidden but so are any overloaded methods in the base
class. The following code shows how shadowing can occur when the `Overrides`
keyword is left out of the overriding method:

```
Public Class Account
    Public Overridable Sub Withdraw(ByVal Amount As Double)
        'implementation code
    End Sub
    Public Overridable Sub Withdraw(ByVal Amount As Double, _
        ByVal MinimumBalance As Double)
        'Implementation code
    End Sub
End Class
```

```
Public Class CheckingAccount
     Inherits Account
     Public Sub Withdraw(ByVal Amount As Double, _
           ByVal MinimumBalance As Double)
           'Implementation code
     End Sub
End Class
```

Although the Integrated Development Environment (IDE) will issue a warning, the code will still compile. If you intend to shadow a base class method, you should explicitly use the Shadows keyword in the definition of the shadowing method of the derived class:

```
Public Shadows Sub Withdraw(ByVal Amount As Double, _
     ByVal MinimumBalance As Double)
      'Implementation code
End Sub
```

Implementing Interfaces

As you saw earlier, you can create an abstract base class that does not contain any implementation code but defines the method signatures that must be used by any class that inherits from the base class. When using an abstract class, the derived classes must provide the implementation code for the inherited methods. You could use another technique to accomplish a similar result. In this case, instead of defining an abstract class, you would define an interface that defines the method signatures.

> **NOTE** *Interfaces can also define properties and events.*

Classes that implement the interface are contractually required to implement the interface signature definition and cannot alter it. This technique is useful to ensure that client code using the classes know what methods are available, how they should be called, and what return values to expect. The following code shows how you declare an interface definition:

```
Public Interface IAccount
     Function GetAccountInfo() As String
End Interface
```

A class implements the interface by using the `Implements` keyword. When a class implements an interface it must provide implementation code for all methods defined by the interface. The following code demonstrates how a `CheckingAccount` class and a `SavingsAccountClass` implement the `IAccount` interface. Notice that the keyword `Implements` indicates the class implements the interface, and it is also used to indicate when a method of the class is implementing a method of the interface:

```
Public Class CheckingAccount
    Implements IAccount
    Public Function GetAccountInfo() As String _
        Implements IAccount.getAccountInfo
        Return "Printing Checking Account Info"
    End Function
End Class
Public Class SavingsAccount
    Implements IAccount
    Public Function GetAccountInfo() As String _
        Implements IAccount.getAccountInfo
        Return "Printing Savings Account Info"
    End Function
End Class
```

Because implementing an interface and inheriting from an abstract base class are similar, you might ask why you should bother using an interface. The main advantage of using interfaces is that a class can implement multiple interfaces. Visual Basic does not support inheritance from more than one class. As a workaround to multiple inheritance, the ability to implement multiple interfaces was introduced. Another advantage to implementing interfaces is that at compile-time clients can instantiate an object instance based on an interface. During runtime any object of a class type that implements the interface can be used. This is the basis for a type of *polymorphism*, which is discussed in the next section.

Understanding Polymorphism

Polymorphism is the ability of objects based on different classes to respond to the same method call using their own unique method implementation. This simplifies client code because the client code does not have to worry about which class type it is referencing as long as the class types implement the same method interfaces. For example, you want all account classes to contain a `GetAccountInfo` method with the same interface definition but different implementations based on account type. Client code could loop through a collection of account-type classes, and the compiler would determine at runtime which specific account-type implementation needs to be executed. If you later add a new account type that implements the `GetAccountInfo` method, you do not have to alter existing client code.

You can achieve polymorphism either by using inheritance or by implementing interfaces. The following code demonstrates the use of inheritance. First you define the base and derived classes:

```
Public MustInherit Class Account
    Public MustOverride Function GetAccountInfo() As String
End Class

Public Class CheckingAccount
    Inherits Account
    Public Overrides Function GetAccountInfo() As String
        Return "Printing Checking Account Info"
    End Function
End Class

Public Class SavingsAccount
    Inherits Account
    Public Overrides Function GetAccountInfo() As String
        Return "Printing Savings Account Info"
    End Function
End Class
```

You can then create a collection class to hold a collection of classes of type `Account`:

```
Imports System.Collections.CollectionBase
Public Class AccountCollection
    Inherits CollectionBase
    Public Sub add(ByVal value As Object)
        list.Add(value)
    End Sub
    Public Sub remove(ByVal value As Object)
        list.Remove(value)
    End Sub
End Class
```

You can then loop through the collection class and call the `GetAccountInfo` method:

```
Dim oAccountCollection As AccountCollection = New AccountCollection()
Dim oCheckAccount As Account = New CheckingAccount()
Dim oSavingsAccount As Account = New SavingsAccount()
oAccountCollection.add(oCheckAccount)
oAccountCollection.add(oSavingsAccount)

Dim oItem as Account
For Each oItem In oAccountCollection
    MsgBox(oItem.GetAccountInfo)
Next
```

You can also achieve a similar result by using interfaces. Instead of inheriting from the base class Account, you would define and implement an IAccount interface:

```
Public Interface IAccount
    Function GetAccountInfo() As String
End Interface

Public Class CheckingAccount
    Implements IAccount
    Public Function GetAccountInfo() As String _
        Implements IAccount.GetAccountInfo
        Return "Printing Checking Account Info"
    End Function
End Class

Public Class SavingsAccount
    Implements IAccount
    Public Function GetAccountInfo() As String _
        Implements IAccount.GetAccountInfo
        Return "Printing Savings Account Info"
    End Function
End Class
```

You can then use the collection class to hold a collection of interfaces of type IAccount:

```
Dim oAccountCollection As AccountCollection = New AccountCollection()
Dim oCheckAccount As IAccount = New CheckingAccount()
Dim oSavingsAccount As IAccount = New SavingsAccount()
oAccountCollection.add(oCheckAccount)
oAccountCollection.add(oSavingsAccount)
```

You can then loop through the collection class and call the GetAccountInfo method:

```
Dim oItem As IAccount
For Each oItem In oAccountCollection
    MsgBox(oItem.GetAccountInfo)
 Next
```

ACTIVITY 7-3. INVESTIGATING POLYMORPHISM

In this activity you will become familiar with the following:

- Creating polymorphism through inheritance

- Creating polymorphism through interfaces

Implementing Polymorphism Using Inheritance

To implement polymorphism using inheritance, follow these steps:

1. Start Visual Studio. On the File menu, choose Open ➢ Project.

2. Navigate to the Activity7_3Starter folder, click the Act7_3.sln file, and then click Open.

3. When the project opens, it will contain a teller form. You will use this form later to test the classes you will create.

4. The project also contains a BankClass.vb file. This file contains code for an AccountCollection class, which you will use to hold a collection of objects declared as type Account.

5. Examine the code for the AccountCollection class. Notice that it inherits from a base class CollectionBase from the System.Collections namespace. This base class included in the Common Language Runtime (CLR) provides functionality for working with strongly typed collections.

6. After the code for the AccountCollection class, add the code to create an abstract base class with a MustOverride method GetAccountInfo that takes no parameters and returns a string:

```
Public MustInherit Class Account
     Public MustOverride Function GetAccountInfo() As String
End Class
```

7. Add code to create two derived classes, CheckingAccount and SavingsAccount. These classes will override the GetAccountInfo method of the base class:

```
Public Class CheckingAccount
     Inherits Account
     Public Overrides Function GetAccountInfo() As String
          Return "Printing Checking Account Info"
     End Function
End Class

Public Class SavingsAccount
     Inherits Account
     Public Overrides Function GetAccountInfo() As String
          Return "Printing Savings Account Info"
     End Function
End Class
```

8. On the Build menu, choose Build Solution and make sure there are no build errors in the Task List window. If there are, fix them and rebuild.

Testing the Polymorphic Method

To test the polymorphic method, follow these steps:

1. Open the frmTeller in the code editor and locate the btnAccountInfo click event code.

2. Instantiate an instance of the `AccountCollection` as type `AccountCollection`:

```
Dim oAccountCollection As AccountCollection = New AccountCollection()
```

3. Instantiate an instance of the `CheckingAccount` and `SavingsAccount` as type `Account`. By instantiating these as the base type class, you are only exposing the common functionality inherited from the base class. You can now work with these objects generically in our client code:

```
Dim oCheckAccount As CheckingAccount = _
      New CheckingAccount()
Dim oSavingsAccount As SavingsAccount = _
      New SavingsAccount()
```

4. Add the `oCheckingAccount` and `oSavingsAccount` to the collection using the `Add` method of the `oAccountCollection`:

```
oAccountCollection.add(oCheckAccount)
oAccountCollection.add(oSavingsAccount)
```

5. Loop through the collection and call the `GetAccountInfo` method of each object in the collection:

```
Dim oItem as Account
For Each oItem In oAccountCollection
      MsgBox(oItem.GetAccountInfo)
Next
```

6. On the Build menu, choose Build Solution and make sure there are no build errors in the Task List window. If there are, fix them and rebuild.

7. On the Debug menu, choose Start to run the project and click the Account Info button. You should see a message box for each object in the collection implementing its own version of the `GetAccountInfo` method.

8. After testing the polymorphism, close the form, which in turn will stop the debugger.

Implementing Polymorphism Using an Interface

To implement polymorphism using an interface, follow these steps:

1. View the code for the BankClass.vb file in the code editor.

2. Comment out the code for the Account, CheckingAccount, and the SavingsAccount classes.

3. Change the Add method of the AccountCollection class so that it accepts items of type IAccount:

```
Public Sub Add(ByVal Item as IAccount)
      List.Add(Item)
End Sub
```

4. Define an interface IAccount that contains the GetAccountInfo method:

```
Public Interface IAccount
      Function GetAccountInfo() As String
End Interface
```

5. Add code to create two classes, CheckingAccount and SavingsAccount. These classes will implement the IAccount interface:

```
Public Class CheckingAccount
      Implements IAccount
      Public Function GetAccountInfo() As String _
          Implements IAccount.GetAccountInfo
          Return "Printing Checking Account Info"
      End Function
End Class
Public Class SavingsAccount
      Implements IAccount
      Public Function GetAccountInfo() As String _
          Implements IAccount.GetAccountInfo
          Return "Printing Savings Account Info"
      End Function
End Class
```

6. On the File menu, choose Save All.

Testing the Polymorphic Method

To test the polymorphic method, follow these steps:

1. Open the frmTeller in the code editor and locate the `btnAccountInfo` click event code.

2. Change the instantiation code for `oItem` so that it is instantiated as type `IAccount`:

   ```
   Dim oItem as IAccount
   ```

3. On the Build menu, choose Build Solution and make sure there are no build errors in the Task List window. If there are, fix them and rebuild.

4. On the Debug menu, choose Start to run the project and click the Account Info button. You should see a message box for each object in the collection implementing its own version of the `GetAccountInfo` method.

5. After testing the polymorphism, close the form, which in turn will stop the debugger.

Summary

In this chapter you looked at the following:

- Creating base classes

- Creating derived classes

- Using base and derived classes in client code

- How access modifiers are used to control inheritance

- Overriding base class methods

- Implementing interfaces

- Implementing polymorphism through inheritance

- Implementing polymorphism through interfaces

This chapter gave you a firm foundation at understanding and implementing two of OOP's most powerful features: inheritance and polymorphism. Being able to implement these features is fundamental to becoming a successful object-oriented programmer regardless of the language implementation chosen.

In the next chapter, you will take a closer look at how the objects in your applications collaborate together. The topics covered include how objects pass messages to one another, how events drive your programs, how data is shared among instances of a class, and how exceptions are handled.

CHAPTER 8

Implementing Object Collaboration

IN THE PREVIOUS CHAPTER you looked at how class hierarchies are created in Visual Basic. The chapter also introduced the concepts of inheritance, polymorphism, and interfaces. In this chapter you will look at how the objects of the application work together to perform the tasks required. You will look at how objects communicate through messaging and how application processing initiates through events. Another important concept reviewed in this chapter is how the objects respond and communicate exceptions that may occur as they carry out their assigned tasks.

After reading this chapter you should be familiar with the following:

- The process of object communication through messaging

- The different types of messaging that can occur

- How objects can respond to events and publish their own events

- How to use delegation in Visual Basic applications

- The process of issuing and responding to exceptions

- Creating shared data and procedures among several instances of the same class

- Issuing message calls asynchronously

Object Communication through Messaging

One of the advantages of Object-Oriented Programming (OOP) is that the applications you create function in much the same way people function in the real world. You can think of your application as an organization similar to a company. In large organizations, the employees have specialized functions they perform. For example, one person is in charge of accounts payable processing, and another is responsible for the accounts receivable. When an employee needs to request a service—paid time off (PTO), for example—the employee (the client) sends a message to her manager (the server). This client-server request can simply involve two objects, or it can be a complex chain of client-server requests. For example, the employee requests the PTO from her manager who in turn checks with the Human Resources (HR) department to see if she has enough accumulated time. In this case, the manager is both a server to the employee and a client to the HR department.

Defining Method Signatures

When a message passes between a client and server, the client may or may not expect a response back. For example, when an employee requests for PTO, she expects a response indicating approval or denial. Other times, a message is sent where no response is expected or required. For example, when accounting issues paychecks, it does not expect everyone in the company to issue a response email thanking them! A common requirement when a message is issued is to include information needed to carry out the request. When an employee requests PTO, her manager expects her to provide him with the dates she is requesting off or he can't service the request. In OOP terminology, you refer to the name of the method (requested service) and the input parameters (client supplied information) as the *method signature.*

The following code demonstrates how methods are defined in Visual Basic (VB). A method that returns a value is defined as a function procedure. If the method does not return a value, then it is defined as a sub procedure:

```
Public Function AddEmployee(ByVal LogonName As String, ...)
    As Integer
      'Code to save data to database.
   ...
End Function
Public Sub Login(ByVal LogonName As String, ...)
      'Code to retrieve data from database.
       ...
End Sub
```

Passing Parameters

When a method is defined in the class you also must indicate how the parameters are passed. If you choose to pass the parameters by value, a copy of the parameter data is passed from the client to the server. The server works with the copy and if changes are made to the data, the server must pass the copy back to the client so that the client can choose to discard the changes or replicate the changes. If you go back to the company analogy, think about the process of updating your employee file. The HR department does not give you direct access to the file. It sends you a copy of the values in the file, you make changes to the copy, and send it back to the HR department. The HR department then decides whether to replicate these changes to your actual file.

Another way you can parameters is by reference. In this case, the client does not pass in a copy of the data but a reference to where the data is located. Using the previous example, this would be like requesting to update your employee data and instead of sending you a copy of the data in your file, HR tells you where the file is located and tells you to go get it and make the changes. In this case, clearly it would be better to pass the parameters by value. The following code shows how you define the method to pass values by reference:

```
Public Function AddEmployee(ByRef LogonName As String, ...) As Integer
        'Code to save data to database.
...
End Function
```

> **NOTE** *Because the default method of passing parameters is by value, the* byVal *keyword is optional and can be omitted.*

In highly distributed applications it is advantageous to pass parameters by value instead of by reference. Passing parameters by reference in this case can cause increased overhead because when the server object must work with parameter information it has to make calls across processing boundaries and the network. Passing values by reference is also less secure when maintaining data integrity. The client is opening up a channel for the data to be manipulated without the client's knowledge or control. The advantage of passing values by reference is if the client and server are in the same process space (they occupy the same cubicle, so to speak) and if there is a clearly established trust relationship between the client and the server. In this situation, there is no real compelling reason not to allow direct access to the memory storage location, and passing the parameters by reference would incur less overhead than passing the parameters by value. The other situation where passing parameters by reference may be advantageous is if the object is a complex data type such as another object. In this case, the overhead of copying the data structure and passing it across process and network boundaries outweighs the overhead of making repeated calls across the network.

> **NOTE** *The .NET Framework addresses this by allowing you to efficiently copy and pass complex data types by serializing and deserializing them in an XML structure.*

Event-Driven Programming

So far you have been looking at messaging between the objects in which the client initiates the message interaction. If you think about how you interact with objects in real life, you often receive messages in response to an event that has occurred. For example, when the sandwich man comes into the building, a message is issued over the intercom informing employees that the event has occurred. This type of messaging is referred to as *broadcast messaging*. The server issues the message, and the clients decide to ignore or respond to the message. Another way this event message could be issued is by the receptionist issuing an email to interested employees when the sandwich man shows up. In this case, the interested employees would subscribe to receive the event message with the receptionist. This type of messaging is often referred to as *subscription-based messaging*.

Applications built with the .NET Framework are object-oriented, event-driven programs. If you trace the client-server processing chains that occur in your applications, you can identify an event that has occurred that kicked off the processing. In the case of Windows applications, the user interacting with a Graphical User Interface (GUI) usually initiates the event. For example, a user might initiate the process of saving data to a database by clicking a button. Classes in applications can also initiate events. A security class could broadcast an event message when an invalid logon is detected. You can also subscribe to external events. You could create a Web service that would issue an event notification when a change occurs in the stock market. You could write an application that subscribes to the service and responds to the event notification.

In VB if you want to issue event messages, you add an event definition to the class definition file. The interface associated with an event procedure is similar to a sub procedure. You can pass parameters with the message notification, but you do not expect a response back. When you want to raise the event, you execute the RaiseEvent statement. The following code shows how you define and raise an event in a server class:

```
Public Class Data
      Public Event DataUpdate(ByVal Msg As String)
      Public Sub SaveInfo()
            Try
                  RaiseEvent DataUpdate("Data has been updated")
            Catch
                  RaiseEvent DataUpdate("Data could not be updated")
            End Try
      End Sub
End Class
```

If a client wants to subscribe to the events of the server it must use the WithEvents keyword when declaring an instance of the server class. The object instance of the server class must also be declared with class-level scope. Once the object instance of the server has been declared, any of the methods of the client class can be used to handle the event as long as the argument list matches that passed by the event message. The following code shows a form class handling an event message issued by the server class:

```
Public Class Form2
      Inherits System.Windows.Forms.Form
      Dim WithEvents oData As Data

      Private Sub oData_DataSaved(ByVal Msg As String) Handles oData.DataUpdate
            MsgBox(Msg)
      End Sub

      Private Sub btnSave_Click(ByVal sender As System.Object, _
                  ByVal e As System.EventArgs) Handles btnSave.Click
            oData = New Data()
            oData.SaveInfo()
      End Sub
End Class
```

> **NOTE** *The Visual Studio form designer uses the* WithEvents *keyword when declaring object instances of Windows controls placed on a form.*

ACTIVITY 8-1. ISSUING AND RESPONDING TO EVENT MESSAGES

In this activity you will become familiar with the following:

- Creating and raising events from a server class

- Handling events from client classes

- Handling GUI events

Adding and Raising Event Messaging in the Class Definition

To add and raise event messaging in the class definition file, follow these steps:

1. Start Visual Studio. On the File menu, choose New ➢ Project.

2. Choose a Windows Application project. Name the project **Act8_1**.

3. A default form is included in the project. Add controls to the form and change the property values, as listed in Table 8-1. Your completed form should look similar to Figure 8-1.

Table 8-1. Form and Control Properties

OBJECT	PROPERTY	VALUE
Form1	Name	frmLogin
	Text	Login
Label1	Name	lblName
	Text	Name:
Label2	Name	lblPassword
	Text	Password:
Textbox1	Name	txtName
	Text	(empty)
Textbox2	Name	txtPassword
	Text	(empty)
Button1	Name	btnLogin
	Text	Log In
Button1	Name	btnClose
	Text	Close

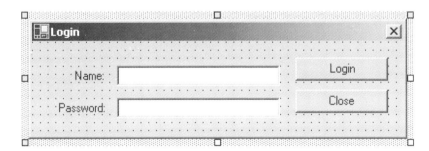

Figure 8-1. The completed form

4. On the Project menu, choose Add Class. Name the class **Employee** and open the Employee class code in the code editor.

5. Inside the class declaration add the following line of code to define the LogLogin event procedure. You will use this event to track employee logins to your application:

```
Public Event LogLogin(ByVal LoginName As String, _
    ByVal Status As Boolean)
```

6. Add the following Login method to the class, which will raise the LogLogin event:

```
Public Sub Login(ByVal strLoginName As String, _
    ByVal strPassword As String)
        'Data normally retrieved from database. Hard coded for demo only
        If strLoginName = "Smith" And strPassword = "js" Then
            RaiseEvent LogLogin(strLoginName, True)
        Else
            RaiseEvent logLogin(strLoginName, False)
        End If
End Sub
```

Receiving Events in the Client Class Using the WithEvents *Declaration*

To receive events in the client class using the WithEvents declaration, follow these steps:

1. Open the frmLogin class code in the code editor.

2. At the top of the form class code, after the inherits System.Windows.Forms.Form statement, declare an object instance of the Employee class including the WithEvents keyword:

```
Private WithEvents oEmployee As Employee
```

3. At the top of the code editor, choose the oEmployee object in the left drop-down list. In the right drop-down list, choose the LogLogin event.

4. In the event handler method oEmployee_LogLogin, add the following code:

   ```
   MsgBox(" Login status: " & Status)
   ```

5. Notice at the end of the method deceleration is the handles keyword, which assigns the method as a handler for the LogLogin event message.

6. At the top of the code editor, choose the btnLogin object in the left drop-down list. In the right drop-down list, choose the click event.

7. In the event handler method btnLogin_Click, add the following code to call the Login method of the Employee object:

   ```
   oEmployee = New Employee()

   oEmployee.Login(txtName.Text, txtPassword.Text)
   ```

8. In the Solution Explorer, select the project node. Right-click the project node and select Properties. In the Property Pages dialog box, change the startup object to **frmLogin**.

9. On the Build menu, choose Build Solution and make sure there are no build errors in the Task List window. If there are, fix them and rebuild.

10. On the Debug menu, choose Start to run the project and test to make sure the LogLogin event message is raised when you log in. Entering a login name of **Smith** and a password of **js** should trigger a login status of true.

11. After testing the LogLogin event, close the form, which in turn will stop the debugger.

Receiving Events in the Client Class Using the AddHandler *Method*

To receive events in the client class using the AddHandler method, follow these steps:

1. Open the frmLogin class code in the code editor.

2. Comment out the Dim oEmployee ... declaration added previously.

3. Delete the following code from the oEmployee_LogLogin method declaration:

```
Handles oEmployee.LogLogin
```

4. Comment out the following line of code in the btnLogin_Click method:

```
oEmployee = New Employee()
```

5. Add the following code after the line of code commented out in step 4:

```
Dim oEmployee As Employee = New Employee()
AddHandler oEmployee.LogLogin, AddressOf oEmployee_LogLogin
```

6. On the Build menu, choose Build Solution and make sure there are no build errors in the Task List window. If there are, fix them and rebuild.

7. On the Debug menu, choose Start to run the project and test to make sure the LogLogin event message is raised when you log in.

8. After testing LogLogin event, close the form, which in turn will stop the debugger.

9. On the File menu, choose Save All.

Handling Multiple Events with One Method

To handle multiple events with one method, follow these steps:

1. Open frmLogin in the GUI editor by right-clicking the frmLogin node in the Solution Explorer and choosing View Code.

2. From the Toolbox add a MainMenu control to the form. Name the top-level menu **mnuFile** with a text of File. Add a submenu with a name of **mnuExit** and enter a text of **Exit**.

3. Open the frmLogin class code in the code editor and locate the btnClose_Click method.

4. Change the name of the method to `FormClose` and add a handler for the `mnuExit` click event:

```
Private Sub FormClose(ByVal sender As System.Object, _
    ByVal e As System.EventArgs) _
            Handles btnClose.Click, mnuExit.Click
    Me.Close()
End Sub
```

5. On the Build menu, choose Build Solution and make sure there are no build errors in the Task List window. If there are, fix them and rebuild.

6. On the Debug menu, choose Start to run the project and test `mnuExit` and `btnClose`.

7. After testing, close the form, which will stop the debugger.

8. Save the project and exit Visual Studio.

Understanding Delegation

Delegation is when you request a service from a server by making a method call. The server then reroutes this service request to another method, which services the request. The delegate class can examine the service request and dynamically determine at runtime where to rout the request. If you return to the company analogy, you can find examples of delegation occurring within the company. When a manager receives a service request, she often delegates it to a member of her department. As a matter of fact, many would argue that a common trait among successful managers is the ability to know when and how to delegate responsibilities.

Using Delegation

When creating a delegated method you define the delegated methods signature. Because the delegate function does not actually service the request, it does not contain any implementation code. The following code shows a delegated method used to compare integer values:

```
Delegate Function CompareInt(ByVal I1 As Integer, _
    ByVal I2 As Integer) As Boolean
```

Once the delegated method's signature is defined, you can then create the methods that will be delegated to. These methods must have the same parameters and return types as the delegated method. The following code shows two methods, which the delegated method will in turn delegate to:

```
Private Function AscendOrder(ByVal I1 As Integer, _
    ByVal I2 As Integer) As Boolean
    If I1 < I2 Then
        Return True
    End If
End Function
Private Function DescendOrder(ByVal I1 As Integer, _
    ByVal I2 As Integer) As Boolean
    If I1 > I2 Then
        Return True
    End If
End Function
```

Once the delegate and its delegating methods have been defined, you are ready to use the delegate. The following code shows a portion of a sorting routine that determines which delegated method to call depending on a SortType passed in as a parameter:

```
Public Sub SortIntegers(ByVal SortDirection As SortType, _
    ByVal intArray() As Integer)
    Dim CheckOrder As CompareInt
    If SortDirection = SortType.Ascending Then
        CheckOrder = New CompareInt(AddressOf AscendOrder)
    Else
        CheckOrder = New CompareInt(AddressOf DescendOrder)
    End If
        'Code contines ...
End Sub
```

Using delegating techniques, the same sorting routine can be called by clients to implement descending and ascending sorting of integers.

Using Delegation to Implement Event Handlers

Another way of implementing event handlers is by using the AddHandler statement, which takes two parameters: the name of the event being handled and the name of the delegating method that will handle the event. The following code shows how to use the AddHandler statement to handle the DataUpdate event message defined in the Data class:

```
Public Class Form1
     Inherits System.Windows.Forms.Form

     Private Sub Save_click(ByVal sender As System.Object, _
        ByVal e As System.EventArgs) Handles btnSave.Click
          Dim oData As Data = New Data()
          AddHandler oData.DataUpdate, AddressOf oData_DataUpdate
          oData.SaveInfo()
     End Sub

     Private Sub oData_DataUpdate(ByVal Msg As String)
          MsgBox(Msg)
     End Sub
End Class
```

The advantage to implementing event handles using this method is that you do not have to declare the class instance variable with class-level scope, and you can dynamically add and remove event handlers at runtime.

ACTIVITY 8-2. IMPLEMENTING DELEGATION IN VB

In this activity you will become familiar with the following:

- Creating and implementing a delegated method

- Filtering event messages in an event handler

Creating Delegated Methods

To create delegated methods, follow these steps:

1. Start Visual Studio. On the File menu, choose New ➢ Project.

2. Choose a Windows Application project. Name the project **Act8_2**.

3. A default form is included in the project. Add controls to the form and change the property values, as listed in Table 8-2. Your completed form should look similar to Figure 8-2.

Table 8-2. Form and Control Properties

OBJECT	PROPERTY	VALUE
Form1	Name	frmSort
	Text	Sort
Textbox1	Name	txtList
	Text	(empty)
Button1	Name	btnSortDesc
	Text	Sort Desc
Button1	Name	btnSortAsc
	Text	Sort Asc

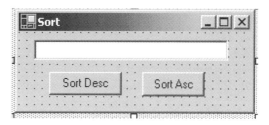

Figure 8-2. Your completed form

4. On the Project menu, choose Add Class. Name the class **Sort** and open the Sort class code in the code editor. You will investigate delegation by creating a method that will sort a list of comma-delimited words in ascending or descending order.

5. Add the following code to create a public enumeration SortType that will be used in the Sort method:

```
Public Enum SortType
    Ascending = 1
    Descending = 2
End Enum
```

6. Create the delegated method signature using the following code. You will delegate to one of two methods depending on the sort direction chosen:

```
Delegate Function CompareStrings(ByVal String1 As String, _
                ByVal String2 As String) As Boolean
```

7. Add a `CompareAscending` and a `CompareDescending` method that will be delegated to in your main Sort method:

```
Private Function CompareAscending(ByVal String1 As String, _
                ByVal String2 As String) As Boolean
    If String.Compare(String1, String2, True) < 1 Then
            Return True
    End If
End Function
Private Function CompareDescending(ByVal String1 As String, _
                ByVal String2 As String) As Boolean
    If String.Compare(String1, String2, True) > 0 Then
            Return True
    End If
End Function
```

8. Create a `SortString` method that will delegate to the correct compare function depending on the sort type requested. This function takes an array of strings, performs a bubble sort, and returns the sorted array to the client:

```
Public Function SortStrings(ByVal SortDirection As SortType, _
                ByVal SortArray() As String) As String()
    ...
End Function
```

9. The first thing you need to do in the Sort function is to determine which direction to implement the sort and point to the appropriate function that must be delegated to:

```
    Dim CheckOrder As CompareStrings
    If SortDirection = SortType.Ascending Then
            CheckOrder = New CompareStrings(AddressOf CompareAscending)
    Else
            CheckOrder = New CompareStrings(AddressOf CompareDescending)
    End If
```

10. The next part of the Sort function will implement a bubble sort on the string array by comparing adjacent values and switching the order if needed:

```
Dim OuterCount, InnerCount As Integer
Dim TempValue As String
For OuterCount = 0 To UBound(SortArray)
        For InnerCount = OuterCount + 1 To UBound(SortArray)
                If Not CheckOrder(SortArray(OuterCount), _
                    SortArray(InnerCount)) Then
                        TempValue = SortArray(OuterCount)
                        SortArray(OuterCount) = SortArray(InnerCount)
                        SortArray(InnerCount) = TempValue
                End If
        Next
Next
Return SortArray
```

11. In the Solution Explorer, select the project node. Right-click the project node and select Properties. In the Property Pages dialog box, change the startup object to frmSort.

12. On the Build menu, choose Build Solution and make sure there are no build errors in the Task List window. If there are, fix them and rebuild.

Testing the Sort Routine and Filtering Events in the Client Class

To test the sort routine and filter events in the client class, follow these steps:

1. Open the frmSort class code in the code editor.

2. Add the following Sort method to the form class code. This method handles either clicking the btnSortAsc or btnSortDes buttons. You can determine which button has been clicked by examining the sender parameter that gets passed in with the event message:

```
Private Sub Sort(ByVal sender As System.Object, _
            ByVal e As System.EventArgs) Handles btnSortDesc.Click, _
            btnSortAsc.Click
    ...
End Sub
```

3. Declare and instantiate an object instance of the Sort class. Declare a string array and populate it by using the Split function to separate a list of strings entered in the textbox. Declare an array of type string to hold the string returned by the SortStrings method:

```
Dim oSort As Sort = New Sort()
Dim _Array() As String = Split(TxtList.Text, ",")
Dim _ReturnArray() As String
```

4. Check the event message sender object and call the SortStrings method of the oSort object and pass the appropriate SortType:

```
If sender Is btnSortAsc Then
    _ReturnArray = oSort.SortStrings(Sort.SortType.Ascending, _Array)
ElseIf sender Is btnSortDesc Then
    _ReturnArray = oSort.SortStrings(Sort.SortType.Descending, _Array)
End If
```

5. Using the Join method, populate the txtList with a comma-delineated list of the sorted array:

```
txtList.Text = Join(_ReturnArray, ",")
```

6. On the Build menu, choose Build Solution and make sure there are no build errors in the Task List window. If there are, fix them and rebuild.

7. On the Debug menu, choose Start to run the project. Test the sorting by entering a comma-delimited list of strings in the textbox and clicking on sort ascending and sort descending button.

8. After testing, then close the form, which in turn will stop the debugger.

9. Save the project and exit Visual Studio.

Handling Exceptions in the .NET Framework

It is important when creating applications that you gracefully handle exceptions that may occur when your applications are processing. Exceptions are things that you do not expect to occur during normal processing but are instead situations that may occur unexpectedly. For example, you may be trying to save data to a database over the network when the connection fails, or a user may be trying to save to the floppy drive without a disk in the drive..

The .NET Framework uses a structured exception-handling mechanism. Some of the benefits of this structured exception handling are common support and structure across all .NET languages, support for the creation of protected blocks of code, the ability to filter exceptions to create efficient robust error handling, and support of termination handlers to guarantee that cleanup tasks are completed regardless of any exceptions that may be encountered. The .NET Framework also provides an extensive number of exception classes used to handle common exceptions that might occur. For example, the `FileNotFoundException` class encapsulates information such as the file name, error message, and the source for an exception that is thrown when an attempt to access a file that does not exist is made. In addition, the .NET Framework allows the creation of application-specific exception classes used to handle common exceptions that may be unique to your application.

Using the Try-Catch Block

When creating code that could end up causing an exception, you should place it in a Try block. Code placed inside the Try block is considered protected. If an exception occurs while the protected code is executing, code processing is transferred to the Catch block where it is handled. Listing 8-1 shows a method of a class that tries to read from a file that does not exist. When the exception is thrown, it is caught in the Catch block.

Listing 8-1. Throwing an Exception

```
Imports System.IO
Public Class Reader
    Private strFilePath As String
    Property FilePath() As String
        Get
            Return strFilePath
        End Get
        Set(ByVal Value As String)
            strFilePath = Value
        End Set
    End Property
    Public Function ReadText() As String
        Dim sr As StreamReader
        Dim strFileText As String
        Try
            sr = File.OpenText(strFilePath)
            strFileText = sr.ReadToEnd()
```

```
            sr.Close()
            Return strFileText
        Catch
            Return "Error! File not found."
        End Try
    End Function
End Class
```

All Try blocks require at least one nested Catch block. You can use the Catch block to catch all exceptions that may occur in the Try block, or you can use it to filter exceptions based on the type of exception. This enables you to dynamically respond to different exceptions based on the exception type. The following code demonstrates filtering exceptions based on the different exceptions that could occur when trying to read a text file from disk:

```
...
Try
    sr = File.OpenText(strFilePath)
    strFileText = sr.ReadToEnd()
    sr.Close()
    Return strFileText
Catch e As DirectoryNotFoundException
    Return e.Message
Catch e As FileNotFoundException
    Return e.Message
Catch
    Return "Error! File not found."
End Try
...
```

Adding a Finally *Block*

Additionally, you can nest a Finally block at the end of the Try block. Unlike the Catch block, the use of the Finally block is optional. The Finally block is for any cleanup code that needs to occur even if an exception is encountered. For example, you may need to close a database connection or release a file. When the code of the Try block is executed and an exception occurs, processing will jump to the appropriate Catch block. After the Catch block executes, then the Finally block will execute. If the Try block executes and no exception is encountered, then the Catch blocks do not execute but the Finally block will still get processed. The following code shows a Finally block being used to close a connection to a SQL Server database:

```
Public Sub MakeConnection()
     Dim myConnString As String = "user id=sa;" &_
               "password=;database=northwind;server=myserver"
     Dim myConnection As New SqlConnection(myConnString)
     Try
          myConnection.Open()
          'Code to interact with data base ...
     Catch myException As SqlException
          Dim myErrors As SqlErrorCollection = myException.Errors
          Dim i As Integer
          For i = 0 To myErrors.Count - 1
               MessageBox.Show("Index #" & i & ControlChars.Cr & _
                         "Error: " & myErrors(i).ToString() & ControlChars.Cr)
          Next I
     Finally
          MyConnection.Close()
     End Try
End Sub
```

Throwing Exceptions

When an exception occurs during code execution that does not fit into one of the predefined system exception classes, you can throw your own exceptions. You normally throw your own exceptions when the error will not cause problems with execution but rather with the processing of your business rules. For example, you could look for an order date that is in the future and throw an invalid date range exception. When you throw an exception, you are creating an instance of the System.Exception class. The following code shows an example of throwing a custom exception:

```
Public Sub LogOrder(ByVal OrderNumber As Long, ByVal OrderDate As Date)
     Try
          If OrderDate > Now() Then
               Throw New Exception("Order date can not be in the future.")
          End If
          'processing code...
     Catch
          'Exception handler code...
     End Try
End Sub
```

Nesting Exception Handling

There may be times when an exception could occur in which you can correct the exception and continue processing the rest of the code in the Try block. For example, a division by zero error may occur, and it would be acceptable to assign the result a value of zero and continue processing. In this case, a Try-Catch block could be nested around the line of code that would cause the exception. After the exception is handled, processing would return to the line of code in the outer Try-Catch immediately after the nested Try block. The following code demonstrates the nesting of one Try block within another:

```
Try
    Try
        Y1 = X1 / X2
    Catch e As DivideByZeroException
        Y1 = 0
    End Try
    'Rest of processing code ...
Catch
    'Outer exception processing....
End Try
```

> **NOTE** *For more information on handling exceptions and the .NET Framework exception classes, refer to Apendix B, "Error Handling in VB .NET."*

Accessing Shared Properties and Methods

When you declare an object instance of a class, it instantiates its own instances of the properties and methods defined by the class. For example, if you had a counting routine that incremented a counter and you instantiated two object instances of the class, the counters of each object would be independent of each other. If you increment one counter, it would have no effect on the other. Normally this object independence is the behavior you want. There are times, however, when you may want different object instances of a class accessing shared variables. For example, you may want to build in a counter that would log how many of the object instances have been instantiated. In this case, you would have to create a shared property value in the class definition. The following code demonstrates how you create a shared property DiscountRate in a class definition:

```
Public Class AccountingUtilities
    Private Shared _TaxRate As Single = 0.06
    Public Shared ReadOnly Property TaxRate() As Single
        Get
                Return _TaxRate
        End Get
    End Property
End Class
```

To access the shared property, you do not create an object instance of the class but refer to the class directly. The following code shows a client accessing the shared DiscountRate defined previously:

```
Public Class Purchase
    Public Function CalculateTax(ByVal PurchasePrice As Double) As Double
        Return PurchasePrice * AccountingUtilities.TaxRate
    End Function
End Class
```

Shared methods are useful if you have utility functions that clients need to access, but do not want the overhead of creating an object instance of a class to gain access to the method. It should be noted that shared methods can only access shared properties. The following code shows a shared method used to count the number of users currently logged into an application:

```
Public Class UserLog
    Private Shared _UserCount As Integer
    Public Shared Sub IncrementUserCount()
        _UserCount += 1
    End Sub
    Public Shared Sub DecrementUserCount()
        _UserCount -= 1
    End Sub
End Class
```

When client code accesses a shared method it does so by referencing the class directly and does not have to create an object instance of the class. The following code demonstrates accessing the shared method defined previously:

```
Public Class User
...
    Public Sub Logon(ByVal UserName As String, ByVal UserPassword As String)
        'code to check logon credentials
```

```
        'if successful ...
        UserLog.IncrementUserCount()
    End Sub
...
End Class
```

Although you may not use shared properties and methods often when creating the classes in your applications, they are useful when creating base class libraries and are used throughout the .NET Framework system classes. The following code demonstrates the use of the Compare method of the System.String class. This is a shared method that compares two strings alphabetically. It returns a positive value if the first string is greater, a negative value if the second string is greater, and zero if the strings are equal:

```
Public Function CheckStringOrderAscending(ByVal String1 As String, _
              ByVal String2 As String) As Boolean
    If String.Compare(String1, String2, True) >= 0 Then
          Return True
    End If
End Function
```

ACTIVITY 8-3. EXCEPTION HANDLING AND SHARED METHODS

In this activity you will become familiar with the following:

- Creating and calling shared methods of a class

- Using structured exception handling in VB

Creating the Shared Methods

To create the shared methods, follow these steps:

1. Start up Visual Studio. On the File menu, choose New ➤ Project.

2. Choose a Windows Application project. Name the project **Act8_3**.

3. A default form is included in the project. Add controls to the form and change the property values, as listed in Table 8-3. Your completed form should look similar to Figure 8-3.

Table 8-3. Form and Control Properties

OBJECT	PROPERTY	VALUE
Form1	Name	frmLogger
	Text	Logger
Textbox1	Name	txtLogPath
	Text	c:\LogTest.txt
Textbox2	Name	txtLogInfo
	Text	Test Message
Button1	Name	btnLogInfo
	Text	Log Info

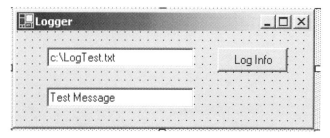

Figure 8-3. The completed logger form

4. On the Project menu, choose Add Class. Name the class **Logger**.

5. Because you will be using the System.IO class within the Logger class, add an Imports statement to the file:

```
Imports System.IO
Public Class Logger
...
End Class
```

6. Add a shared LogWrite function to the class that will write information to a log file. To open the file you will create a FileStream object. A StreamWriter object will be created to write the information to the file:

```
Public Shared Function LogWrite(ByVal LogFilePath As String, _
                ByVal LogInfo As String) As String
```

```
            Dim oFileStream As FileStream = New FileStream(LogFilePath, _
                    FileMode.Open, FileAccess.Write)
            Dim oStreamWriter As StreamWriter = NewStreamWriter(oFileStream)
            oFileStream.Seek(0, SeekOrigin.End)
            oStreamWriter.WriteLine(Now)
            oStreamWriter.WriteLine(LogInfo)
            oStreamWriter.WriteLine()
            oStreamWriter.Close()
            Return "Info logged"
        End Function
```

7. Open frmLogger in the code editor. In the right object drop-down list, choose btnLogInfo. In the left drop-down list, choose the click event. Add the following code that causes the LogWrite method of the Logger class and displays the results in the form's text property:

```
Private Sub btnLogInfo_Click(ByVal sender As System.Object, _
            ByVal e As System.EventArgs) Handles btnLogInfo.Click
        Me.Text = Logger.LogWrite(txtLogPath.Text, txtLogInfo.Text)
End Sub
```

8. Notice that because you designated the WriteLog method as shared, the client does not have to create an object instance of the Logger class. Shared methods are accessed directly through a class reference.

9. In the Solution Explorer, select the project node. Right-click the project node and select Properties. In the Property Pages dialog box, change the startup object to frmLogger.

10. On the Build menu, choose Build Solution and make sure there are no build errors in the Task List window. If there are, fix them and rebuild.

11. On the Debug menu, choose Run. When the form launches, click the LogInfo button. Do not worry—you should get an unhandled exception message of type System.IO.FileNotFoundException. Choose Break and stop the debugger.

Creating the Structured Exception Handler

To create the structured exception handler, follow these steps:

1. Open the Logger class code in the code editor.

2. Locate the `WriteLog` method and add a Try-Catch block around the current code. In the `Catch` block, return a string stating the logging failed:

```
Try
        Dim oFileStream As FileStream = New FileStream _
            (strLogFilePath, FileMode.Open, FileAccess.Write)
        ... rest of code
Catch
    Return "Logging failed!"
End Try
```

3. On the Build menu, choose Build Solution and make sure there are no build errors in the Task List window. If there are, fix them and rebuild.

4. On the Debug menu, choose Run. When the form launches, click the LogInfo button. This time you should not get the exception message because it was handled by the `WriteLog` method. You should see the message *Login Failed!* in the form's caption. Close the form to stop the debugger.

Filtering Exceptions

To filter exceptions, follow these steps:

1. Alter the `Catch` block to return different messages depending on what exception is thrown:

```
Catch e As FileNotFoundException
    Return "Logging failed! Could not find the file."
Catch e As IOException
    Return "Logging failed! No disk in drive."
Catch
    Return "Logging failed!"
End Try
```

2. On the Build menu, choose Build Solution and make sure there are no build errors in the Task List window. If there are, fix them and rebuild.

3. On the Debug menu, choose Start to run the project and test the `FileNotFoundException` catch by clicking the Log Info button. Test the IO exception by changing the file path to the A drive and clicking the log

info button. These errors should be caught and the appropriate message presented in the form's caption.

4. After testing, close the form, which in turn will stop the debugger.

5. Using Notepad, create the LogTest.txt file on the C drive and close the file.

6. On the Debug menu, choose Start to run the project and test the WriteLog method by clicking the log info button. This time the form's caption should indicate the log write was successful.

7. Stop the debugger and open the LogTest.txt file using Notepad and verify the information was logged.

8. Save the project and exit Visual Studio.

Asynchronous Messaging

When objects interact by passing messages back and forth, they can pass the message synchronously or asynchronously. When a client object makes a synchronous message call to a server object, the client suspends processing and waits for a response back from the server before continuing. Synchronous messaging is the easiest to implement and is the default type of messaging implemented in the .NET Framework. There are some instances, however, where it can be an inefficient way of passing messages. For example, the synchronous messaging model is not well suited for long-running file reading and writing, making service calls across slow networks, and message queuing in disconnected client scenarios. To more effectively handle these types of situations, the .NET Framework provides the plumbing needed to pass messages between objects asynchronously. When a client object passes a message asynchronously, the client can continue to process. After the server completes the message request, the response information will be sent back to the client.

If you think about it, you interact with objects in the real world both synchronously and asynchronously. A good example of synchronous messaging is when you are in the checkout line at the grocery store. When the clerk cannot determine the price of one of the items, he calls the manager for a price check and suspends the checkout process until a result is returned. An example of an asynchronous message call is when the clerk notices that he is running low on change. He alerts the manager that he will need change soon, but he can continue to process his customer's items until the change arrives.

In the .NET Framework, when you want to call a method of the server object asynchronously, you first need to create a delegate. Instead of making the call directly to the server, the call is passed to the delegate. When a delegate is created, the compiler also creates two methods you can use to interact with a server class asynchronously. These methods are called `BeginInvoke` and `EndInvoke`. The `BeginInvoke` method takes the parameters defined by the delegate plus an `AsyncCallback` delegate, which is used to pass a callback method that the server will call and return information to the client when the asynchronous method completes. Another parameter that can be sent in to the `BeginInvoke` method is a context object that the client can use to keep track of the context of the asynchronous call. When the client calls the `BeginInvoke` method, it returns a reference to an object that implements the `IAsynchResult` interface. The `BeginInvoke` method also starts the execution of the asynchronous method call on a different thread from the main thread used by the client when initiating the call. The `EndInvoke` method takes the parameters and the `IasyncResult` object returned by the `BeginInvoke` method and blocks the thread used by the `BeginInvoke` method until a result is returned. When the results are returned by the asynchronous method, the `EndInvoke` method intercepts the results and passes them back to the client thread that initiated the call.

> **NOTE** *It is interesting to note that the method of the server class is not altered to enable a client to call its methods asynchronously. It is up to the client to decide whether to call the server asynchronously and implement the functionality required to make the call.*

The following code demonstrates the process needed to make a call to a server method asynchronously. In this example, the client code is making a call to a server method over a slow connection to read log information. The first step is to define a delegate type that will be used to make the call:

```
Private Delegate Function AsyncReadLog(ByVal FilePath As String) As String
```

The next step is to declare a variable of the delegate type and instantiate it passing in the address of the method you are calling asynchronously:

```
Private LogReader As AsyncReadLog = New AsyncReadLog(AddressOf Logger.LogRead)
```

> **NOTE** *Because the* `LogRead` *method of the* `Logger` *class is a shared method, you can call it directly.*

You then declare a variable of type `AsyncCallBack` and instantiate it, passing in the address of the method that you have set up to process the results of the asynchronous call. The `AsyncCallBack` class is a member of the `System.Runtime.Remoting.Messaging` namespace:

```
Dim aCallBack As AsyncCallback = New AsyncCallback(AddressOf Me.LogReadCallBack)
```

You are now ready to call the server method asynchronously by implementing the `BeginInvoke` method of the delegate type. You have to declare a variable of type `IAsyncResult` to capture the return value and pass the parameters required by the server method and a reference to the `AsyncCallback` object declared previously:

```
Dim ar As IAsyncResult = _
    LogReader.BeginInvoke(txtLogPath.Text, aCallBack, Nothing)
```

You can now implement the call back method in the client, which needs to accept an input parameter of type `IAsyncCallback` that will be passed to it. Inside this method you will make a call to the delegate's `EndInvoke` method. This method takes the same parameters passed into the `BeginInvoke` method as well as the `IAsyncCallBack` object type returned by the `BeginInvoke` method. In this case you are displaying the results of the call in a message box:

```
Public Sub LogReadCallBack(ByVal ar As IAsyncResult)
    MsgBox(LogReader.EndInvoke(txtLogPath.Text, ar))
End Sub
```

ACTIVITY 8-4. CALLING METHODS ASYNCHRONOUSLY

In this activity you will become familiar with the following:

- Creating shared methods

- Calling methods asynchronously

Creating the Shared Method and Calling It Synchronously

To create the shared method and call it synchronously, follow these steps:

1. Start Visual Studio. On the File menu, choose Open ➤ Project.

2. Open the solution file you completed in Act8_3.

3. Add the following buttons to the frmLogger form, as shown in Table 8-4. Figure 8-4 shows the completed form.

Table 8-4. Form and Control Properties

OBJECT	PROPERTY	VALUE
Button1	Name	btnSyncRead
	Text	Sync Read
Button2	Name	btnAsyncRead
	Text	Async Read
Button3	Name	btnMessage
	Text	Message

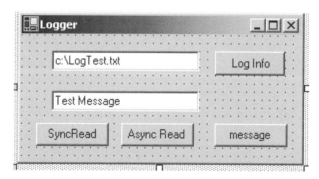

Figure 8-4. The completed logger form

4. Open the class Logger in the code editor.

5. Recall that because you are using the System.IO namespace within the Logger class, you added an Imports statement to the file. You are also going to use System.Threading namespace, so add an Imports statement to include this namespace:

```
Imports System.IO
Imports System.Threading
Public Class Logger
...
End Class
```

6. Add a shared LogRead function to the class that will read information from a log file. To open the file, you will create a FileStream object. A StreamReader object will be used to read the information from the file. You are also using the Thread class to suspend processing for three seconds to simulate a long call across a slow network.

```
Public Shared Function LogRead(ByVal FilePath As String) As String
    Dim sr As StreamReader
    Dim _FileText As String
    Try
        sr = File.OpenText(FilePath)
        strFileText = sr.ReadToEnd()
        sr.Close()
        Thread.Sleep(3000)
        Return _FileText
    Catch e As DirectoryNotFoundException
        Return e.Message
    Catch e As FileNotFoundException
        Return e.Message
    Catch
        Return "Error! File not found."
    End Try
End Function
```

7. Open frmLogger in the code editor. In the right object drop-down list, choose btnSyncRead. In the left drop-down list, choose the click event. Add code that calls the LogRead method of the Logger class and displays the results in a message box:

```
Private Sub btnSyncRead_Click(ByVal sender As System.Object, _
            ByVal e As System.EventArgs) Handles btnSyncRead.Click
    MsgBox(Logger.LogRead(txtLogPath.Text))
End Sub
```

8. Notice that because you designated the LogRead method as shared, the client does not have to create an object instance of the Logger class. Shared methods are accessed directly through a class reference.

9. Open frmLogger in the code editor. In the right object drop-down list, choose btnMessage. In the left drop-down list, choose the click event. Add code that displays a message box:

```
Private Sub btnMessage_Click(ByVal sender As System.Object, _
            ByVal e As System.EventArgs) Handles btnMessage.Click
    MsgBox("Hello, Asynchronous World!")
End Sub
```

10. On the Build menu, choose Build Solution and make sure there are no build errors in the Task List window. If there are, fix them and rebuild.

11. On the Debug menu, choose Run. When the form launches, click the Sync Read button. After clicking the Sync Read button, try clicking the Message button. You should not get a response when clicking the Message button because you called the ReadLog method synchronously. After the ReadLog method returns a result, then the message button will respond when clicked.

12. When you have finished testing, close the form, which will in turn stop the debugger.

Calling a Method Asynchronously

To call a method asynchronously, follow these steps:

1. Open the frmLogger class code in the code editor.

2. After the line containing the Inherits statement at the beginning of the class file, add code to create a delegate function definition that will be used to make the asynchronous call:

```
Private Delegate Function AsyncReadLog _
    (ByVal FilePath As String) As String
```

3. On the next line, declare a LogReader variable of the delegate type and instantiate it passing the address of the LogRead method of the Logger class:

```
Private LogReader As AsyncReadLog = _
    New AsyncReadLog(AddressOf Logger.LogRead)
```

4. Create a callback method that will be used to retrieve the results of the asynchronous message call. This method needs to accept a parameter of type IAsyncResult:

```
Public Sub LogReadCallBack(ByVal ar As IAsyncResult)
    ...
End Sub
```

5. At the top of the code editor, in the right object drop-down list, choose btnAsyncRead. In the left drop-down list, choose the `click` event. Add code that declares a variable of type `AsyncCallback` and instantiate it passing in the address of the `LogReadCallBack` method you created. On the next line of code, call the `BeginInvoke` method of the `LogReader` delegate, passing in the file path and the `AsyncCallBack` variable. Capture the return value in a variable of type `IasyncResult`:

```
Private Sub btnAsyncRead_Click(ByVal sender As System.Object, _
               ByVal e As System.EventArgs) Handles btnAsyncRead.Click
    Dim aCallBack As AsyncCallback = New AsyncCallback _
               (AddressOf Me.LogReadCallBack)
    Dim ar As IAsyncResult = LogReader.BeginInvoke _
        (txtLogPath.Text, aCallBack, Nothing)
End Sub
```

6. Add code to the `LogReadCallback` method that calls the `EndInvoke` method of the `LogReader` delegate, passing in the file path and the `IAsyncResult` parameter. Display the results in a message box:

```
Public Sub LogReadCallBack(ByVal ar As IAsyncResult)
    MsgBox(LogReader.EndInvoke(ar))
End Sub
```

7. On the Build menu, choose Build Solution and make sure there are no build errors in the Task List window. If there are, fix them and rebuild.

8. On the Debug menu, choose Run. When the form launches, click the Async Read button. After clicking the Async Read button, try clicking the Message button. This time, you should get a response when clicking the Message button because you called the `ReadLog` method asynchronously.

9. When you have finished testing, close the form, which will in turn stop the debugger.

10. Save the project and exit Visual Studio.

Summary

In this chapter you did the following:

- Examined how objects communication through messaging

- Investigated the different types of messaging that can occur between a client and server

- Discussed the process involved in publishing and handling events

- Examined how and when to use delegation in a VB application

- Looked at how to implement structured exception handling

- Examined the process of creating shared attributes and methods in a class

- Discussed how a client implements asynchronous messaging calls to a server

This chapter is the final chapter in a series of three that introduced you to the various OOP constructs such as classes, inheritance, and polymorphism as they are implemented in VB code. You have been introduced to and practiced using Visual Studio. You should also have a firm understanding of how class structures and object collaboration are implemented in a VB application. You are now ready to put the pieces together and develop a working application. The next chapter is the first in a series in which you will revisit the Unified Modeling Language (UML) models you developed for the Office-Supply Ordering (OSO) case study in Chapter 4, "Designing OOP Solutions: A Case Study." You will transform these models into an OSO application. In the process, you will investigate data access using ADO.NET, creating a Windows Form-based GUI, and creating a Web Form-based GUI.

Part Three

Developing Applications
with Visual Basic .NET

CHAPTER 9

OSO Application Revisited: Implementing the Business Logic

DURING THE PAST THREE CHAPTERS you looked at the various object-oriented programming constructs such as classes, inheritance, and polymorphism as they are implemented in Visual Basic code. You have been introduced to and practiced using the Visual Studio integrated development environment. You should also have a firm understanding of how class structures and object collaboration are implemented in a Visual Basic application.

You are now ready to put the pieces together and develop a working application. In this chapter you will revisit the Office-Supply Ordering application you first started designing in Chapter 4, "Designing OOP Solutions: A Case Study." You are now ready to implement the business logic in Visual Basic code. Because most business applications involve working with and updating data in a backend database, you will first look at how the .NET Framework provides you with the functionality to work with relational data. Once you are familiar with working with relational data in the .NET Framework, you will construct and test the classes that will implement the business logic of the Office-Supply Ordering application.

After reading this chapter you should be familiar with the following:

- Transitioning from the logical design phase to the physical design phase

- Separating the application logic into distinct tiers

- Establishing a connection to a database using the Connection object

- Using a Command object to execute SQL queries

- Using a Command object to execute stored procedures

- Retrieving records with the DataReader object

- Populating a DataSet using a DataAdapter object

- Establishing relationships between tables in a `DataSet`

- Editing and updating data in a `DataSet`

- Populating a `DataSet` from an Extensible Markup Language structure

- Persisting a `DataSet` to an Extensible Markup Language structure

Revisiting Application Design

When designing applications, you can generally classify the design process into three distinct phases. The conceptual design is the first phase, which constitutes the discovery phase of the process. The conceptual design phase involves a considerable amount of collaboration and communication between the users of the system and the system designers. The system designers must gain a complete understanding of the business processes that the proposed system will encompass. Using scenarios and use cases, you define the functional requirements of the system. A common understanding and agreement on system functionality and scope among the developers and users of the system is the required outcome of this phase.

The second phase of the design process is the logical design. During the logical design phase, you work out the details about the structure and organization of the system. This phase consists of the development and identification of the business objects and classes that will compose the system. Unified Modeling Language (UML) class diagrams identify the system objects. You identify and document the attributes and behaviors of the system objects. You also develop and document the structural interdependencies of these objects using the class diagrams. Using sequence and collaboration diagrams, you discover and identify the interactions and behavioral dependencies between the various system objects. The outcome of this phase is the application object model. The application object model is independent of any implementation-specific technology and deployment architecture.

The third phase of the design process is the physical design. During the physical design phase, you transform the application object model into an actual system. You evaluate and decide upon specific technologies and infrastructures. You do cost analysis and determine any constraints. Issues such as programmer experience and knowledge base, current implementation technologies, and legacy system integration will all influence your decisions during the physical design. You must also analyze security concerns, network infrastructure, and scalability requirements.

When designing a distributed application, you normally separate the logical architectural structure from the physical architectural structure. By separating the architectural structure in this way, it is much easier to maintain and update the application. You can make any physical architectural changes (to increase scalability, for example) with minimal impact. The logical architectural design of an application is separated into three tiers. Users interact with the presentation tier, which is responsible for presenting data to the user and providing a way for the user to initiate business service requests. The business logic tier encapsulates and implements the business logic of an application. It is responsible for performing calculations, processing data, and controlling application logic and sequencing. The data tier is responsible for managing the access to and storage of information that must be persisted and shared among various users and business processes.

One of the main functions of the business logic tier is retrieving and processing data. Before you implement the Office-Supply Ordering (OSO) application's business logic tier, you need to look more closely at how the .NET Framework provides the ability to retrieve and work with data structures. This functionality is encapsulated in a set of .NET namespaces commonly referred to as ADO.NET.

Introducing ADO.NET

A majority of applications developed for businesses need to interact with a data storage device. Data storage can occur in many different forms. Data can be maintained in a flat file system, as is the case with many traditional mainframe systems. It can also be maintained in a relational database management system, such as SQL Server, Oracle, or Sybase. You can also maintain data in a hierarchical textual file structure, as is the case with XML. To access and work with data in a consistent way across these various data stores, the .NET Framework provides a set of classes organized into the `System.Data` namespace. This collection of classes is commonly referred to as ADO.NET.

Looking at the history of Microsoft's data access technologies reveals an evolution from a connected model to a disconnected one. When developing traditional two-tier client-server applications prevalent in the 1980s and early 1990s, it was often more efficient to open a connection with the database, work with the data implementing server-side cursors, and closing the connection when finished working with the data. The problem with this approach became apparent in the late 1990s as companies tried to evolve their data-driven applications from traditional two-tier client-server applications to multitier Web-based models. It became apparent that opening and holding a connection open until processing was complete is not scalable. *Scalability* is the ability of an application to handle an increasing number of simultaneous clients without a noticeable degradation of performance.

Another problem with the traditional data access technologies developed during this time was the lack of interoperability. Systems with a high degree of interoperability can easily exchange data back and forth between one and other regardless of the implementation technologies of the various systems. Traditional data access technologies rely on proprietary methods of data exchange. Using these techniques it is hard for a system built using Microsoft technologies such as ADO (pre-.NET) and DCOM to exchange data with a system built using Java technologies such as JDBC and CORBA. The industry as a whole realized it was in the best interest of all parties to develop standards—such as Simple Object Access Protocol (SOAP) and Extensible Markup Language (XML)—for exchanging between disparate systems. Microsoft has embraced these standards and has incorporated support of the standards into the .NET Framework.

Microsoft has designed ADO.NET to be highly scalable and interoperable. To achieve scalability, Microsoft has designed ADO.NET around a disconnected model. A connection is made to the database, the data and meta-data are retrieved and cashed locally, and the connection is closed. To achieve a high level of interpretability, Microsoft has embraced XML as the main mechanism for transferring data. XML is based on open standards and is being supported by many different segments of the software industry. By exposing data natively as XML, it has become much easier to exchange data with components, applications, and business partners who may not be using Microsoft technologies. Transporting data using XML over Hypertext Transfer Protocol (HTTP) also alleviates many of the problems associated with passing binary information between the various tiers of an application and through firewall security.

Working with Data Providers

To establish a connection and work with a specific data source such as SQL Server, you must work with the appropriate .NET provider classes. The SQL Server provider classes are located in the System.Data.SQLClient namespace. Other data providers exist such as the OLEDB data provider classes located in the System.Data.OLEDB namespace. As time goes on you can expect many more native providers will be added to the .NET Framework. Each of these providers implement a similar class structure used to work with the data source. Table 9-1 summarizes the main classes of the System.Data.SQLClient provider namespace.

Table 9-1. Classes in the `System.Data.SqlClient` *Namespace*

CLASS	RESPONSIBILITY
SqlConnection	Establishes a connection and a unique session with the database
SqlCommand	Represents a Transact-SQL statement or stored procedure to execute at the database
SqlDataReader	Provides a means of reading a forward-only stream of rows from the database
SqlDataAdapter	Used to fill a DataSet and update changes back to the database
SqlParameter	Represents a parameter used to pass information to and from stored procedures
SqlTransaction	Represents a Transact-SQL transaction to be made in the database
SqlError	Collects information relevant to a warning or error returned by the database server
SqlException	The exception that is thrown when a warning or error is returned by the database server

A similar set of classes exists in the `System.Data.OLEDB` provider namespace. For example, instead of the `SqlConnection` class, there is an `OleDbConnection` class.

Establishing a Connection

The first step to retrieving data from a database is to establish a connection. A connection is established using a `Connection` object based on the type of provider being used. To establish a connection to SQL Server you will instantiate a `Connection` object of type `SqlConnection`. You also need to provide the `Connection` object with a `ConnectionString`. The `ConnectionString` consists of a series of semicolon-delineated name-value pairs that provide information needed to connect to the database server. Some of the information commonly passed by the `ConnectionString` is the name of the server, the name of the database, and security information. The following code demonstrates a `ConnectionString` used to connect to a SQL Server database.

```
"Data Source=TestServer;Initial Catalog=Pubs;User ID=Dan;Password=training"
```

The attributes you need to provide through the `ConnectionString` are dependent on the data provider you are using. The following code demonstrates a `ConnectionString` used to connect to an Access database:

```
"Provider=Microsoft.Jet.OleDb.4.0;Data Source=D:\Data\Northwind.mdb"
```

> **NOTE** *You also need to use a* `Connection` *object of type* `OleDbConnection`.

The next step is to invoke the `Open` method of the `Connection` object. This will result in the `Connection` object loading the appropriate driver and opening a connection to the data source. Once the connection is open, you can work with the data. When you are done interacting with the database it is important you invoke the `Close` method of the `Connection` object. When a `Connection` object falls out of scope or is garbage collected, the connection is not implicitly released.
Listing 9-1 demonstrates the process of opening a connection to the Pubs database in SQL Server, working with the data, and closing the connection.

Listing 9-1. Establishing a Connection

```vb
Imports System.Data
Imports System.Data.SqlClient
Imports System.Windows.Forms
Public Class SqlData
    Public Sub MakeConnection()
        Dim oPubConnection As SqlConnection
        Dim sConnString As String
        Try
            sConnString = "Data Source=(local);Initial Catalog=Pubs;" & _
                        "User ID=sa;Password="
            oPubConnection = New SqlConnection(sConnString)
            oPubConnection.Open()
            MessageBox.Show(oPubConnection.State.ToString)
        Catch oEx As Exception
            MessageBox.Show(oEx.Message)
        Finally
            oPubConnection.Close()
        End Try
    End Sub
End Class
```

Executing a Command

Once a database connection is established and opened, you can execute SQL statements against the database. A Command object stores and executes command statements against the database. You can use the Command object to execute any valid SQL statement understood by the data store. In the case of SQL Server, these can be Data Manipulation Language statements (Select, Insert, Update, and Delete), Data Definition Language statements (Create, Alter, and Drop), or Data Control Language statements (Grant, Deny, and Revoke). The CommandText property of the Command object holds the SQL Statement that will be submitted. The Command object contains three methods for submitting the CommandText to the database depending on what is returned. If records are returned, as is the case when a Select statement is executed, then you can use the ExecuteReader. If a single value is returned—for example, the results of a Select Count aggregate function—you should use the ExecuteScalar method. When no records are returned from a query—for example, an Insert statement— you should use the ExecuteNonQuery method. Listing 9-2 demonstrates using a Command object to execute a SQL statement against the Pubs database that returns the number of employees.

Listing 9-2. Executing a Command

```
Public Function CountEmployees() As Integer
    Dim oPubConnection As SqlConnection
    Dim sConnString As String
    Dim oSqlCommand As SqlCommand
    Try
        sConnString = "Data Source=(local);Initial Catalog=Pubs;" & _
                    "User ID=sa;Password="
        oPubConnection = New SqlConnection(sConnString)
        oPubConnection.Open()
        oSqlCommand = New SqlCommand()
        oSqlCommand.Connection = oPubConnection
        oSqlCommand.CommandText = "Select Count(emp_id) from employee"
        Return oSqlCommand.ExecuteScalar
    Catch oEx As Exception
        MessageBox.Show(oEx.Message)
    Finally
        oPubConnection.Close()
    End Try
End Function
```

Using Stored Procedures

In many application designs, instead of executing a SQL statement directly, clients must execute *stored procedures*. Stored procedures are an excellent way to encapsulate the database logic, increase scalability, and enhance the security of multitiered applications. To execute a stored procedure, you use the Command object. When executing a stored procedure, you set the CommandType property of the Command object to StoredProcedure and the CommandText property to the name of the stored procedure. Listing 9-3 demonstrates executing a stored procedure that returns the number of employees in the Pubs database.

Listing 9-3. Executing a Stored Procedure

```
Public Overloads Function CountEmployees() As Integer
    Dim oPubConnection As SqlConnection
    Dim sConnString As String
    Dim oSqlCommand As SqlCommand
    Try
        sConnString = "Data Source=(local);Initial Catalog=Pubs;" & _
                    "User ID=sa;Password="
        oPubConnection = New SqlConnection(sConnString)
        oPubConnection.Open()
        oSqlCommand = New SqlCommand()
        oSqlCommand.Connection = oPubConnection
        oSqlCommand.CommandText = "GetEmployeeCount"
        oSqlCommand.CommandType = CommandType.StoredProcedure
        Return oSqlCommand.ExecuteScalar
    Catch oEx As Exception
        MessageBox.Show(oEx.Message)
    Finally
        oPubConnection.Close()
    End Try
End Function
```

When executing a stored procedure, you often must supply input parameters. You may also need to retrieve the results of the stored procedure through output parameters. To work with parameters, you need to instantiate a parameter object of type SqlParameter. You then add it to the Parameters collection of the Command object. When constructing the parameter, you supply the name of the parameter and the SQL Server data type. For some data types you also supply the size. If the parameter is an output, input-output, or return parameter, then you must indicate the parameter direction. Listing 9-4 demonstrates calling a stored procedure that accepts an input parameter of a letter. The procedure passes back a count of the employees whose last name starts with the letter. The count is returned in the form of an output parameter.

Listing 9-4. Calling a Stored Procedure

```
Public Overloads Function CountEmployees(ByVal LInitial As String) As Integer
    Dim oPubConnection As SqlConnection
    Dim sConnString As String
    Dim oSqlCommand As SqlCommand
    Try
        sConnString = "Data Source=(local);Initial Catalog=Pubs;" & _
                    "User ID=sa;Password="
        oPubConnection = New SqlConnection(sConnString)
        oPubConnection.Open()
        oSqlCommand = New SqlCommand()
        oSqlCommand.Connection = oPubConnection
        oSqlCommand.CommandText = "GetEmployeeCountbyLInitial"
        oSqlCommand.CommandType = CommandType.StoredProcedure
        Dim oInputParam As SqlParameter = _
            oSqlCommand.Parameters.Add("@LInitial", SqlDbType.Char, 1)
      oInputParam.Value = LInitial
        Dim oOutPutParam As SqlParameter = _
            oSqlCommand.Parameters.Add("@EmployeeCount", SqlDbType.Int)
        oOutPutParam.Direction = ParameterDirection.Output
        oSqlCommand.ExecuteNonQuery()
        Return oOutPutParam.Value
    Catch oEx As Exception
        MessageBox.Show(oEx.Message)
    Finally
        oPubConnection.Close()
    End Try
End Function
```

Using the `DataReader` *Object to Retrieve Data*

A `DataReader` object accesses data through a forward-only, read-only stream. There are many instances when you want to loop through a set of records and process the results sequentially without the overhead of maintaining the data in a cache. A good example of this would be loading a list or array with the values returned from the database. After declaring an object of type `SqlDataReader`, you instantiate it by invoking the `ExecuteReader` method of a `Command` object. The `Read` method of the `DataReader` object accesses the records returned. The `Close` method of the `DataReader` object is called after the records have been processed.

Listing 9-5 demonstrates using a DataReader object to retrieve a list of names and return it to the client.

Listing 9-5. Using the DataReader Object

```
Public Function ListNames() As ArrayList
    Dim oPubConnection As SqlConnection
    Dim sConnString As String
    Dim oSqlCommand As SqlCommand
    Dim _NameArray As ArrayList
    Dim oDataReader As SqlDataReader
    Try
        sConnString = "Data Source=(local);Initial Catalog=Pubs;" & _
                    "User ID=sa;Password="
        oPubConnection = New SqlConnection(sConnString)
        oPubConnection.Open()
        oSqlCommand = oPubConnection.CreateCommand
        oSqlCommand.CommandText = "Select lname from employee"
        oDataReader = oSqlCommand.ExecuteReader
        _NameArray = New ArrayList()
        Do Until oDataReader.Read = False
            _NameArray.Add(oDataReader("lname"))
        Loop
        Return _NameArray
    Catch oEx As Exception
        MessageBox.Show(oEx.Message)
    Finally
        oDataReader.Close()
        oPubConnection.Close()
    End Try
End Function
```

Using the DataAdapter to Retrieve Data

In many cases you need to retrieve a set of data from the database, work with the data, and update any changes to the data back to the database. In that case, you use a DataAdapter as a bridge between the data source and the in-memory cache of the data. This in-memory cache of data is contained in a DataSet, which is a major component of the ADO.NET architecture.

> **NOTE** *The DataSet object is discussed in greater detail shortly.*

To retrieve a set of data from a database, you instantiate a DataAdapter object. You set the SelectCommand property of the DataAdapter to an existing Command object. You then execute the Fill method, passing the name of a DataSet object to fill. Listing 9-6 demonstrates using a DataAdapter to fill a DataSet and passing the DataSet back to the client.

Listing 9-6. Using a DataAdapter

```
Public Function GetEmployeeInfo() As DataSet
    Dim oPubConnection As SqlConnection
    Dim sConnString As String
    Dim oSqlCommand As SqlCommand

    Dim oDataAdapter As SqlDataAdapter
    Try
        sConnString = "Data Source=(local);Initial Catalog=Pubs;" & _
                      "User ID=sa;Password="
        oPubConnection = New SqlConnection(sConnString)
        oPubConnection.Open()
        oSqlCommand = oPubConnection.CreateCommand
        oSqlCommand.CommandText = _
            "Select emp_id,lname,Hire_Date from employee"
        oDataAdapter = New SqlDataAdapter()
        oDataAdapter.SelectCommand = oSqlCommand
        Dim datEmployeeInfo As DataSet = New DataSet()
        oDataAdapter.Fill(datEmployeeInfo)
        Return datEmployeeInfo
    Catch oEx As Exception
        MessageBox.Show(oEx.Message)
    Finally
        oPubConnection.Close()
    End Try
End Function
```

You may find that you need to retrieve a set of data by executing a stored procedure as opposed to passing in a SQL statement. Listing 9-7 demonstrates executing a stored procedure that accepts an input parameter and returns a set of records. The records are loaded into a DataSet object and returned to the client.

Listing 9-7. Executing a Stored Procedure

```
Public Overloads Function GetEmployeeInfo(ByVal LInitial As String) As DataSet
    Dim oPubConnection As SqlConnection
    Dim sConnString As String
    Dim oSqlCommand As SqlCommand
    Dim oDataAdapter As SqlDataAdapter
```

```
    Try
        sConnString = "Data Source=(local);Initial Catalog=Pubs;" & _
                "User ID=sa;Password="
        oPubConnection = New SqlConnection(sConnString)
        oPubConnection.Open()
        oSqlCommand = oPubConnection.CreateCommand
        oSqlCommand.CommandText = "GetEmployeeInfobyInitial"
        oSqlCommand.CommandType = CommandType.StoredProcedure
        Dim oInputParam As SqlParameter = _
            oSqlCommand.Parameters.Add("@LInitial", SqlDbType.Char, 1)
        oInputParam.Value = LInitial
        oDataAdapter = New SqlDataAdapter()
        oDataAdapter.SelectCommand = oSqlCommand
        Dim datEmployeeInfo As DataSet = New DataSet()
        oDataAdapter.Fill(datEmployeeInfo)
        Return datEmployeeInfo
    Catch oEx As Exception
        MessageBox.Show(oEx.Message)
    Finally
        oPubConnection.Close()
    End Try
End Function
```

ACTIVITY 9-1. RETRIEVING DATA

In this activity you will become familiar with the following:

- Establishing a connection to a SQL Server database

- Executing queries through a Command object

- Retrieving data with a DataReader object

- Executing a stored procedure using a Command object

> **NOTE** *For the activities in this chapter to work, you must be logged on under a Windows account that has been given the appropriate rights in SQL Server. You may have to alter the* ConnectionString *depending on your settings.*

Creating a Connection and Executing SQL Queries

To create a connection and execute SQL queries, follow these steps:

1. Start Visual Studio. On the File menu, choose New ➤ Project.

2. Choose Windows Application under the Visual Basic Projects folder. Rename the project to **Act9_1** and click the OK button.

3. After the project opens, add a new class to the project named **Author**.

4. Open the Author class code in the code editor.

5. Add an Imports statement at the top of the file to import the SQLClient namespace:

```
Imports System.Data.SqlClient
```

6. Add code to declare a private class level variable of type SQLConnection:

```
Private cnPubs As SqlConnection
```

7. Create a class constructor that instantiates the cnPubs Connection object and set up the ConnectionString property:

```
Public Sub New()
    cnPubs = New SqlConnection()
    cnPubs.ConnectionString = _
        ("Integrated Security=True;Data Source=LocalHost; _
"Initial Catalog=Pubs")
End Sub
```

8. Add a method to the class that will use a Command object to execute a query to count the number of authors in the authors table. Because you are only returning a single value, you will use the ExecuteScalar method of the Command object:

```
Public Function GetAuthorCount() As Integer
    Try
        Dim cmdAuthors As New SqlCommand()
        cmdAuthors.Connection = cnPubs
        cmdAuthors.CommandText = "Select count(*) from authors"
        cnPubs.Open()
        Return cmdAuthors.ExecuteScalar
```

```
        Catch ex As SqlException
            Debug.WriteLine(ex.Message)
        Finally
            cnPubs.Close()
        End Try
    End Function
```

9. Add a button to Form1. Change the Name property of the button to **btnCount** and change the Text property to **Get Count**.

10. Add the following code to the button-click event procedure, which will execute the GetAuthorCount method defined in the Author class:

```
Dim oAuthor As New Author()
MessageBox.Show(oAuthor.GetAuthorCount.ToString)
```

11. Build the project and fix any errors. Once the project builds, run the project in debug mode and test the GetAuthorCount method.

Using the DataReader *Object to Retrieve Records*

To use the DataReader object to retrieve records, follow these steps:

1. Open the Author class code in the code editor.

2. Add a public function to the class definition called GetAuthorList that returns an ArrayList:

```
Public Function GetAuthorList() As ArrayList
End Function
```

3. Add the following code to create procedural scoped variables of type SqlCommand, SqlDataReader, and ArrayList:

```
Dim cmdAuthors As New SqlCommand()
Dim drAuthorList As SqlDataReader
Dim alAuthorsList As New ArrayList()
```

4. Add the following Try-Catch block, which executes a SQL Select statement to retrieve the author last names. A DataReader object then loops

through the records and creates an array list that gets returned to the client:

```
Try
        cmdAuthors.Connection = cnPubs
        cmdAuthors.CommandText = "Select au_lname from authors"
        cnPubs.Open()
        drAuthorList = cmdAuthors.ExecuteReader
        Do While drAuthorList.Read = True
            alAuthorsList.Add(drAuthorList.GetString(0))
        Loop
Catch ex As SqlException
        Debug.WriteLine(ex.Message)
Finally
        cnPubs.Close()
End Try
Return alAuthorsList
```

5. Build the project and fix any errors.

6. Add a ListBox to Form1 and change the `Name` property to **lstAuthors**.

7. Open the `Form1` class code in the code editor. In the left drop-down list choose `(Base Class Events)`. In the right drop-down list, choose `Form1_Load`.

8. Add the following code to the `Form1_Load` event procedure. This code calls the `GetAuthorList` of the `Author` class, which returns an `ArrayList` of author names. The elements of the `ArrayList` are then added to the `lstAuthor`:

```
Private Sub Form1_Load(ByVal sender As Object, _
      ByVal e As System.EventArgs) _
                    Handles MyBase.Load
    Dim i As Integer
    Dim oAuthor As New Author()
    Dim alAuthorList As New ArrayList()
    alAuthorList = oAuthor.GetAuthorList
    For i = 0 To (alAuthorList.Count - 1)
        lstAuthors.Items.Add(alAuthorList.Item(i))
    Next
End Sub
```

9. Build the project and fix any errors.

10. Run the project and test to make sure the list is filled when the form loads.

Executing a Stored Procedure Using a Command Object

To execute a stored procedure using a Command object, follow these steps:

1. Open the Author class code in the code editor.

2. Add a public function that overloads the GetAuthorList function by accepting an integer parameter named Royalty. This function will call the stored procedure byroyalty in the Pubs database. This procedure takes an integer input of royalty percentage and returns a list of author IDs with the percentage:

```
Public Function GetAuthorList(Royalty as Integer) As ArrayList
End Function
```

3. Add the following code to create procedural scoped variables of type SqlCommand, SqlDataReader, ArrayList, and SqlParameter:

```
Dim cmdAuthors As New SqlCommand()
Dim drAuthorList As SqlDataReader
Dim alAuthorsList As New ArrayList()
Dim parRoyalty As New SqlParameter()
```

4. Add the following Try-Catch block, which executes a stored procedure to retrieve the author IDs that have a certain royalty percentage. The royalty percentage is passed into the stored procedure by way of the Parameter collection. A DataReader object then loops through the records and create an array list that gets returned to the client:

```
Try
        cmdAuthors.Connection = cnPubs
        cmdAuthors.CommandType = CommandType.StoredProcedure
        cmdAuthors.CommandText = "byroyalty"
        parRoyalty.ParameterName = "@percentage"
        parRoyalty.Direction = ParameterDirection.Input
```

```
        parRoyalty.SqlDbType = SqlDbType.Int
        parRoyalty.Value = Royalty
        cmdAuthors.Parameters.Add(parRoyalty)
        cnPubs.Open()
        drAuthorList = cmdAuthors.ExecuteReader
        Do While drAuthorList.Read = True
            alAuthorsList.Add(drAuthorList.GetString(0))
        Loop
    Catch ex As SqlException
        Debug.WriteLine(ex.Message)
    Finally
        cnPubs.Close()
    End Try
    Return alAuthorsList
```

5. Build the project and fix any errors.

6. Add a Button control to Form1. Change the Name property of the button to **btnRoyaltyList**. Change the Text property of the button to **Get Royalty List**.

7. Double-click the btnRoyaltyList in the Form1 designer window. The btnRoyaltyList_Click event procedure will be displayed.

8. Add the following code to the btnRoyaltyList_Click event procedure. This code calls the overloaded GetAuthorList of the Author class, which returns an ArrayList of author IDs with a royalty percentage of 50. The elements of the ArrayList are then added to the lstAuthor:

```
Private Sub btnRoyaltyList_Click(ByVal sender As System.Object, _
    ByVal e As System.EventArgs) Handles
                      btnRoyaltyList.Click
    Dim i As Integer
    Dim oAuthor As New Author()
    Dim alAuthorList As New ArrayList()
    alAuthorList = oAuthor.GetAuthorList(50)
    lstAuthors.Items.Clear()
    For i = 0 To (alAuthorList.Count - 1)
        lstAuthors.Items.Add(alAuthorList.Item(i))
    Next
End Sub
```

9. Build the project and fix any errors. Run the application in debug mode and test the code.

10. After testing, stop the debugger and exit Visual Studio.

Working with `DataSet` Objects

A `DataSet` is an in-memory cache of data. It provides a consistent relational programming model for working with data regardless of the data source. You can think of a `DataSet` as a mini-relational database, including the data tables and the relational integrity constraints between the tables. There are several ways to create a `DataSet`. The most obvious method is to populate a `DataSet` from an existing relational database management system (RDBMS) such as a SQL Server database. As mentioned previously, a `DataAdapter` object provides the bridge between the RDBMS and the `DataSet`. By using a `DataAdapter` object, the `DataSet` is totally independent from the data source. Although you need to use a specific set of provider classes to load the `DataSet` object, you work with a `DataSet` with the same set of .NET Framework classes regardless of how the `DataSet` was created and populated. The `System.Data` namespace contains the framework classes for working with `DataSet` objects. Table 9-2 lists some of the classes contained in the `System.Data` namespace.

Table 9-2. Some Members of the `System.Data` *Namespace*

CLASS	DESCRIPTION
DataSet	Collection of `DataTable` and `DataRelation` objects. Organizes an in-memory cache of relational data.
DataTable	Collection of `DataColumn`, `DataRow`, and `Constraint` objects. Organizes records and fields related to a data entity.
DataColumn	Represents the schema of a column in a `DataTable`.
DataRow	Represents a row of data in a `DataTable`.
Constraint	Represents a constraint that can be enforced on `DataColumn` objects.
ForeignKeyConstraint	Used to enforce referential integrity of a parent/child relationship between two `DataTable` objects.
UniqueConstraint	Used to enforce uniqueness of a `DataColumn` or set of `DataColumns`. This is required to enforce referential integrity in a parent/child relationship.
DataRelation	Represents a parent/child relation between two `DataTable` objects.

Populating a DataSet *from a SQL Server Database*

To retrieve data from a database, you set up a connection with the database using a Connection object. After a connection is established, you create a Command object to retrieve the data from the database. If you are retrieving data from multiple tables, you may want to create a separate Command object for each table. You then create a DataAdapter to fill the DataSet. You set the previously created Command object to the SelectComand property of the DataAdapter. If you have multiple Select commands, create a separate DataAdapter for each one. The final step is to fill the DataSet with the data by executing the Fill method of the DataAdapter. Listing 9-8 demonstrates filling a DataSet with data from the publishers table and the titles table of the Pubs database.

Listing 9-8. Populating a DataSet

```
Public Overloads Function GetBookInfo() As DataSet
    Dim oPubConnection As SqlConnection
    Dim sConnString As String
    Dim oSqlCommPubs As SqlCommand
    Dim oSqlCommTitles As SqlCommand
    Dim oDataAdapterPubs As SqlDataAdapter
    Dim oDataAdapterTitles As SqlDataAdapter
    Try
        sConnString = "Data Source=(local);Initial Catalog=Pubs;" & _
                    "User ID=sa;Password="
        oPubConnection = New SqlConnection(sConnString)
        oPubConnection.Open()
        'Create command to retrieve pub info
        oSqlCommPubs = New SqlCommand()
        oSqlCommPubs.Connection = oPubConnection
        oSqlCommPubs.CommandText = "Select pub_id,pub_name from publishers"
        'Create Data Adapter for pub info
        oDataAdapterPubs = New SqlDataAdapter()
        oDataAdapterPubs.SelectCommand = oSqlCommPubs
        'Create command to retrieve title info
        oSqlCommTitles = New SqlCommand()
        oSqlCommTitles.Connection = oPubConnection
        oSqlCommTitles.CommandText = _
            "Select pub_id,title,price,ytd_sales from titles"
        'Create Data Adapter for title info
        oDataAdapterTitles = New SqlDataAdapter()
        oDataAdapterTitles.SelectCommand = oSqlCommTitles
        'Create and fill a Data Set
        Dim datBookInfo As DataSet = New DataSet()
```

```
            oDataAdapterPubs.Fill(datBookInfo, "Publishers")
            oDataAdapterTitles.Fill(datBookInfo, "Titles")
            Return datBookInfo
        Catch oEx As Exception
            MessageBox.Show(oEx.Message)
        Finally
            oPubConnection.Close()
        End Try
    End Function
```

Establishing Relationships between Tables in a DataSet

In an RDBMS system, referential integrity between tables is enforced through a primary key and foreign key relationship. Using a DataRelation object you can enforce data referential integrity between the tables in the DataSet. The DataRelation object contains an array of DataColumn objects that define the common field(s) between the parent table and the child table used to establish the relation. Essentially, the field identified in the parent table is the primary key, and the field identified in the child table is the foreign key. When establishing a relationship, create two DataColumn objects for the common column in each table. Next, create a DataRelation object; pass a name for the DataRelation, and pass the DataColumn objects to the constructor of the DataRelation object. The final step is to add the DataRelation to the Relations collection of the DataSet object. Listing 9-9 demonstrates establishing a relation between the publishers and the titles tables of the datBookInfo created in Listing 9-8.

Listing 9-9. Establishing DataTable Relations

```
'create a DataRelation to link the two tables.
Dim drPub_Title As DataRelation
Dim dcPub_PubId As DataColumn
Dim dcTitle_PubId As DataColumn
'Get the parent and child columns of the two tables.
dcPub_PubId = datBookInfo.Tables("Publishers").Columns("pub_id")
dcTitle_PubId = datBookInfo.Tables("Titles").Columns("pub_id")
' Create the DataRelation and add it to the collection.
drPub_Title = New System.Data.DataRelation _
("PublishersToTitles", dcPub_PubId, dcTitle_PubId)
datBookInfo.Relations.Add(drPub_Title)
```

Editing Data in the DataSet

Clients often need to be able to update a DataSet. They may need to add records, delete records, or update the information of an existing record. Because DataSet objects are disconnected by design, the changes made to the DataSet are not automatically propagated back to the database. The changes are held locally until the client is ready to replicate the changes back to the database. To replicate the changes, the Update method of the DataAdapter is invoked. The Update method determines what changes have been made to the records and implements the appropriate SQL command (Update, Insert, or Delete) that has been defined to replicate the changes back to the database.

To demonstrate the process of updating a DataSet, you will construct an Author class that will pass a DataSet containing author information to a client when the GetData method is invoked. The Author class will accept a DataSet containing changes made to the author information and replicate the changes back to the Pubs database when its UpdateData method is invoked. The first step is to define the class and include an Imports statement for the namespaces that will be referenced:

```
'// Declare namespace references
Imports System.Data
Imports System.Data.SqlClient
Public Class Author
End Class
```

Define class-level variables for SQLConnection, SQLDataAdapter, and DataSet objects:

```
'// Declare class level variables
    Private m_oConn As SqlConnection
    Private m_oDAPubs As SqlDataAdapter
    Private m_oDSPubs As DataSet
```

In the class constructor, a Connection object is initialized:

```
Public Sub New()
    Dim oSelCmd As SqlCommand
    Dim oUpdCmd As SqlCommand

    '// set up connection
    Dim sConnString As String
        sConnString = "Data Source=(local);Initial Catalog=Pubs;" & _
```

```
                              "User ID=sa;Password="
    m_oConn = New SqlConnection(sConnString)
```

Then create a `Select` `Command` object:

```
'// set up the select command
Dim sSQL As String
sSQL = "Select au_id, au_lname, au_fname from authors"
oSelCmd = New SqlCommand(sSQL, m_oConn)
oSelCmd.CommandType = CommandType.Text
```

Next you create an `Update` Command. The command text references parameters in the command's `Parameters` collection that will be created next:

```
'// set up the update command
sSQL = "Update authors set au_lname = @au_lname, au_fname = @au_fname" _
            & " where au_id = @au_id"
oUpdCmd = New SqlCommand(sSQL, m_oConn)
oUpdCmd.CommandType = CommandType.Text
```

A `Parameter` object is added to the `Command` object's `Parameter` collection for each `Parameter` in the `Update` statement. The `Add` method of the `Parameters` collection is passed information on the name of the `Parameter`, the SQL data type, size, and the source column of the `DataSet`:

```
oUpdCmd.Parameters.Add("@au_id", SqlDbType.VarChar, 11, "au_id")
oUpdCmd.Parameters.Add("@au_lname", SqlDbType.VarChar, 40, "au_lname")
oUpdCmd.Parameters.Add("@au_fname", SqlDbType.VarChar, 40, "au_fname")
```

The final step is to create and set up the `DataAdapter` object. Set the `SelectCommand` and `UpdateCommand` properties to the appropriate `SQLCommand` objects:

```
    '// set up the data adapter
    m_oDAPubs = New SqlDataAdapter()
    m_oDAPubs.SelectCommand = oSelCmd
    m_oDAPubs.UpdateCommand = oUpdCmd
End Sub
```

Now that the `SQLDataAdapter` has been set up and created in the class constructor, the `GetData` and `UpdateData` methods will use the `DataAdapter` to get and update the data from the database:

```
Public Function GetData() As DataSet
    m_oDSPubs = New DataSet()
    m_oDAPubs.Fill(m_oDSPubs, "Authors")
    Return m_oDSPubs
End Function
Public Sub SaveData(ByVal DSChanges As DataSet)
    m_oDAPubs.Update(DSChanges, "Authors")
End Sub
```

In a similar fashion you could implement the InsertCommand and the DeleteCommand properties of the DataAdapter to allow clients to insert new records or delete records in the database.

> **NOTE** *For simple updates to a single table in the data source, the .NET Framework provides a* CommandBuilder *class to automate the creation of the* InsertCommand, UpdateCommand, *and* DeleteCommand *properties of the* DataAdapter.

Converting between Relational DataSet Objects and Hierarchical XML Files

One of the most powerful features of ADO.NET is its tight integration with XML. When an ADO.NET DataSet is transferred from a client to a server (or vice versa), it is persisted in XML structures. The ability to load XML files into a relational DataSet structure and to persist relational DataSet objects as XML structures is fundamental to the .NET Framework. The DataSet class includes the ReadXML method to load an existing XML document into a DataSet object. The following function reads author data from an existing XML file and returns it to the client in the form of a DataSet:

```
Public Function LoadDataFromXML() As DataSet
    Dim ds As DataSet = New DataSet()
    ds.ReadXml("c:\Authors.xml", XmlReadMode.ReadSchema)
    Return ds
End Function
```

You can just as easily persist a DataSet to an XML file by using the WriteXml method of the DataSet class. The following method accepts a DataSet from the client and writes the data and the schema of the DataSet to a file:

```
Public Sub SaveDataAsXML(ByVal ds As DataSet)
    ds.WriteXml("c:\Authors.xml", XmlWriteMode.WriteSchema)
End Sub
```

ACTIVITY 9-2. WORKING WITH *DATASET* OBJECTS

In this activity you will become familiar with the following:

- Populating a DataSet from a SQL Server database

- Editing data in a DataSet

- Updating changes from the DataSet to the database

- Establishing relationships between tables in a DataSet

Populating a DataSet *from a SQL Server Database*

To populate a DataSet from a SQL Server database, follow these steps:

1. Start Visual Studio. On the File menu, choose New ➤ Project.

2. Choose Windows Application under the Visual Basic Projects folder. Rename the project to **Act9_2** and click the OK button.

3. After the project opens, add a new class to the project named **Author**.

4. Open the Author class code in the code editor.

5. Add an Imports statement at the top of the file to import the SQLClient namespace:

   ```
   Imports System.Data.SqlClient
   ```

6. Add code to declare private class level variables of type SQLConnection, SqlDataAdapter, and DataSet:

   ```
   Private cnPubs As SqlConnection
   Private daPubs As SqlDataAdapter
   Private dsPubs As DataSet
   ```

7. Create a class constructor that instantiates the cnPubs Connection object and set up the ConnectionString property:

```
Public Sub New()
    cnPubs = New SqlConnection()
    cnPubs.ConnectionString = _
        ("Integrated Security=True;Data Source=LocalHost; _
"Initial Catalog=Pubs")
```

8. Add code to set up a SqlCommand object that will execute a select query to retrieve author information:

```
Dim strSQL As String
Dim oSelCmd As SqlCommand
strSQL = "Select au_id, au_lname, au_fname from authors"
oSelCmd = New SqlCommand(strSQL, cnPubs)
```

9. Add code to instantiate the DataAdapter and set its SelectCommand property to the SqlCommand object created in step 8:

```
    daPubs = New SqlDataAdapter()
    daPubs.SelectCommand = oSelCmd
End Sub
```

10. Add code to create a method of the Author class called GetData that will use the DataAdapter object to fill the DataSet and return it to the client:

```
Public Function GetData() As DataSet
    dsPubs = New DataSet()
    daPubs.Fill(dsPubs, "Authors")
    Return dsPubs
End Function
```

11. Build the project and fix any errors.

12. Add the following controls to Form1 and set the properties as listed in Table 9-3.

Table 9-3. Form1 Controls

CONTROL	PROPERTY	VALUE
DataGrid	Name	dgAuthors
	AllowNavigation	False
Button	Name	btnGetDS
	Text	Get DS
Button	Name	btnUpdate
	Text	Update

13. Add the following declaration after the Inherits System.Windows.Forms.Form statement located at the top of the Form1 class code. This code creates a class-level DataSet object:

```
Private m_oDSPubs As DataSet
```

14. Add the following code to the btnGetDS click event procedure, which will execute the GetData method defined in the Author class. The DataSet returned by the method is passed to the class-level DataSet object m_dsPubs:

```
Private Sub btnGetDS_Click(ByVal sender As System.Object, _
            ByVal e As System.EventArgs) Handles btnGetDS.Click
    Dim oAuthor As Author = New Author()
    m_oDSPubs = oAuthor.GetData
    dgAuthors.DataSource = m_oDSPubs.Tables("Authors")
End Sub
```

15. Build the project and fix any errors. Once the project builds, run the project in debug mode and test the GetData method. After testing stop the debugger.

Editing and Updating a DataSet to a SQL Server Database

To edit and update a DataSet to a SQL Server database, follow these steps:

1. Open the Author class code in the code editor.

2. At the end of the class constructor (in other words, Sub New), add code to set up a SqlCommand object that will execute an Update query to update author information:

```
Dim oUpdCmd As SqlCommand
strSQL = "Update authors set au_lname = @au_lname, au_fname = " _
                        & "@au_fname where au_id = @au_id"
oUpdCmd = New SqlCommand(strSQL, cnPubs)
```

3. Add code to add the update parameters to the Parameters collection of the SqlCommand object created in step 2:

```
oUpdCmd.Parameters.Add("@au_id", SqlDbType.VarChar, 11, "au_id")
oUpdCmd.Parameters.Add("@au_lname", SqlDbType.VarChar, 40, "au_lname")
oUpdCmd.Parameters.Add("@au_fname", SqlDbType.VarChar, 40, "au_fname")
```

4. Add code to set the DataAdapter object's Update Command property to the SqlCommand object created in step 2:

```
    daPubs.UpdateCommand = oUpdCmd
End Sub
```

5. Add code to create a method of the Author class called UpdateData that will use the Update method of the DataAdapter object to update changes made to the DataSet to the Pubs database:

```
Public Function UpdateData(ByVal DSChanged As DataSet) As Boolean
    Try
        daPubs.Update(DSChanged, "Authors")
        Return True
    Catch ex As Exception
```

```
            Return False
        End Try
    End Function
```

6. Build the project and fix any errors.

7. Open the Form1 class code in the code editor.

8. Add the following code to the btnUpdate click event procedure, which
    will execute the UpdateData method defined in the Author class. By using
    the GetChanges method of the DataSet object, only data that has changed
    is passed for updating:

```
Private Sub btnUpdate_Click(ByVal sender As System.Object, _
                ByVal e As System.EventArgs) Handles btnUpdate.Click
    Dim oAuthor As Author = New Author()
    If m_oDSPubs Is Nothing Then Exit Sub
    MsgBox(oAuthor.UpdateData(m_oDSPubs.GetChanges))
End Sub
```

9. Build the project and fix any errors. Once the project builds, run the
    project in debug mode and test the Update method. First click the
    Get DS button. Change the last name of several authors and click the
    Update button. Click the Get DS button again to retrieve the changed
    values back from the database. After testing, stop the debugger.

Establishing Relationships between Tables in *a* DataSet

To establish relationships between tables in a DataSet, follow these steps:

1. Add a new class named **Orders** to the project.

2. Open the Orders class code in the code editor.

3. Add an Imports statement at the top of the file to import the SQLClient
    namespace:

```
Imports System.Data.SqlClient
```

4. Add code to declare private class-level variables of type SQLConnection,
    SqlDataAdapter, and DataSet:

```
Private cnPubs As SqlConnection
Private DAOrders As SqlDataAdapter
Private DAOrderDetails As SqlDataAdapter
Private DSOrders As DataSet
```

5. Create a class constructor that instantiates the cnPubs Connection object and set up the ConnectionString property:

```
Public Sub New()
    cnPubs = New SqlConnection()
    cnPubs.ConnectionString = _
            ("Integrated Security=True;Data Source=LocalHost; _
"Initial Catalog=Northwind")
```

6. Add code to set up a SqlCommand object that will execute a Select query to retrieve order information:

```
Dim oSelCmd As SqlCommand
Dim strSQL As String
strSQL = "Select OrderID, OrderDate from Orders"
oSelCmd = New SqlCommand(strSQL, cnPubs)
```

7. Add code to instantiate the DataAdapter and set its SelectCommand property to the SqlCommand object created in step 6:

```
DAOrders = New SqlDataAdapter()
DAOrders.SelectCommand = oSelCmd
```

8. Repeat steps 6 and 7 to add code to set up a DataAdapter to retrieve order details:

```
    strSQL = "Select OrderID, ProductID, Quantity from [Order Details]"
    oSelCmd = New SqlCommand(strSQL, cnPubs)
    DAOrderDetails = New SqlDataAdapter()
    DAOrderDetails.SelectCommand = oSelCmd
End Sub
```

9. Add code to create a method of the Orders class called GetData that will use the DataAdapter objects to fill the DataSet, establish a table relation, and return the DataSet to the client:

```
Public Function GetData() As DataSet
    DSOrders = New DataSet()
    DAOrders.Fill(DSOrders, "Orders")
```

```
        DAOrderDetails.Fill(DSOrders, "OrderDetails")
        Dim drOrders As New DataRelation("Orders_OrderDetails", _
            DSOrders.Tables("Orders").Columns("OrderID"), _
            DSOrders.Tables("OrderDetails").Columns("OrderID"))
        DSOrders.Relations.Add(drOrders)
        Return DSOrders
    End Function
```

10. Build the project and fix any errors.

11. Add a second form to the project. Add the following controls to Form2 and set the properties as listed in Table 9-4.

Table 9-4. Form2 Controls

CONTROL	PROPERTY	VALUE
DataGrid	Name	dgOrders
	AllowNavigation	True
Button	Name	btnGetDS
	Text	Get DS

12. Add the following declaration after the `Inherits` `System.Windows.Forms.Form` statement located at the top of the `Form2` class code. This code creates a class-level `DataSet` object:

```
    Private m_oDSOrders As DataSet
```

13. Add the following code to the `btnGetDS` click event procedure, which will execute the `GetData` method defined in the `Orders` class. The `DataSet` returned by the method is passed to the class-level `DataSet` object `m_dsPubs`:

```
Private Sub btnGetDS_Click(ByVal sender As System.Object, _
        ByVal e As System.EventArgs) Handles btnGetDS.Click
    Dim oOrders As Orders = New Orders()
    m_dsOrders = oOrders.GetData
    dgOrders.SetDataBinding(m_dsOrders, "Orders")
End Sub
```

14. Build the project and fix any errors.

15. Change the startup object of the project to Form2. Run the project in debug mode and test the GetData method. When the grid loads, you should be able to drill down to the order details of each order row in the grid.

16. After testing, stop the debugger and exit Visual Studio.

Building the OSO Application's Business Logic Tier

Now that you are familiar with the System.Data and the System.Data.SQLClient namespaces, you are ready to build the OSO application's business logic tier. First let's review the OSO application's class diagram that you created in Chapter 4, "Designing OOP Solutions: A Case Study" (see Figure 9-1).

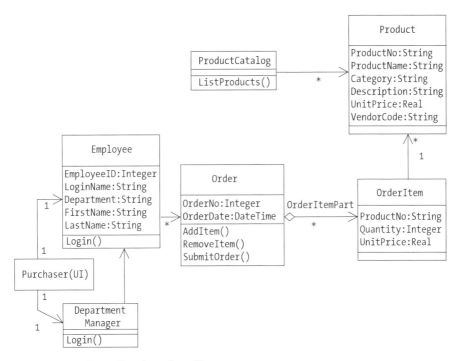

Figure 9-1. OSO application class diagram

You also must review the structure of the database that will comprise the data tier of the OSO application. Figure 9-2 shows the database diagram for the OSO application. This database will be implemented in a SQL Server 2000 database.

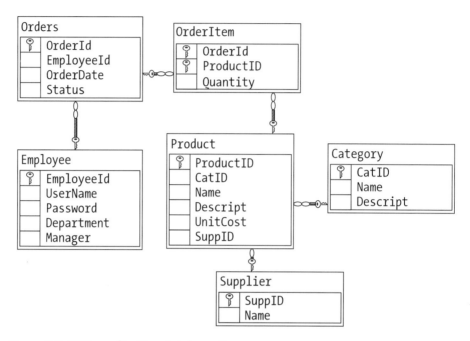

Figure 9-2. OSO application database diagram

The first class you are going to construct is the ProductCatalog class. The purpose of this class is to encapsulate the functionality of retrieving a listing of the available products in the database. You also want the ability to view the products based on the category to which they belong. The information you need is in two database tables: the catalog table and the products table. These two tables are related through the CatID field. When a client requests the product catalog information, a DataSet will be created and returned to the client. This service will be provided in the ProductCatalog class's GetProductInfo method (see Listing 9-10).

Listing 9-10. ProductCatalog *Class*

```
'/// Retrieves information on product categories and products
'/// Returns information as a dataset object
Imports System.Data.SqlClient
Public Class ProductCatalog
    Private m_conn As SqlConnection
    Private m_dsProducts As New DataSet()
```

```
    Public Function GetProductInfo() As DataSet
        Try
            'Get the Category info
            Dim strSQL As String = "select CatID, Name, Descript from Category"
            Dim cmdSelCatagory As SqlCommand = New SqlCommand(strSQL, m_conn)
            Dim daCatagory As SqlDataAdapter =
New SqlDataAdapter(cmdSelCatagory)
            daCatagory.Fill(m_dsProducts, "Category")
            'Get the product info
            strSQL = "Select ProductID,CatID,Name,Descript,UnitCost _
"from Product"
            Dim cmdSelProductInfo As SqlCommand =
New SqlCommand(strSQL, m_conn)
            Dim daProductInfo As SqlDataAdapter = _
                New SqlDataAdapter(cmdSelProductInfo)
            daProductInfo.Fill(m_dsProducts, "Product")
            'Set up the table relation
            Dim drCat_Prod As New DataRelation _
                    ("drCat_Prod", _
                    m_dsProducts.Tables("Category").Columns("CatID"), _
                    m_dsProducts.Tables("Product").Columns("CatID"))
             m_dsProducts.Relations.Add(drCat_Prod)
        Catch ex As Exception
            Debug.WriteLine(ex.ToString)
        End Try
        Return m_dsProducts
    End Function
    Public Sub New()
        m_conn = New SqlConnection()
        m_conn.ConnectionString = "Integrated Security=True;" & _
                    "Data Source=LocalHost;Initial Catalog=OfficeSupply"
    End Sub
End Class
```

The next class you need to construct is the OrderItem class, which will hold information pertaining to an order item of an order. The quantity, product ID, and price will be exposed as read/write properties. The subtotal of the order item will be calculated and exposed as a read only property of the class (see Listing 9-11).

Listing 9-11. OrderItem *Class*

```
'/// Used to hold line item information for orders.
'/// toString method has been overriden to provide order
'/// item info in an XML structure.
```

```
Public Class OrderItem
    Private m_ProductID As String
    Private m_Quantity As Integer
    Private m_UnitPrice As Double
    Private m_SubTotal As Double

    Public Property ProductID() As String
        Get
            Return m_ProductID
        End Get
        Set(ByVal Value As String)
            Value = m_ProductID
        End Set
    End Property
    Public Property Quantity() As Integer
        Get
            Return m_Quantity
        End Get
        Set(ByVal Value As Integer)
            m_Quantity = Value
        End Set
    End Property
    Public Property UnitPrice() As Double
        Get
            Return m_UnitPrice
        End Get
        Set(ByVal Value As Double)
            m_UnitPrice = Value
        End Set
    End Property
    Public ReadOnly Property SubTotal()
        Get
            Return m_SubTotal
        End Get
    End Property

    Public Sub New(ByVal ProductID As String, _
        ByVal UnitPrice As Double, ByVal Quantity As Integer)

        m_ProductID = ProductID.Trim
        m_UnitPrice = UnitPrice
```

```
            m_Quantity = Quantity
            m_SubTotal = m_UnitPrice * m_Quantity
    End Sub
        Public Overrides Function toString() As String
            Dim xml As String
            xml = "<OrderItem"
            xml &= " ProductID='" & m_ProductID & "'"
            xml &= " Quantity='" & m_Quantity & "'"
            xml &= " />"
            Return xml
        End Function
End Class
```

An Order class will encapsulate the process of adding items to an order and removing items from an order. Order items will be held in an ArrayList object. The ArrayList class is part of the System.Collections namespace and provides the functionality for working with a list of objects. The list of order items is exposed to clients through a read-only property that returns an array list of OrderItem objects (see Listing 9-12).

Listing 9-12. Order *Class*

```
'/// Used to process orders.
'/// Items can be added or removed.
'/// The total cost of the order is calculated.
'/// When the order is placed it is sent as XML
'/// to the dbOrder class for processing.
Public Class Order
    Private m_alOrderItems As New ArrayList()
    Public ReadOnly Property OrderItems() As ArrayList
        Get
            Return m_alOrderItems
        End Get
    End Property
    Public Sub AddItem(ByVal Value As OrderItem)
        Dim oItem As OrderItem
        For Each oItem In m_alOrderItems
            If oItem.ProductID = Value.ProductID Then
                oItem.Quantity += Value.Quantity
                Exit Sub
            End If
```

```
                Next
                m_alOrderItems.Add(Value)
        End Sub
        Public Sub RemoveItem(ByVal ProductID As String)
            Dim oItem As OrderItem
            For Each oItem In m_alOrderItems
                If oItem.ProductID = ProductID Then
                    m_alOrderItems.Remove(oItem)
                    Exit Sub
                End If
            Next
        End Sub
        Public Function GetOrderTotal() As Double
            If m_alOrderItems.Count = 0 Then
                Return 0.0
            Else
                Dim oItem As OrderItem
                Dim total As Double
                For Each oItem In m_alOrderItems
                    total += oItem.SubTotal
                Next
                Return total
            End If
        End Function
        Public Function PlaceOrder(ByVal EmployeeID As Integer) As Integer
            Dim xmlOrder As String
            xmlOrder = "<Order EmployeeID='" & EmployeeID.ToString & "'>"
            Dim oItem As OrderItem
            For Each oItem In m_alOrderItems
                xmlOrder &= oItem.ToString
            Next
            xmlOrder &= "</Order>"

            Dim odbOrder As New dbOrder()
            Return odbOrder.PlaceOrder(xmlOrder)
        End Function
End Class
```

When a client is ready to submit an order, the PlaceOrder method of the Order class will be called. The client will pass the employee ID into the method and receive an order number as a return value. The PlaceOrder method of the Order class will pass the order information in the form of an XML string to the dbOrder class for processing. It has been decided to create a separate class to process the order information and pass it into data storage. This will enable you to more effectively decouple the data tier from the business logic tier. The dbOrder class contains the PlaceOrder method that receives an XML order string from the Order class and passes it into a stored procedure in the SQL Server database. The stored procedure updates the database and passes back the order number. This order number is then returned to the Order class, which in turn passes it back to the client. Listing 9-13 contains the code used to define the dbOrder class.

Listing 9-13. dbOrder *Class*

```
'/// Persists order data to the database.
'/// Uses the up_PlaceOrder stored procedure
Imports System.Data.SqlClient
Public Class dbOrder
    Public Function PlaceOrder(ByVal xmlOrder As String) As Integer
        Dim cn As SqlConnection = New SqlConnection()
        cn.ConnectionString = _
            "Integrated Security=True;Data Source=localhost;" & _
            "Initial Catalog=OfficeSupply"
        Try
            Dim cmd As SqlCommand = cn.CreateCommand()
            cmd.CommandType = CommandType.StoredProcedure
            cmd.CommandText = "up_PlaceOrder"

            Dim inParameter As New SqlParameter()
            inParameter.ParameterName = "@xmlOrder"
            inParameter.Value = xmlOrder
            inParameter.DbType = DbType.String
            inParameter.Direction = ParameterDirection.Input
            cmd.Parameters.Add(inParameter)

            Dim ReturnParameter As New SqlParameter()
            ReturnParameter.ParameterName = "@OrderID"
            ReturnParameter.Direction = ParameterDirection.ReturnValue
            cmd.Parameters.Add(ReturnParameter)
```

```
                Dim intOrderNo As Integer
                cn.Open()
                cmd.ExecuteNonQuery()
                cn.Close()
                intOrderNo = cmd.Parameters("@OrderID").Value
            Return intOrderNo
        Catch ex As Exception
                Debug.WriteLine(ex.ToString)
            End Try
    End Function
End Class
```

The final class that you need to construct is the Employee class (see Listing 9-14). This class will encapsulate the process of verifying an employee before an order can be placed. The Login method of the Employee class will verify the login credentials of an employee attempting to submit a purchase order. Once an employee has been verified, the Login method will return the EmployeeID to the client.

Listing 9-14. Employee Class

```
'/// Used to verify employees and provide the employee
'/// id so employees can place an order.
Imports System.Data.SqlClient
Public Class Employee
    Private m_LoginAttempt As Integer
    Public Function Login(ByVal UserName As String, _
        ByVal Password As String) As Integer
        Dim conn As SqlConnection = New SqlConnection()
        Try
            conn.ConnectionString = "Integrated Security=True;" & _
                    "Data Source=LocalHost;Initial Catalog=OfficeSupply"
            conn.Open()
            Dim comm As SqlCommand = New SqlCommand()
            Dim userID As Integer
            comm.Connection = conn
            comm.CommandText = "Select EmployeeID from Employee" & _
                " where UserName='" _
                & UserName & "' and Password='" & Password & "'"
            userID = comm.ExecuteScalar()
            If userID > 0 Then
```

```
                Return userID
            Else
                m_LoginAttempt += 1
                If m_LoginAttempt >= 3 Then
                    Throw New Exception("Too many invalid attemps!")
                End If
                Return -1
            End If
        Catch ex As Exception
            Debug.WriteLine(ex.ToString)
        Finally
            conn.Close()
        End Try
    End Function
End Class
```

Now that you have created the business logic classes for this part of the application, you should revise the class diagram to more accurately reflect the classes developed up to this point. It is important to remember that the class diagram was developed to help you plan the development of the classes and the relationships between those classes. As you develop and test the classes in the implementation phase, it is natural and almost inevitable that the class structure of the application will evolve. Figure 9-3 represents the current class structure of the OSO application's business logic tier.

ACTIVITY 9-3. REVIEWING AND TESTING THE OSO APPLICATION'S BUSINESS LOGIC TIER

In this activity you will become familiar with the following:

- Installing the OSO database

- Reviewing the OSO application's business logic class structure

- Testing the OSO application's business logic

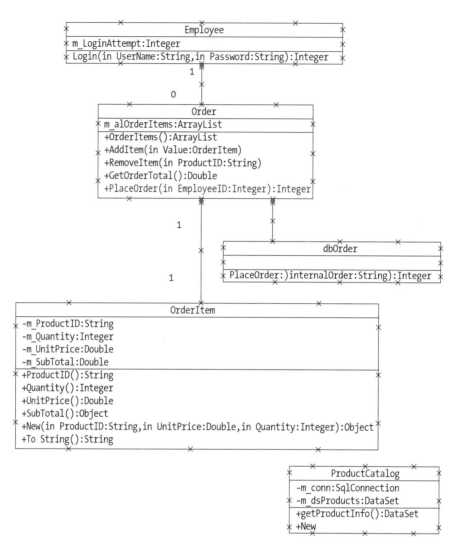

Figure 9-3. OSO business logic class diagram

Setting Up the Office Supply Database

To set up the office-supply database, follow these steps:

1. Start Visual Studio. On the File menu, choose Open ➤ Project.

2. Navigate to the OSODataBase folder and open it.

3. Select the OSODataBase solution file and click Open.

4. In the Solution Explorer you should see a `Database References` node. Select the node, right-click, and select New Database Reference.

5. In the Data Link Properties dialog box, select your SQL Server or use localhost if it is installed locally. Use a valid security context that has administrator rights on the server. Select the master database and test the connection.

6. After establishing the connection, click OK to close the dialog box.

7. In the Solution Explorer right-click the `OfficeSupplyDB_Schema.sql` file and select Run. In the Run On dialog box, choose the reference you created in step 5 and click OK.

8. Repeat step 7 for the `up_PlaceOrder.sql` and `OfficeSupply_DataLoad.sql` files.

9. Repeat step 7 for the `Test.sql` file and make sure the product information is displayed in the Output window.

10. After running the script, close the application.

Testing the OSO Application Business Logic

To test the OSO application business logic, follow these steps:

1. On the File menu, choose Open ➤ Project.

2. Navigate to the `OSOBusTier` folder and open it.

3. Select the `OSOBusTier` solution file and click Open.

4. The project contains the OSO business logic classes and a form that you will use to test the classes.

5. Add the following controls to Form1 and set the properties as listed in Table 9-5.

Table 9-5. Form1 Control Property Settings

CONTROL	PROPERTY	VALUE
Label	Text	UserName
TextBox	Name	txtUserName
	Text	[blank]
Label	Text	Password
TextBox	Name	txtPassword
	Text	[blank]
Button	Name	btnLogin
	Text	Login

6. Add the following code to the btnLogin click event procedure. This will execute the Login method defined in the Employee class and display the EmployeeID passed back in a message box:

```
Private Sub btnLogin_Click(ByVal sender As System.Object, _
        ByVal e As System.EventArgs) Handles btnLogin.Click
    Dim oEmployee As New Employee()
    MsgBox(oEmployee.Login(txtUserName.Text, _
txtPassword.Text).ToString)
End Sub
```

7. Build the project and fix any errors.

8. Run the project in debug mode. To test the Login method, enter a user name of **jsmith** and a password of **js**. After logging, a message box containing an Employee ID of 2 should be displayed.

9. After testing stop the debugger.

10. Add the following additional controls to Form1 and set the properties as listed in Table 9-6.

Table 9-6. Form1 Control Property Settings

CONTROL	PROPERTY	VALUE
DataGrid	Name	dgProducts
Button	Name	btnGetProducts
	Text	Get Products

11. Add the following code to the btnGetProducts click event procedure. This will execute the GetProductInfo method defined in the ProductCatalog class and display the DataSet passed back in the DataGrid:

```
Private Sub btnGetProducts_Click(ByVal sender As System.Object, _
    ByVal e As System.EventArgs) Handles btnGetProducts.Click
    Dim oProducts As New ProductCatalog()
    dgProducts.DataSource = _
oProducts.getProductInfo.Tables("Category")
End Sub
```

12. Build the project and fix any errors.

13. Run the project in debug mode. Click the Get Product button. A hierar-chical DataSet of categories and products should be displayed in the grid. Navigate through the DataSet.

14. After testing, stop the debugger.

Testing the Order Class

To test the Order class, follow these steps:

1. Add a Button control to Form1. Change the Name property to **btnTestOrder** and the Text property to **Test Order**.

2. Add the following code to the btnTestOrder click event procedure. This code will create an order and add order items. A message box will display the order items in the order as an XML node. Another message box will display the total cost of the order. A final message box will display the order number of the order returned from the database when the order is placed:

```
Dim oOrder As New Order()
oOrder.AddItem(New OrderItem("ACM-10414", 3.79, 2))
oOrder.AddItem(New OrderItem("ACM-10414", 3.79, 4))
oOrder.AddItem(New OrderItem("OIC-5000", 1.99, 2))
oOrder.AddItem(New OrderItem("MMM-6200", 3.9, 2))

Dim i As Integer
For i = 0 To oOrder.OrderItems.Count - 1
    MessageBox.Show(oOrder.OrderItems.Item(i).ToString)
Next

MessageBox.Show(oOrder.GetOrderTotal.ToString)
MessageBox.Show(oOrder.PlaceOrder(1).ToString)
```

3. Build the project and fix any errors.

4. Run the project in debug mode. Click the Test Order button. A series of message boxes should be displayed showing the order information described in step 2.

5. After testing, stop the debugger and close Visual Studio.

Summary

In this chapter you did the following:

- Looked at transitioning from the logical design phase to the physical design phase

- Established a connection to a database using the Connection object

- Used a `Command` object to execute SQL queries and stored procedures

- Retrieved records with the `DataReader` object

- Populated a `DataSet` using a `DataAdapter` object

- Established relationships between tables in a `DataSet`

- Persisted changed data in a `DataSet` back to the database

- Reviewed and tested the OSO application's business logic tier

This chapter is the first in a series of three aimed at introducing you to building the various tiers of an OOP application. To implement the application's business logic, you learned about ADO.NET. You looked at the various classes that make up the `System.Data.SqlClient` namespace. These classe are used to retrieve and update data stored in a SQL Server database. You also examined the `System.Data` namespace classes that work with disconnected data.

In the next chapter you will look at implementing the interface tier of an application. You will implement the user interface through traditional Windows Forms. Along the way you will take a closer look at the classes and namespaces of the .NET Framework used to implement rich Windows Forms-based user interfaces.

CHAPTER 10

Developing Windows Applications

I**N THE PREVIOUS CHAPTER** you looked at developing the business logic layer of an application. To implement the business logic you worked with the classes contained in the System.Data namespace. These classes retrieve and work with relational data, which is a common requirement of many business applications. You are now ready to look at how users will interact with your application. Users interact with an application through the user interface layer. The user interface layer in turn interacts with the business logic layer, which in turn interacts with the data storage layer. This chapter covers building a "traditional" user interface consisting of Windows Forms. In the next chapter, you will look at creating a Web interface for an application.

After reading this chapter you should be familiar with the following:

- Working with forms and controls

- The inheritance hierarchy of forms and controls

- Responding to form and control events

- Constructing base and derived forms

- Working with and creating modal dialog forms

- Data binding controls contained in a Windows Form

Windows Forms Fundamentals

Forms are objects with a visual interface and are painted on the screen to provide users the ability to interact with programs. Just like all objects you work with in object-oriented languages, forms expose properties, methods, and events. The form's *properties* define the appearance of the form; for example, a form's BackColor property determines the background color of the form. The *methods* of a form define its behaviors; for example, a form object has a Hide method that causes its visual interface to be hidden from the user. The form's *events* define interactions with the user (or other objects); for example, the MouseDown event could initiate an action when the user clicks the right mouse button on the form.

Controls are components with visual interfaces that provide users with a way to interact with the program. A form is a special type of control, called a *container control*. A container control hosts other controls. There are many different types of controls you can place on Windows Forms. Some of the more common controls used on forms are TextBoxes, Labels, OptionButtons, ListBoxes, and CheckBoxes, just to name a few. In addition to the controls provided by the .NET Framework, you can also create your own custom controls or purchase controls from third-party vendors.

Understanding Windows Forms Inheritance Hierarchy

If you trace the inheritance chain of form classes, you can see that the Form class you create in a Windows application inherits from the Form class, which is part of the System.Windows.Forms namespace. This class is where the common functionality required by all Windows Forms is defined. For example, the form's FormBorderStyle property is defined in this class, and it determines how the outer edge of the form appears. One of the methods defined in the System.Windows.Forms.Form class is the Activate method. The Activate method brings the form to the front if it is contained in the active application, or it flashes the window caption if the application is not the active application. A MenuStart event is defined in the System.Windows.Forms.Form class. This event is raised when the user clicks any menu item in the form's menu.

If you trace the inheritance chain of Windows Forms further, you discover that the Form class inherits functionality from the ContainerControl class, which provides management functionality for controls that function as a container for other controls. The ContainerControl class inherits from the ScrollableControl class, which provides support for autoscrolling behavior. The ScrollableControl class inherits from the Control class, which provides the basic functionality required by classes that display information to the user. Although tracing this hierarchy is not necessary to add and use Windows Forms (or controls, which have a similar hierarchy) in your application, it is beneficial to understand this hierarchy exists and how the forms you construct gain their built-in functionality. Figure 10-1 shows the hierarchical chain of a Windows Form as represented in the Class View of Visual Studio. Figure 10-2 illustrates the hierarchical chain of a TextBox control, as represented in the Object Browser window of Visual Studio.

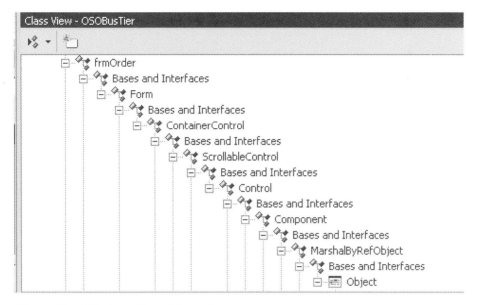

Figure 10-1. Windows Form hierarchy

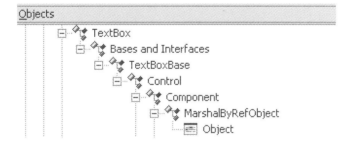

Figure 10-2. TextBox control hierarchy

Using the Visual Studio Form Designer

Although it is quite possible to create your forms entirely through code using a text editor, you will probably find this process quite tedious and not the most productive use of your time. Thankfully, the Visual Studio Integrated Development Environment (IDE) includes an excellent visual Form Designer. Using the designer you can drag and drop controls onto the form from the Toolbox and set control properties using the Properties window. Figure 10-3 shows a form being designed in Visual Studio.

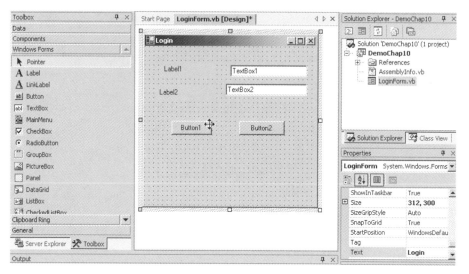

Figure 10-3. Visual Studio Form Designer

If you look at the code for the form class file, you will see a region marked as Windows Form Designer–Generated Code. This region contains the class constructor code, destructor code, and the code needed to construct and manage the controls contained on the form:

```
Public Class LoginForm
    Inherits System.Windows.Forms.Form

#Region " Windows Form Designer generated code "

End Class
```

Although it is generally not a good idea to alter the code contained in this region directly, it is beneficial to look at the code in this region to gain an understanding of what the code is doing. The code for the form being designed in Figure 10-3 is shown in Listing 10-1 with the Windows Form Designer region expanded.

Listing 10-1. Windows Form Designer–Generated Code
```
Public Class LoginForm
    Inherits System.Windows.Forms.Form

#Region " Windows Form Designer generated code "

    Public Sub New()
```

```
        MyBase.New()

        'This call is required by the Windows Form Designer.
        InitializeComponent()

        'Add any initialization after the InitializeComponent() call

End Sub

'Form overrides dispose to clean up the component list.
Protected Overloads Overrides Sub Dispose(ByVal disposing As Boolean)
    If disposing Then
        If Not (components Is Nothing) Then
            components.Dispose()
        End If
    End If
    MyBase.Dispose(disposing)
End Sub

'Required by the Windows Form Designer
Private components As System.ComponentModel.IContainer

'NOTE: The following procedure is required by the Windows Form Designer
'It can be modified using the Windows Form Designer.
'Do not modify it using the code editor.
Friend WithEvents Label1 As System.Windows.Forms.Label
Friend WithEvents Label2 As System.Windows.Forms.Label
Friend WithEvents txtName As System.Windows.Forms.TextBox
Friend WithEvents txtPassword As System.Windows.Forms.TextBox
Friend WithEvents btnOK As System.Windows.Forms.Button
Friend WithEvents btnCancel As System.Windows.Forms.Button
<System.Diagnostics.DebuggerStepThrough()> Private Sub InitializeComponent()
    Me.Label1 = New System.Windows.Forms.Label()
    Me.Label2 = New System.Windows.Forms.Label()
    Me.txtName = New System.Windows.Forms.TextBox()
    Me.txtPassword = New System.Windows.Forms.TextBox()
    Me.btnOK = New System.Windows.Forms.Button()
    Me.btnCancel = New System.Windows.Forms.Button()
    Me.SuspendLayout()
    '
    'Label1
    '
    Me.Label1.Location = New System.Drawing.Point(24, 32)
```

```
Me.Label1.Name = "Label1"
Me.Label1.Size = New System.Drawing.Size(96, 20)
Me.Label1.TabIndex = 0
Me.Label1.Text = "Name:"
'
'Label2
'
Me.Label2.Location = New System.Drawing.Point(24, 64)
Me.Label2.Name = "Label2"
Me.Label2.Size = New System.Drawing.Size(104, 20)
Me.Label2.TabIndex = 1
Me.Label2.Text = "Password:"
'
'txtName
'
Me.txtName.Location = New System.Drawing.Point(144, 32)
Me.txtName.Name = "txtName"
Me.txtName.Size = New System.Drawing.Size(144, 20)
Me.txtName.TabIndex = 2
Me.txtName.Text = ""
'
'txtPassword
'
Me.txtPassword.Location = New System.Drawing.Point(144, 64)
Me.txtPassword.Name = "txtPassword"
Me.txtPassword.Size = New System.Drawing.Size(144, 20)
Me.txtPassword.TabIndex = 3
Me.txtPassword.Text = ""
'
'btnOK
'
Me.btnOK.Location = New System.Drawing.Point(64, 104)
Me.btnOK.Name = "btnOK"
Me.btnOK.Size = New System.Drawing.Size(72, 24)
Me.btnOK.TabIndex = 4
Me.btnOK.Text = "OK"
'
'btnCancel
'
Me.btnCancel.Location = New System.Drawing.Point(160, 104)
Me.btnCancel.Name = "btnCancel"
Me.btnCancel.Size = New System.Drawing.Size(72, 24)
Me.btnCancel.TabIndex = 5
Me.btnCancel.Text = "Cancel"
```

```
        '
        'LoginForm
        '
        Me.AutoScaleBaseSize = New System.Drawing.Size(5, 13)
        Me.ClientSize = New System.Drawing.Size(304, 157)
        Me.Controls.AddRange(New System.Windows.Forms.Control() _
            {Me.btnCancel, Me.btnOK, Me.txtPassword, Me.txtName, Me.Label2,
Me.Label1})
        Me.Name = "LoginForm"
        Me.Text = "Login"
        Me.ResumeLayout(False)

    End Sub

#End Region

End Class
```

The first part of the code in this region is the constructor for the Form class:

```
Public Sub New()
        MyBase.New()

        'This call is required by the Windows Form Designer.
        InitializeComponent()

        'Add any initialization after the InitializeComponent() call

End Sub
```

In the constructor of the form a call to the base class constructor is made. This is important because of the hierarchy chain of Windows Forms discussed previously. Any required constructor code for the base classes is handled here. After the base class construction is processed, a call is made to the InitializeComponent sub procedure that has been added to the class code. Just above this sub procedure, a container object is declared. The container object is used to keep track of the various components added to the form. It encapsulates the functionality for adding, removing, and retrieving components. After the container object is instantiated, the various component objects (controls) added to the form are declared:

```
    'Required by the Windows Form Designer
    Private components As System.ComponentModel.IContainer
```

```
'NOTE: The following procedure is required by the Windows Form Designer
'It can be modified using the Windows Form Designer.
'Do not modify it using the code editor.
Friend WithEvents Label1 As System.Windows.Forms.Label
Friend WithEvents Label2 As System.Windows.Forms.Label
Friend WithEvents txtName As System.Windows.Forms.TextBox
Friend WithEvents txtPassword As System.Windows.Forms.TextBox
Friend WithEvents btnOK As System.Windows.Forms.Button
Friend WithEvents btnCancel As System.Windows.Forms.Button
```

Because these declarations are made outside of any procedure blocks, they have class-level scope. The `Friend` keyword makes these controls accessible from anywhere within the current application or assembly. The `WithEvents` keyword allows these controls to raise events. After the control declarations, the `InitializeComponent` sub procedure instantiates the various components. A call is made to `SuspendLayout` method of the form to halt the layout of the controls until the initial properties have been set. The initial properties of the controls are then set (the ones you set in the designer's Properties window), and the controls are added to the control collection of the form. The final step of the `InitalizeComponet` sub procedure is a call to the `ResumeLayout` method to resume laying out the form (see Listing 10-2).

Listing 10-2. Initializing Form Components

```
<System.Diagnostics.DebuggerStepThrough()> Private Sub InitializeComponent()
    Me.Label1 = New System.Windows.Forms.Label()
    Me.Label2 = New System.Windows.Forms.Label()
    Me.txtName = New System.Windows.Forms.TextBox()
    Me.txtPassword = New System.Windows.Forms.TextBox()
    Me.btnOK = New System.Windows.Forms.Button()
    Me.btnCancel = New System.Windows.Forms.Button()
    Me.SuspendLayout()
    '
    'Label1
    '
    Me.Label1.Location = New System.Drawing.Point(24, 32)
    Me.Label1.Name = "Label1"
    Me.Label1.Size = New System.Drawing.Size(96, 20)
    Me.Label1.TabIndex = 0
    Me.Label1.Text = "Name:"
    '
    'Label2
    '
    Me.Label2.Location = New System.Drawing.Point(24, 64)
```

```
        Me.Label2.Name = "Label2"
        Me.Label2.Size = New System.Drawing.Size(104, 20)
        Me.Label2.TabIndex = 1
        Me.Label2.Text = "Password:"
        '
        'txtName
        '
        Me.txtName.Location = New System.Drawing.Point(144, 32)
        Me.txtName.Name = "txtName"
        Me.txtName.Size = New System.Drawing.Size(144, 20)
        Me.txtName.TabIndex = 2
        Me.txtName.Text = ""
        '
        'txtPassword
        '
        Me.txtPassword.Location = New System.Drawing.Point(144, 64)
        Me.txtPassword.Name = "txtPassword"
        Me.txtPassword.Size = New System.Drawing.Size(144, 20)
        Me.txtPassword.TabIndex = 3
        Me.txtPassword.Text = ""
        '
        'btnOK
        '
        Me.btnOK.Location = New System.Drawing.Point(64, 104)
        Me.btnOK.Name = "btnOK"
        Me.btnOK.Size = New System.Drawing.Size(72, 24)
        Me.btnOK.TabIndex = 4
        Me.btnOK.Text = "OK"
        '
        'btnCancel
        '
        Me.btnCancel.Location = New System.Drawing.Point(160, 104)
        Me.btnCancel.Name = "btnCancel"
        Me.btnCancel.Size = New System.Drawing.Size(72, 24)
        Me.btnCancel.TabIndex = 5
        Me.btnCancel.Text = "Cancel"
        '
        'LoginForm
        '
        Me.AutoScaleBaseSize = New System.Drawing.Size(5, 13)
        Me.ClientSize = New System.Drawing.Size(304, 157)
        Me.Controls.AddRange(New System.Windows.Forms.Control() _
            {Me.btnCancel, Me.btnOK, Me.txtPassword, Me.txtName, Me.Label2,
Me.Label1})
```

```
Me.Name = "LoginForm"
Me.Text = "Login"
Me.ResumeLayout(False)

End Sub
```

In addition to the Sub New constructor, the Windows Form Designer region contains a Dispose method. This method calls the Dispose method of the component's object, which in turn loops through the controls in the container collection and calls the Dispose method of the controls. Once the controls have been properly disposed, a call is made to the form's base class so that the required cleanup code can be processed up through the form inheritance chain:

```
'Form overrides dispose to clean up the component list.
Protected Overloads Overrides Sub Dispose(ByVal disposing As Boolean)
    If disposing Then
        If Not (components Is Nothing) Then
            components.Dispose()
        End If
    End If
    MyBase.Dispose(disposing)
End Sub
```

Handling Windows Form and Control Events

Windows graphical user interface (GUI) programs are based on an event-driven model. Events are actions initiated by a user or the system—for example, a user clicking a button or a SqlConnection object issuing a StateChange event. Event-driven applications execute code in response to the various events that occur. To respond to an event an event handler is created that will execute when an event occurs. The .NET Framework uses delegation to bind an event with the event handler procedures written to respond to the event. A delegation object maintains an invocation list of methods that have subscribed to receive notification when the event occurs. When an event occurs—for example, a button click—the control will raise the event by invoking the delegate for the event, which in turn will call the event handler methods that have subscribed to receive the event notification. Although this sounds complicated, the framework classes do most of the work for you.

Adding Form Event Handlers

The easiest way to add a form event handler is to use the drop-down list boxes at the top of the Code Editor. In the left drop-down box, choose the (Base Class Events) option, as shown in Figure 10-4.

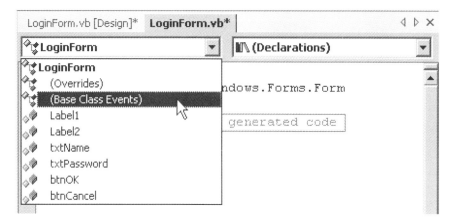

Figure 10-4. Choosing a control

In the right drop-down list, select the event you want to handle, as shown in Figure 10-5.

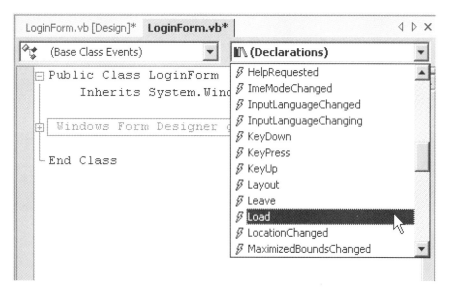

Figure 10-5. Choosing an event

As you can see from the list, there are many different form events that can be responded to. Part of your education is to investigate these various events to determine when they fire, what information they pass to the method handlers, and any dependencies they may have on other events.

After choosing the form event, the code editor inserts an event handler method. The following code shows the event handler method inserted for the Form_Load event. The Form_Load event occurs before the form is displayed the first time.

```
Private Sub LoginForm_Load(ByVal sender As Object, _
        ByVal e As System.EventArgs) Handles MyBase.Load

End Sub
```

By convention, the name of the event handler method is the name of the object issuing the event followed by an underscore character (_) and the name of the event. The actual name of the event handler, however, is unimportant. It is the Handles keyword that adds this method to the invocation list of the event's delegation object.

All event handlers must provide two parameters that will be passed to the method when the event is fired. The first parameter is the sender, which represents the object that initiated the event. The second parameter, of type System.EventArgs, is an object used to pass any information specific to a particular event. For example, the MouseDown event passes information on which button was clicked and the coordinates of the mouse cursor when it was clicked. The following code demonstrates checking which button was pressed in a form's MouseDown event handler:

```
Private Sub LoginForm_MouseDown(ByVal sender As Object, _
        ByVal e As System.Windows.Forms.MouseEventArgs) _
Handles MyBase.MouseDown
    If e.Button = MouseButtons.Right Then
            'implementation code goes here
    End If
End Sub
```

Adding Control Event Handlers

You add control event handlers the same way you added the form event handlers using the drop down lists at the top of the code editor. The right drop-down list selects the control and the left drop-down list selects the event to handle. Figure 10-6 demonstrates adding an event handler for a button click event.

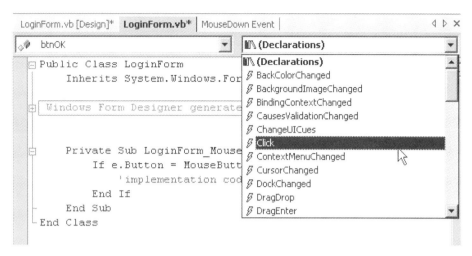

Figure 10-6. Adding a button click event handler

Because the .NET Framework uses delegates for event notification, you can handle multiple events with the same method. The only requirement is that the events being handled have the same signatures. For example, you could handle a button Click event and a menu Click event with the same event handler, but you could not handle a button Click event and a button KeyPress event using the same method. The following code demonstrates handling the MouseHover event of a Label and a TextBox using the same handler method. The sender parameter is interrogated to determine which control fired the event:

```
Private Sub Label1_MouseHover(ByVal sender As Object, _
        ByVal e As System.EventArgs) _
        Handles Label1.MouseHover, txtName.MouseHover
    If sender.Name = "Label1" Then
        MsgBox(sender.GetType.AssemblyQualifiedName)
    ElseIf sender.Name = "txtName" Then
        MsgBox(sender.GetType.Name)
    End If
End Sub
```

In the following activity you will investigate working with forms and controls by constructing a simple menu viewer application. It will allow users to load and view memo documents.

In this activity you will become familiar with the following:

- Creating a Windows Form–based GUI application

- Working with Menu, Status Bar, and Dialog controls

- Working with `Control` events

Creating the Memo Viewer Interface

To create the memo viewer interface, follow these steps:

1. Start Visual Studio. On the File menu, choose New ➤ Project.

2. Choose a Windows Application under the Visual Basic Projects folder. Rename the project to **Act10_1** and click the OK button.

3. Add a RichTextBox control to Form1 and set the properties as listed in Table 10-1.

Table 10-1. Form and Control Properties

CONTROL	PROPERTY	VALUE
Form1	Name	frmMemoViewer
	Text	Memo Viewer
RichTextBox1	Name	rtbMemo
	Text	[empty]
	Dock	Fill (click in center)
	ReadOnly	True

4. Add a MainMenu control to the form. The MainMenu control will show up in the component tray below the form. The component tray displays controls that do not present the user with a visual interface at runtime. Figure 10-7 shows a MainMenu control displayed in the component tray.

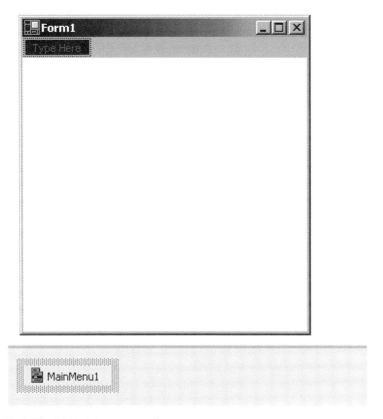

Figure 10-7. The MainMenu control

5. To create a MenuItem, type **File** in the Type Here box located at the top of the form. Then press the Enter key. Click back on the File menu and in the Properties window and change the Name property to **miFile**. Complete the menu items for the form as indicated in Table 10-2.

Table 10-2. Menu Items

NAME	TEXT	TOP MENU
miFile	File	
miOpen	Open	miFile
miClose	Close	miFile
miExit	Exit	miFile
miView	View	
miStatusbar	Statusbar	miView

6. Using the Properties window, change the Checked property of the miStatusBar control to **True**.

7. Add a StatusBar to the form and change the Name property to **sbViewer**. Click the Panels property located in the Properties window. Click again on the ellipses that are presented. This will display the StatusBarPanels Collection Editor dialog box, as shown in Figure 10-8.

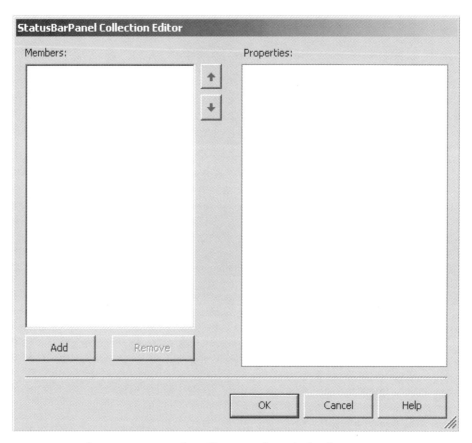

Figure 10-8. The StatusBarPanels Collection Editor dialog box

8. Clicking the Add button will add a panel to the collection and present the properties for the panel. Add two panels and set the properties as listed in Table 10-3.

Table 10-3. StatusBar Panel Properties

PANEL	PROPERTY	VALUE
StatusBarPanel1	Name	sbpFile
	Text	[empty]
	AutoSize	Spring
StatusBarPanel2	Name	sbpDate
	Text	[empty]
	AutoSize	Contents

9. After closing the StatusBarPanels Collection Editor dialog box, change the ShowPanels property of the StatusBar control to **True**.

10. Add an OpenFileDialog control to the form. This control will be displayed in the component tray below the form. Change the property values as shown in Table 10-4.

Table 10-4. OpenFileDialog Properties

PROPERTY	VALUE
Name	ofdMemoViewer
Filter	memo files|*.memo
InitialDirectory	c:\Memos\
Title	Open Memo Files

11. Switch to the code editor for the frmMemoViewer form. In the left drop-down list, choose the (Base Class Events) option. In the right drop-down list, select Load. Add the following code to display a message and the date in the StatusBar control:

```
sbViewer.Panels(0).Text = "Ready to load file..."
sbViewer.Panels(1).Text = System.DateTime.Today.ToShortDateString()
```

12. Build the solution and fix any errors.

13. Right-click the project in the Solution Explorer and select Properties. Change the startup object to frmMemoViewer.

14. On the Debug menu, choose Start. When the form displays, the status bar should contain the message and today's date. After testing, stop the debugger.

Coding the Menu Click Events

To code the menu click events, follow these steps:

1. Switch to the code editor for the frmMemoViewer form. In the left drop-down list, choose miOpen. In the right drop-down list, select Click event. Add the following code to open a memo file and load it into the rtbMemo control:

```
ofdMemoViewer.ShowDialog()
rtbMemo.LoadFile(ofdMemoViewer.FileName, RichTextBoxStreamType.PlainText)
sbViewer.Panels(0).Text = ofdMemoViewer.FileName
```

2. Add the following code to a miClose click event procedure to clear the rtbMemo control and reset the text in the first panel of the status bar:

```
rtbMemo.Clear()
sbViewer.Panels(0).Text = "Ready to load file  "
```

3. Add the following code to a miExit click event procedure to close the form:

```
Me.Close()
```

4. Add the following code to a miStatusBar click event procedure to toggle the visibility of the status bar:

```
miStatusBar.Checked = Not miStatusBar.Checked
sbViewer.Visible = miStatusBar.Checked
```

5. Build the solution and fix any errors.

6. Create a Memos folder on the C drive. Using Notepad create a text file containing a test message. Save the file to the Memos folder. Using Windows Explorer, rename the file to **Test.memo**.

7. On the Debug menu, choose Start. Test the application by loading the `Test.memo` file. Try changing the memo message. You should not be able to because the rtbMemo control was set to read-only. After viewing the file, close it using the Close menu. Toggle the visibility of the status bar using the StatusBar menu located under the View menu. Exit the application using the Exit menu.

8. After testing the application, exit Visual Studio.

Working with Form-Based Inheritance

Because forms are classes in the .NET Framework, you can create your own base forms to encapsulate standard functionality in your applications. Derived forms can then inherit from the base form and gain access to this built-in functionality or override it if necessary. Derived forms inherit not only the methods of the base form but also the visual aspects as well. This can be handy when creating forms for an application that need to convey a common look and feel experience to the users.

Creating the base form is no different from creating a regular form. Simply add a form to the project and place the controls on the form. Set the required properties and add any methods needed. Once the controls and methods have been set up, you need to determine how derived forms can access and alter the control properties and methods of the base form. You must mark any methods that can be overridden by derived forms as overridable. You can alter the access modifiers of the controls to restrict how they can be altered in the derived form. Table 10-5 summarizes the various modifiers and the implication of each. By default, most controls added to a form are designated with the `Friend` modifier.

Table 10-5. Access Modifiers of the Base Form

MODIFIER	IMPLICATION ON INHERITED FORM
Public	Control may be resized and moved. All other classes can modify the properties.
Protected	Control may be resized and moved. Derived forms can modify the properties.
Friend	Control cannot be resized and moved. All classes within the same assembly can modify the properties.
Private	Control cannot be resized and moved. Only the base form can modify the properties.

Figure 10-9 demonstrates the effect the access modifier has on the derived implementation of a control. The Label controls marked as `Public` and `Protected` can be resized and moved as indicated by the sizing handles on the borders. The labels marked as `Private` and `Friend` cannot be resized or moved as indicated by the absence of the resizing handles.

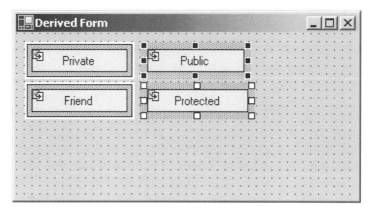

Figure 10-9. Control access on the derived form

Working with the event handlers of the inherited controls on the derived form can be a little tricky. The following base form class code creates a private event handler for the `MouseHover` event of a private control:

```
Private Sub lblPrivate_MouseHover(ByVal sender As Object, _
            ByVal e As System.EventArgs) Handles lblPrivate.MouseHover
    MessageBox.Show("Hello from Base")
End Sub
```

When you hover over the control in the derived form, you get the message *Hello from Base*.

Even though the control was declared as private, you can still override its `MouseHover` event implementation in the derived class. If you declare the event procedure as `Public Overridable` in the base class and create an `Overrides` procedure in the derived class, hovering over the control in the derived form reveals the overridden message *Hello from derived*:

```
'Base class code
Public Overridable Sub lblPrivate_MouseHover(ByVal sender As Object, _
          ByVal e As System.EventArgs) Handles lblPrivate.MouseHover
          MessageBox.Show("Hello from Base")
End Sub
'Derived class code
Public Overrides Sub lblPrivate_MouseHover(ByVal sender As Object, _
          ByVal e As System.EventArgs)
     MessageBox.Show("Hello from Derived")
End Sub
```

The key to this working is the event handler was defined in the base form and marked as being overridable. Without doing this, the derived form would not have access to the private inherited control's events.

When a control on the base form is marked as Public or Protected, a derived form can create event handlers for the controls even if the base form does not. The following code demonstrates creating an event handler for an inherited control marked as protected:

```
'Derived class code
Private Sub lblProtected_MouseHover(ByVal sender As Object, _
     ByVal e As System.EventArgs) Handles lblProtected.MouseHover
     MessageBox.Show("Hello from derived")
End Sub
```

The final scenario you will look at is what happens when you handle the event in both the derived class and the base class. When you do this, you are actually creating to separate event handlers for the same event (this is referred to as *multicasting*):

```
'Base class code
Private Sub lblProtected_MouseHover(ByVal sender As Object, _
     ByVal e As System.EventArgs) Handles lblProtected.MouseHover
     MessageBox.Show("Hello from Base")
End Sub
'Derived class code
Private Sub lblProtected_MouseHover(ByVal sender As Object, _
     ByVal e As System.EventArgs) Handles lblProtected.MouseHover
MessageBox.Show("Hello from derived")
End Sub
```

When the mouse is hovered over the label in the derived form, both event handler methods are executed.

Creating and Using Dialog Boxes

Dialog boxes are special forms often used in Windows Form–based GUI applications. A dialog box often displays information or retrieves information from the user of the application. The difference between a normal form and a dialog box is that a dialog box is displayed modally. A modal form prevents the user from performing other tasks within the application until the dialog box has been dismissed. When you start a new project in Visual Studio, you are presented with a New Project dialog box, as shown in Figure 10-10.

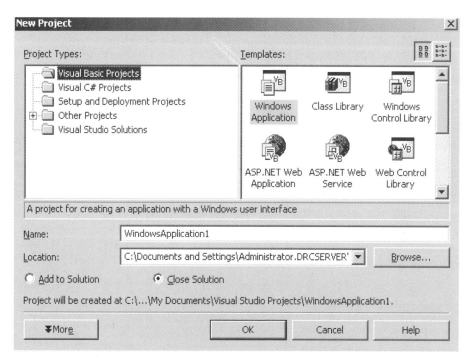

Figure 10-10. The New Project dialog box

You can also use dialog boxes to present the user with critical information and query them for a response. If you try to run an application in debug mode and a build error is encountered, the Visual Studio IDE presents you with a dialog box asking whether you want to continue (see Figure 10-11).

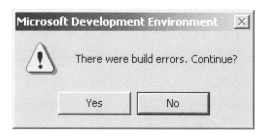

Figure 10-11. Displaying critical information using a dialog box

Presenting a MessageBox to the User

The dialog box shown in Figure 10-11 is a special predefined type called
a MessageBox. The MessageBox class is part of the System.Windows.Forms namespace. The MessageBox class can display a standard Windows message dialog box.
Because the MessageBox class is marked as shared, you do not create a new
instance of the class. To display a MessageBox to the user you call the shared Show
method of the MessageBox class as you have been doing in many of the examples:

```
MessageBox.Show("File Saved")
```

The Show method is overloaded so that you can optionally show a MessageBox
icon, show a title, change the buttons displayed, set the default button, and indicate the form to display it in front of. The only required setting is the text message
that will be displayed on the form. Figure 10-12 shows the MessageBox displayed
by the previous code.

Figure 10-12. A basic MessageBox

The following code calls the Show method using all the parameters.
Figure 10-13 shows the resulting MessageBox that gets displayed. For more information on the various parameters and settings available, look up the MessageBox
class in the help file:

```
MessageBox.Show(Me, "Are you sure you want to quit?", _
            "Closing Application", MessageBoxButtons.OKCancel, _
            MessageBoxIcon.Warning, MessageBoxDefaultButton.Button2, _
            MessageBoxOptions.RightAlign)
```

Figure 10-13. A more complex MessageBox

Retrieving the MessageBox Dialog Box Result

Many times you will use a MessageBox to query for a response to a question. The
user indicates the response by clicking the corresponding button. The result is
passed back as the return value of the MessageBox.Show method in the form of
a DialogResult enumeration. The following code demonstrates capturing the
dialog result and canceling the closing of the form depending on the result:

```
Private Sub Form1_Closing(ByVal sender As Object, _
        ByVal e As System.ComponentModel.CancelEventArgs) _
Handles MyBase.Closing
    Dim mbResult As DialogResult
    mbResult = MessageBox.Show("Are you sure you want to quit?", _
        "Closing Application", MessageBoxButtons.OKCancel, _
        MessageBoxIcon.Warning, MessageBoxDefaultButton.Button2)
    If mbResult = DialogResult.Cancel Then
        e.Cancel = True
    End If
End Sub
```

Creating a Custom Dialog Box

One of the most exciting features about the .NET Framework is its extensibility.
Although there are many types of dialog boxes, you can use "right-out-of-the-
box" ones for such things as printing, saving files, and loading files, just to name

a few. You can also build our own custom dialog boxes. The first step in creating a custom dialog box is to add a Windows Form to the application. Next, add any controls needed to interact with the user. Figure 10-14 shows a dialog box created to verify a user's identity. The `border` style has been set to `FixedDialog`, and the `ControlBox`, `MaximizeBox`, and `MinimizeBox` properties have been set to `false`.

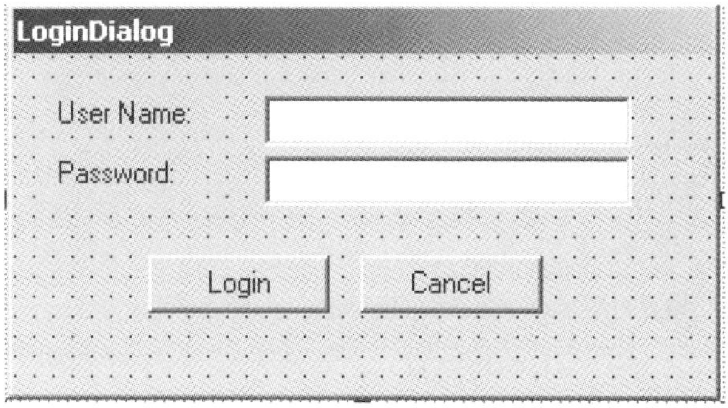

Figure 10-14. Creating a custom dialog box

To determine which button a user clicked to dismiss the form, the `DialogResult` property of the buttons on the form are set to the appropriate `DialogResult` enumeration. This `DialogResult` enumeration gets passed back to the parent form when the button is clicked. For example, the `DialogResult` property of the Login button in Figure 10-14 has been set to `OK`.

To display the dialog box, the `ShowDialog` method of the form is called. This method will display the dialog box modally, which means the user cannot interact with any other forms until the dialog box has been dismissed. Once the user clicks a button to dismiss the form, the form becomes hidden and the `DialogResult` enumeration is passed back to the parent form. The following code demonstrates the process of showing the Login dialog box and inspecting `DialogResult` that is returned:

```
Dim dlgLogin As New LoginDialog()
Dim mbResult As DialogResult
mbResult = dlgLogin.ShowDialog()
If mbResult = DialogResult.OK Then
     'verification code here
Else
     MessageBox.Show("You could not be verified.")
End If
dlgLogin.Dispose()
```

When the user dismisses a form that has been shown as a dialog box, it is hidden and not closed. Because of this behavior, you need to call the `Dispose` method of the form when you no longer need an instance of it as demonstrated by the last line of the code block shown previously. Because the dialog box is hidden when control returns to the calling form, you can interrogate the properties of the controls to retrieve the information the user entered. The following code demonstrates passing user information to the `Verify` method of an `Employee` class:

```
Dim dlgLogin As New LoginDialog()
Dim mbResult As DialogResult
Dim oEmployee As New Employee()
Dim bVerify As Boolean
mbResult = dlgLogin.ShowDialog()
If mbResult = DialogResult.OK Then
    bVerify = oEmployee.Verify (dlgLogin.txtUserName.Text, _
                    dlgLogin.txtPassword.Text)
Else
    MessageBox.Show("You could not be verified.")
End If
dlgLogin.Dispose()
```

Another way of retrieving the user information from the dialog box is to create a class or structure to hold the information and expose it as a property of the dialog form. The following code creates a `LoginInfo` structure, which is used to pass the information back to the parent form:

```
Public Structure LoginInfo
    Public UserName As String
    Public Password As String
End Structure
```

Next, a property of the dialog form of type `LoginInfo` is created to hold the user's information:

```
Public ReadOnly Property dlgInfo() As LoginInfo
    Get
        Dim UserInfo As New LoginInfo()
        UserInfo.UserName = txtUserName.Text
        UserInfo.Password = txtPassword.Text
        Return UserInfo
    End Get
End Property
```

When the user dismisses the dialog box, this property is interrogated to
retrieve the dialog information:

```
Dim dlgLogin As New LoginDialog()
Dim mbResult As DialogResult
Dim oEmployee As New Employee()
Dim bVerify As Boolean
Dim dlgInfo As LoginInfo
mbResult = dlgLogin.ShowDialog()
If mbResult = DialogResult.OK Then
    dlgInfo = dlgLogin.dlgInfo
    bVerify = oEmployee.Verify(dlgInfo.UserName, dlgInfo.Password)
Else
    MessageBox.Show("You could not be verified.")
End If
dlgLogin.Dispose()
```

ACTIVITY 10-2. WORKING WITH FORM INHERITANCE AND DIALOG BOXES IN A WINDOWS FORM-BASED GUI

In this activity you will become familiar with the following:

- Implementing form–based inheritance

- Using `MessageBox` dialog boxes

- Creating custom dialog boxes and retrieving user information

Creating an Inherited Form

To create an inherited form, follow these steps:

1. Start Visual Studio. On the File menu, choose Open ➤ Project.

2. Navigate to the `Act10_1.sln` file and click the Open button.

3. Right-click the project node in the Solution Explorer. From the context
   menu, choose Add ➤ Add InheritedForm. In the Add New Item dialog
   box, change the name of the form to **frmMemoEditor** and click Open.
   You will be presented with the Inheritance Picker dialog box, as shown in
   Figure 10-15.

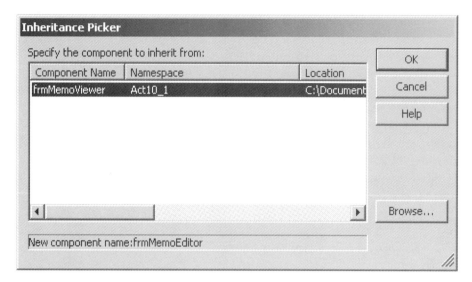

Figure 10-15. Inheritance Picker dialog box

4. In the Inheritance Picker dialog box, select the frmMemoViewer form and click OK.

5. Double-click the frmMenuEditor node in the Solution Explorer to open the form in the Form Designer. Select the form in the Properties window. Notice that you can change the properties of the form. This is because the base form class was declared with the Public modifier. Change the Text property of the form to **Memo Editor**.

6. Select the rtbMemo control in the Property Editor window. Notice that you cannot change the properties of rtbMemo control. This is because the rtbMemo control was declared with the Friend modifier in the base class.

7. Double-click the frmMemoViewer node in the Solution Explorer to open the form in the Form Design Editor. Select the rtbMemo control in the Property Editor window. Change the Modifiers property of the rtbMemo control to **Public**.

8. Notice that the Task List window is displayed with a message stating that the project needs to be rebuilt. This must be done so that the designer can reflect the changes in the inherited frmMemoEditor form. Rebuild the solution.

9. Double-click the frmMemoEditor node in the Solution Explorer to redisplay the form in the Form Design Editor. Select the rtbMemo control in the Property Editor window. Notice that you now have access to the properties of the control. Change the ReadOnly property to **False**.

10. Add a second MainMenu control to the frmMemoEditor. Click the MainMenu2 that appears in the component tray. Create the menu items listed in Table 10-6. Figure 10-16 shows how the menu should look.

Table 10-6. Menu Items

NAME	TEXT	TOP MENU
miFile2	File	
miNew	New	miFile2
miSave	Save	miFile2

Figure 10-16. Menu layout of frmMenuEditor

11. In the Property Editor window, select the frmMemoEditor in the drop-down list. Change the Menu property to **MainMenu1**.

12. Switch to the code editor for frmMemoEditor. In the right drop-down list, select the (Base Class Events) option, and in the left drop-down list, select the Load event. Add the following code, which merges the menu items for display:

```
miFile.MergeMenu(miFile2)
```

13. Build the solution and fix any errors.

14. Right-click the project in the Solution Explorer and select Properties. Change the startup object to **frmMemoEditor**.

15. On the Debug menu choose Start. Test the application by loading the Test.memo file. Try changing the memo message. You should now be able to because the rtbMemo control's ReadOnly property was overriden and changed to False. After viewing the file, close it using the Close menu. Toggle the visibility of the status bar using the StatusBar menu located under the View menu. Exit the application using the Exit menu.

Adding an Application Closing Dialog Box

To add a dialog box that closes the application, follow these steps:

1. Switch to the code editor for frmMemoViewer. In the right drop-down list, select miOpen, and in the left drop-down list, select the Click event. Change the name of the event handler method and the access modifier as shown in the following code. You will override this method in the inherited frmMemoEditor class:

```
Public Overridable Sub OpenMemo(ByVal sender As Object, _
        ByVal e As System.EventArgs) Handles miOpen.Click
    ofdMemoViewer.ShowDialog()
    rtbMemo.LoadFile(ofdMemoViewer.FileName ,_
        RichTextBoxStreamType.PlainText)
    sbViewer.Panels(0).Text = ofdMemoViewer.FileName
End Sub
```

2. Switch to the code editor for frmMemoEditor. In the right drop-down list, select the (Overrides) list, and in the left drop-down list, select OpenMemo. Add code to the overridden OpenMemo method that calls the base class's OpenMemo method. Change the rtbMemo's Modified property back to **false**. This was set to True by the initial file load:

```
Public Overrides Sub OpenMemo(ByVal sender As Object, ByVal e As
System.EventArgs)
    MyBase.OpenMemo(sender, e)
    rtbMemo.Modified = False
End Sub
```

3. In the code editor for frmMemoEditor, use the left drop-down list to select the (Base Class Events) option. In the right drop-down list, select the Closing event. Add the following code to the event handler method. This code checks whether there are unsaved changes and aborts the event by changing the Cancel event argument to True:

```
If rtbMemo.Modified Then
        MessageBox.Show("You must save changes before closing.")
        e.Cancel = True
End If
```

4. Build the solution and fix any build errors.

5. On the Debug menu, choose Start. Test the application by loading the Test.memo file. Do not make any changes and click on the menu Exit. The application should close.

6. Repeat step 5, but add some text to the memo. This time you will get the message and the closing will be canceled. After testing, switch back to the Visual Studio IDE and stop the debugger.

7. Alter the code in the frmMemoEditor_Closing event handler method to give the user the option of closing without saving:

```
If rtbMemo.Modified Then
        Dim Response As DialogResult
        Response = MessageBox.Show _
            ("You have unsaved changes. Exit without saving?", _
            "Closing Application", MessageBoxButtons.YesNo, _
            MessageBoxIcon.Warning)
        If Response = DialogResult.No Then
                e.Cancel = True
        End If
End If
```

8. On the Debug menu, choose Start. Test the application by loading the Test.memo file. Do not make any changes and click on the menu Exit. The application should close.

9. Repeat step 8, but add some text to the memo.. This time you will get a MessageBox dialog box giving you the option to cancel closing the application. After testing, stop the debugger and exit Visual Studio.

Data Binding in Windows Form-Based GUIs

Once you have retrieved the data from the business logic tier, you must present it to the user. The user may need to read through the data, edit the data, add records, or delete records. Many of the controls placed on a form can display the data to the user. The choice of what control to use often depends on the data type, what kind of data manipulation is required, and the interface design. Some common controls used to present data are TextBoxes, DataGrids, Labels, ListBoxes, CheckBoxes, and Calendars. When different fields of a data source are presented to the user in different controls (for example, a first name TextBox and last name TextBox), it is important that the controls remain synchronized to show the same record.

The .NET Framework encapsulates much of the complexity of synchronizing controls to a data source through a process called *data binding*. Every Windows container control such as a form has a BindingContext object associated with it. The BindingContext object keeps track of and communicates with the CurrencyManager object collection. Each data source being bound to by the controls on the form has an associated CurrencyManager. The CurrencyManager is responsible for maintaining synchronization between the bound controls and the data source. When you want to navigate between rows in a data source, a call is made to set the Position property of the associated currency manager. This call is not made directly to the CurrencyManager but is made to the BindingContext object, which is responsible for brokering the call to the appropriate CurrencyManager. When the CurrencyManager issues a PositionChanged event, each control associated with CurrencyManager is updated to reflect the data contained in the new position of the data source.

The following code demonstrates binding the Text property of two TextBox controls and a DateTimePicker control to different fields of the same data source:

```
txtFirstName.DataBindings.Add("Text", dsEmployeeInfo, "Employee.fname")
txtLastName.DataBindings.Add("Text", dsEmployeeInfo, "Employee.lname")
dtpHireDate.DataBindings.Add("Text", dsEmployeeInfo, "Employee.Hire_Date")
```

Although it is not obvious, the form's BindingContext object assigns the controls to the same ConcurrencyManager object based on the fact that they are bound to the same data source. After binding the controls on the form you can move to different records in the data source by setting the Position property of the BindingContext object. When the Position property of the BindingContext is set, any bound controls are updated accordingly. The following code will display the next record in the data source when the btnNext button is clicked:

```
Me.BindingContext(dsEmployeeInfo, "Employee").Position += 1
```

As you can see, binding to a data source and moving through records is fairly painless using the .NET Framework. An interesting point to note is that although you bound the previous controls to a `DataSet` object, in the .NET Framework you can bind to any object that implements the `IList` interface. This opens up the possibility of binding to arrays, collections, and other structures as well.

Controls such as Labels and TextBoxes are referred to as *simple-bound* controls. Simple-bound controls are limited to displaying one record of the data source at a time. Controls such as the DataGrid, ListBox, and ComboBox support *complex data binding*. Complex binding is the ability to bind and display more than one record at a time. In this case you can bind the control using its `DataSource` property. The following code demonstrates binding a ListBox control to an array list of names:

```
lstNames.DataSource = alNames
```

Some data sources may contain multiple elements, such as dataset containing multiple tables. If a DataGrid control is bound to such a data source it will display all the elements and allow the user to navigate between them. In many cases you may want to limit the display to a single element in the data source. You can accomplish this by setting the `DataMember` property of the DataGrid to the name of the element. The following code shows how to limit the display of a DataGrid control to a single table in a `DataSet`:

```
DataGrid1.DataSource = dsTitleAuthor
DataGrid1.DataMember = "Titles"
```

ACTIVITY 10-3. BINDING CONTROLS IN A WINDOWS FORM

In this activity you will become familiar with the following:

- Working with simple-bound controls

- Working with complex-bound controls

- Creating a master/detail form

Implementing Simple Bound Controls

To implement simple-bound controls, follow these steps:

1. Start Visual Studio. On the File menu, choose Open ➢ Project.

2. Navigate to the `Act10_3Starter.sln` file and click Open.

3. This file contains a `PubDB` class that encapsulates the functionality of retrieving records from the Publisher database in SQL Server.

4. View the code for the `GetBookInfo` method of the `PubDB` class. This method returns a `DataSet` containing book information. You will implement simple-binding using this `DataSet`.

5. Add the following controls to Form1 and set the properties as listed in Table 10-7.

Table 10-7. Form1 and Control Property Values

CONTROL	PROPERTY	VALUE
Form1	Name	frmBookInfo
	Text	Book Information
TextBox1	Name	txtTitle
	Text	[empty]
TextBox2	Name	txtSales
	Text	[empty]
DateTimePicker1	Name	dtpPubDate
	Format	Short
Button1	Name	btnNext
	Text	Next
Button2	Name	btnPrevious
	Text	Prev

6. Switch to the code editor for the frmBookInfo class. Declare a class-level variable to hold a DataSet:

```
Private dsBookInfo As DataSet
```

7. Create a sub procedure called BindControls. This procedure will call the GetBookInfo method and store the DataSet returned in a class-level DataSet variable. After retrieving the DataSet, the controls are bound to their related column in the DataSet.

```
Private Sub BindControls()
    Dim oPubDB As New PubDB()
    dsBookInfo = oPubDB.GetBookInfo
    txtTitle.DataBindings.Add("Text", dsBookInfo, "Books.title")
    txtSales.DataBindings.Add("Text", dsBookInfo, "Books.ytd_Sales")
    dtpPubDate.DataBindings.Add("Value", dsBookInfo, "Books.pubdate")
End Sub
```

8. Create a Form_Load event handler that calls the BindControls method:

```
Private Sub frmBookInfo_Load(ByVal sender As Object, _
            ByVal e As System.EventArgs) Handles MyBase.Load
    BindControls()
End Sub
```

9. Change the startup object of the project to the frmBookInfo class.

10. Press the F5 key to run the project in the debugger. After the form loads, you should see the values for the first book record in the controls.

11. After testing, stop the debugger.

12. Switch to the code editor for the frmBookInfo class. Add the following button-click event handler methods to implement the ability to move through the records:

```
Private Sub btnPrevious_Click(ByVal sender As Object, _
            ByVal e As System.EventArgs) Handles btnPrevious.Click
    Me.BindingContext(dsBookInfo, "Books").Position -= 1
End Sub
```

```
Private Sub btnNext_Click(ByVal sender As Object, _
        ByVal e As System.EventArgs) Handles btnNext.Click
    Me.BindingContext(dsBookInfo, "Books").Position += 1
End Sub
```

13. Press the F5 key to run the project in the debugger. After the form loads, test the Next and Prev buttons.

14. After testing, stop the debugger.

Implementing Complex-Bound Controls

To implement complex-bound controls, follow these steps:

1. Add a second form to the project named **frmPubInfo**. Add the following controls to the form and set the properties as listed in Table 10-8.

Table 10-8. Form and Control Property Values

CONTROL	PROPERTY	VALUE
Form	Name	frmPubBookInfo
	Text	Publisher-Book Information
ComboBox1	Name	cboPubInfo
	DropDownStyle	DropDownList
	Text	[empty]
DataGrid1	Name	dgBookInfo
	AllowNavigation	False

2. View the code for the GetPubBookInfo method of the PubDB class. This method calls two methods: one that returns a DataSet containing publisher information and one that returns a DataSet containing book information. The two DataSet objects are merged together, and a DataRelation is added that relates publishers to the books they publish. The merged DataSet is returned to the caller. You will use this to create a master/detail display.

3. Switch to the code editor for the `frmPubInfo` class. Declare a class-level variable to hold a `DataSet`:

```
Private dsPubBookInfo As DataSet
```

4. Create a sub procedure called `BindControls`. This procedure will call the `GetPubBookInfo` method and store the `DataSet` returned in a class-level `DataSet` variable. The ComboBox control's and DataGrid control's `DataSource` properties are set to the `DataSet`. The `DisplayMember` and `ValueMember` properties are then set to the appropriate column objects. The `DataMember` property of the `DataGrid` is set to the `DataRelation` that relates the book information to the publisher information:

```
Private Sub BindControls()
    Dim oPubDB As New PubDB()
    dsPubBookInfo = oPubDB.GetPubBookInfo
    cboPubInfo.DataSource = dsPubBookInfo
    cboPubInfo.ValueMember = "Publishers.pub_id"
    cboPubInfo.DisplayMember = "Publishers.pub_name"
    dgBookInfo.DataSource = dsPubBookInfo
    dgBookInfo.DataMember = "Publishers.PubBookKey"
End Sub
```

5. Create a `Form_Load` event handler that calls the `BindControls` method:

```
Private Sub frmPubBookInfo_Load(ByVal sender As Object, _
            ByVal e As System.EventArgs) Handles MyBase.Load
    BindControls()
End Sub
```

6. Change the startup object of the project to the `frmPubBookInfo` class.

7. Press the F5 key to run the project in the debugger. After the form loads, you should see publisher names in the ComboBox and the related books displayed in the DataGrid. Choosing a different publisher in the ComboBox should automatically update the DataGrid with the related book information.

8. After testing, stop the debugger.

Creating the OSO Application's Windows Form-Based GUI

In the following sections you will review the design and code used to build the Windows Form–based GUI for the Office-Supply Ordering (OSO) application. After reviewing the design and code, you will add the forms (which have been pre-built for you) to the OSO business logic application project and test the user interface.

Displaying Products

The first goal of the user interface is to present information about the products that can be ordered. The product information is presented in a DataGrid control. The user will view products in a particular category by selecting the category in a ComboBox control. Figure 10-17 shows the OSO order form with the controls added.

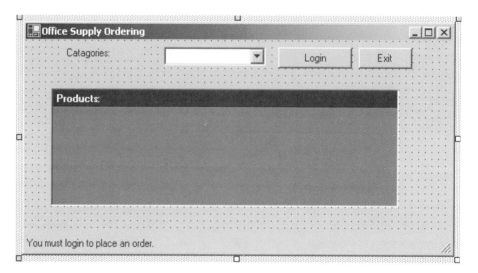

Figure 10-17. The OSO order form

The properties of the form and controls have been set to the values shown in Table 10-9.

Table 10-9. Order Form and Control Property Values

CONTROL	PROPERTY	VALUE
Form	Name	frmOrder
	Text	Office Supply Ordering
ComboBox	Name	cboProductCategories
	DropDownStyle	DropDownList
DataGrid	Name	dgProducts
	AllowNavigation	False
	CaptionText	Products:
Button	Name	btnExit
	Text	Exit
Button	Name	btnLogin
	Text	Login
StatusBar	Name	sbOSO
	Text	You must login to place an order.

You place the following code at the top of the form class after the Inherits statement. These variables have class-level scope and will be used in the various methods of the form.

```
Private EmployeeID As Integer
Private dsProdCat As DataSet
Private oOrder As Order
Private oOrderItemDlg As New dlgOrderItem()
Private oLoginDlg As New dlgLogin()
```

A Form_Load event handler creates an instance of the ProductCatalog class and uses its GetProductInfo method to load a local DataSet object. This DataSet is used as the DataSource for the ComboBox and the DataGrid. The DisplayMember property of the ComboBox is set to the Name column of the Category table contained in the DataSet. The DataMember property of the DataGrid is set to the relation drCat_Prod, which has been defined in the DataSet. By setting the

DataMember to the relation, when the user selects a category in the ComboBox, the DataGrid will display the related products:

```
Private Sub frmOrder_Load(ByVal sender As Object, _
        ByVal e As System.EventArgs) Handles MyBase.Load
    Dim oProdCat As New ProductCatalog()
    dsProdCat = oProdCat.getProductInfo
    cboProductCategories.DataSource = dsProdCat
    cboProductCategories.DisplayMember = "Category.Name"

    dgProducts.DataSource = dsProdCat
    dgProducts.DataMember = "Category.drCat_Prod"
End Sub
```

The controls for implementing the ordering functionality are placed in a Panel control. The Panel control is enabled after the user has logged in. Figure 10-18 shows the order form with the order Panel control added.

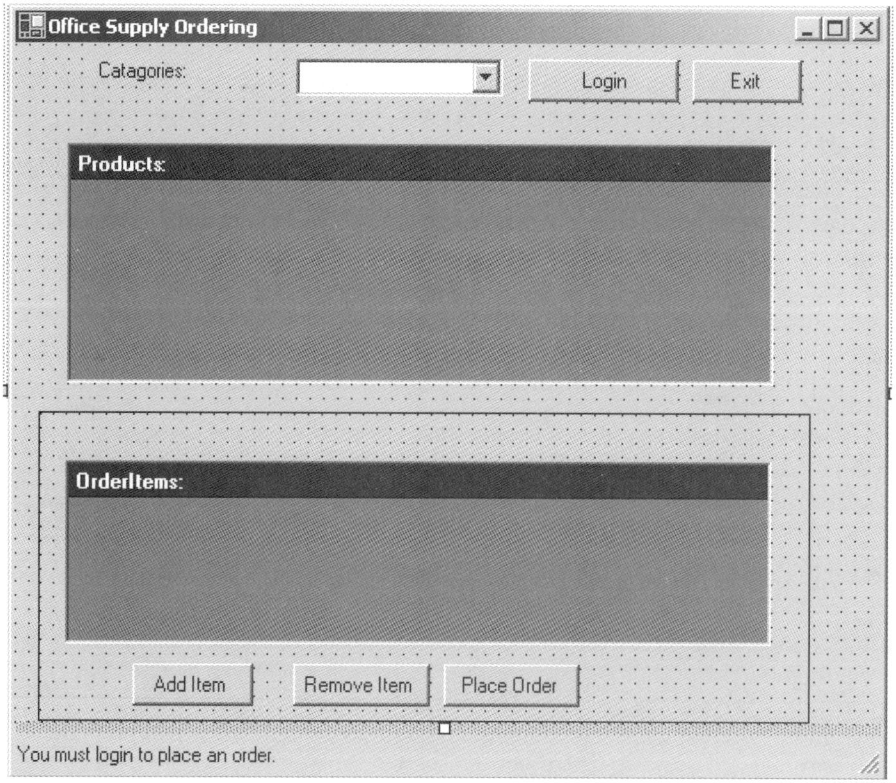

Figure 10-18. The order Panel control added to the order form

The properties of the panel and controls have been set to the values in Table 10-10.

Table 10-10. Panel and Control Property Values

CONTROL	PROPERTY	VALUE
Panel	Name	pnlOrder
	BorderStyle	FixedSingle
	Enabled	False
DataGrid	Name	dgOrder
	AllowNavigation	False
	CaptionText	OrderItems:
Button	Name	btnAddItem
	Text	Add Item
Button	Name	btnRemoveItem
	Text	Remove Item
Button	Name	btnPlaceOrder
	Text	Place Order

Validating Employees

To implement the employee login functionality, the user is presented with a custom dialog form (see Figure 10-19).

The properties of the form and controls have been set to the values in Table 10-11.

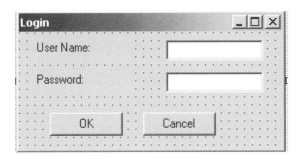

Figure 10-19. The login dialog form

Table 10-11. Login Form and Control Property Values

CONTROL	PROPERTY	VALUE
Form	Name	dlgLogin
	FormBorderStyle	FixedDialog
	Text	Login
	StartPosition	CenterParent
Label	Name	Label1
	Text	User Name:
Label	Name	Label2
	Text	Password:
TextBox	Name	txtName
	Text	[Blank]
TextBox	Name	txtPassword
	Text	[Blank]
	PasswordChr	*
Button	Name	btnOK
	Text	OK
	DialogResult	OK
Button	Name	btnCancel
	Text	Cancel
	DialogResult	Cancel

In Listing 10-3, btnLogin_Click event handler displays the Login dialog form and checks the result returned. If the OK button was pressed, then the Login method of the Employee object is called for verification. If the employee is validated, a new instance of the Order class is created and the order controls are enabled.

Listing 10-3. btnLogin_Click *Event Handler*

```
Private Sub btnLogin_Click(ByVal sender As System.Object, _
          ByVal e As System.EventArgs) Handles btnLogin.Click
    Dim oEmployee As New Employee()
    Dim strUserName As String
```

```
    Dim strPassword As String

    If oLoginDlg.ShowDialog(Me) = DialogResult.OK Then
        strUserName = oLoginDlg.txtName.Text
        strPassword = oLoginDlg.txtPassword.Text
        EmployeeID = oEmployee.Login(strUserName, strPassword)
        If EmployeeID > 0 Then
            sbOSO.Text = "You are logged in as employee number " & EmployeeID
            pnlOrder.Enabled = True
            oOrder = New Order()
        Else
            MessageBox.Show("You could not be verified. Please try again.")
            pnlOrder.Enabled = False
        End If
    End If
End Sub
```

Adding Order Items

When a user clicks the Add Item button, the code in Listing 10-4 presents the user with an Order Item dialog box containing the selected product information. The user then selects the item quantity and clicks the OK button to add the order item to the order. The Order Item grid is bound to the `OrderItem` property of the `Order` object, which contains an array of `OrderItem` objects.

Listing 10-4. `btnAddItem_Click` *Event Handler*

```
Private Sub btnAddItem_Click(ByVal sender As Object, _
              ByVal e As System.EventArgs) Handles btnAddItem.Click
    Dim strProdID As String
    Dim dblUnitPrice As Double
    Dim intQuantity As Integer
    Dim intRowIndex As Integer
    intRowIndex = dgProducts.CurrentRowIndex
    strProdID = dgProducts.Item(intRowIndex, 0)
    dblUnitPrice = dgProducts.Item(intRowIndex, 4)

    oOrderItemDlg.txtProductID.Text = strProdID
    oOrderItemDlg.txtUnitPrice.Text = dblUnitPrice.ToString
    If oOrderItemDlg.ShowDialog(Me) = DialogResult.OK Then
        intQuantity = oOrderItemDlg.nupQuantity.Value
        oOrder.AddItem(New OrderItem(strProdID, dblUnitPrice, intQuantity))
        dgOrder.DataSource = Nothing
```

```
        dgOrder.DataSource = oOrder.OrderItems
    End If
End Sub
```

Figure 10-20 shows the Order Item dialog form.

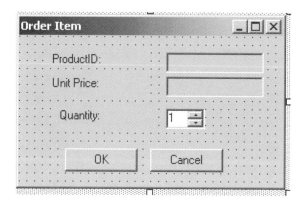

Figure 10-20. The Order Item dialog form

The properties of the form and controls have been set to the values shown in Table 10-12.

Table 10-12. Order Item Dialog Form and Control Properties

CONTROL	PROPERTY	VALUE
Form	Name	dlgOrderItem
	FormBorderStyle	FixedDialog
	Text	Order Item
	StartPosition	CenterParent
Label	Name	Label1
	Text	ProductID:
Label	Name	Label2
	Text	Unit Price:
Label	Name	Label3
	Text	Quantity:
TextBox	Name	txtProductID

Table 10-12. Order Item Dialog Form and Control Properties (continued)

CONTROL	PROPERTY	VALUE
	Text	[Blank]
	ReadOnly	True
TextBox	Name	txtUnitPrice
	Text	[Blank]
	ReadOnly	True
NumericUpDown	Name	nupQuantity
	Minimum	1
	Maximum	5
Button	Name	btnOK
	Text	OK
	DialogResult	OK
Button	Name	btnCancel
	Text	Cancel
	DialogResult	Cancel

Removing Items

When a user clicks the Remove Item button, the following event handler passes the ProductID of the item to the RemoveItem method of the Order object. This method removes the OrderItem from the OrderItem array:

```
Private Sub btnRemoveItem_Click(ByVal sender As Object, _
          ByVal e As System.EventArgs) Handles btnRemoveItem.Click
    Dim strProdID As String
    Dim intRowIndex As Integer
    intRowIndex = dgOrder.CurrentRowIndex
    strProdID = dgOrder.Item(intRowIndex, 3)
    oOrder.RemoveItem(strProdID)
    dgOrder.DataSource = Nothing
    dgOrder.DataSource = oOrder.OrderItems
End Sub
```

Placing an Order

When a user is ready to place an order, the btnPlaceOrder_click event handler
runs. This method calls the PlaceOrder method of the Order object and displays
the OrderNumber returned to the user:

```
Private Sub btnPlaceOrder_Click(ByVal sender As System.Object, _
            ByVal e As System.EventArgs) Handles btnPlaceOrder.Click
    Dim intOrderNumber As Integer
    intOrderNumber = oOrder.PlaceOrder(EmployeeID)
    sbOSO.Text = "The order has been placed. The order number is " _
        & intOrderNumber
End Sub
```

Testing the OSO Windows GUI

To test the OSO Windows GUI, follow these steps:

1. Start Visual Studio.

2. On the File menu choose Open ➢ Project.

3. Navigate to the OSOBusTier folder and open it.

4. Select the OSOBusTier solution file and click Open.

5. The project contains the OSO business logic classes and the test form
   that you used to test the classes in Chapter 9, "OSO Application
   Revisited: Implementing the Business Logic."

6. Select the project node in the Solution Explorer. Right-click and select
   Add ➢ Add Existing Item. Navigate to the OSOGUIForms folder and
   select the dlgLogin.vb, dlgOrderItem.vb, and the frmOrder.vb files, and
   click Open.

7. Change the project startup object to frmOrder. Press the F5 key to launch
   the debugger. Verify that the product information is updated in the grid
   when the category is changed in the ComboBox.

8. Click on the Login button and enter a username of **jsmith** and a password of **js**. You should be validated as an employee. Add some items to
   the order. Place the order and note the OrderID value is returned.

9. After testing the OSO Windows GUI. stop the debugger and exit Visual Studio.

Summary

In this chapter you did the following:

- Worked with forms and controls

- Looked at the inheritance hierarchy of forms and controls

- Responded to form and control events

- Constructed base and derived forms

- Implemented modal dialog forms

- Worked with data binding of Windows controls

- Reviewed and tested the OSO application's Windows GUI layer

In this chapter you looked at implementing the interface tier of an application. You implemented the user interface through a traditional Windows Forms–based application frontend. Along the way you took a closer look at the classes and namespaces of the .NET Framework used to implement rich Windows Forms–based user interfaces. In the next chapter you will revisit implementing the UI tier of a .NET application. Instead of implementing the GUI using Windows Forms, you will implement the GUI as an ASP.NET application using Web Forms. Along the way you will take a closer look at the namespaces available for creating Web-based GUI applications and the techniques involved in implementing the classes contained in these namespaces.

CHAPTER 11

Developing Web Applications

IN THE PREVIOUS CHAPTER you looked at developing a "traditional" Windows Form–based graphical user interface (GUI). Although a Windows Form–based interface gives a programmer the ability to easily build an extremely rich user interface, including advanced control functionality, enhanced graphics capabilities, and visual inheritance, it is not always practical to assume users will be able to access your programs through a Windows-based interface. With the proliferation of intranets, the Internet, and mobile devices, many applications need to allow users the ability to access the interface through a variety of browsers. This chapter covers building a Web-based user interface consisting of Web Forms that can be rendered in any Hypertext Markup Language–compliant browser. If you experience a sense of *deja vu* while reading this chapter, it is by design. Microsoft has implemented Web Form interface design and programming using an object model that is remarkably similar to the one used to design and program Windows Form–based interface.

After reading this chapter you should be familiar with the following:

- Working with Web Forms and controls

- The inheritance hierarchy of Web Forms and controls

- Responding to Web Form and control events

- Data binding controls contained in a Web Form

Web Form Fundamentals

Web Forms act as containers for controls with a visual interface for interacting with users of the application. The advantage of a Web Form over a traditional Windows Form is its ability to allow users to interact with programs remotely through any Hypertext Markup Language (HTML)-compliant browser. A Web application can expose its services to a variety of different client configurations using different operating systems and browsers.

A Web Form consists of two parts: the visual interface and the programming logic. The visual interface consists of a text file containing HTML markup tags, include files, processing directives, and client side scripting blocks. This text file is given the default extension of `.aspx` and is referred to as a *page*. It is this page that acts as a container for the text and controls that will be displayed in the browser. Figure 11-1 shows the `.aspx` file for a Web Form containing a TextBox control, a Button control, and a Label control. When the Web Form is compiled. the code is combined into a new class file dynamically. This file is then compiled into a new class that inherits from `System.Web.UI.Page` class. It is this class code that executes when the `.aspx` page is requested.

```
<%@ Page Language="vb" AutoEventWireup="false"
    Codebehind="WebForm1.aspx.vb" Inherits="WebDemoCh11.WebForm1"%>
<!DOCTYPE HTML PUBLIC "-//W3C//DTD HTML 4.0 Transitional//EN">
<HTML>
    <HEAD>
        <title>WebForm1</title>
        <meta content="Microsoft Visual Studio.NET 7.0" name="GENERATOR">
        <meta content="Visual Basic 7.0" name="CODE_LANGUAGE">
        <meta content="JavaScript" name="vs_defaultClientScript">
        <meta content="http://schemas.microsoft.com/intellisense/ie5"
            name="vs_targetSchema">
    </HEAD>
    <body MS_POSITIONING="GridLayout">
        <form id="Form1" method="post" runat="server">
            <asp:textbox id="txtName" style="Z-INDEX: 101; LEFT: 131px; POSITION: absolute; TOP: 87px"
                runat="server">
            </asp:textbox>
            <asp:button id="btnSubmit" style="Z-INDEX: 102; LEFT: 131px; POSITION: absolute; TOP: 143px"
                runat="server" Height="25px" Width="90px" Text="Submit">
            </asp:button>
            <asp:label id="Label1" style="Z-INDEX: 103; LEFT: 28px; POSITION: absolute; TOP: 85px"
                runat="server" Height="22px" Width="77px">
                Name:
            </asp:label>
        </form>
    </body>
</HTML>
```

Figure 11-1. Code contained in the `.aspx` *file*

Looking at the page directive at the top of the page reveals the second piece of the Web Form, which is referred to as the *code-behind file* and is indicated by the `.aspx.vb` extension. The code-behind file contains a class file where code is placed to handle any necessary events exposed by the page or controls contained within the page. The following class code is contained in the code-behind file linked to the `.aspx` file of Figure 11-1:

```
Public Class WebForm1
    Inherits System.Web.UI.Page
    Protected WithEvents txtName As System.Web.UI.WebControls.TextBox
    Protected WithEvents btnSubmit As System.Web.UI.WebControls.Button
    Protected WithEvents Label1 As System.Web.UI.WebControls.Label
```

```
    Private Sub btnSubmit_Click(ByVal sender As Object, _
            ByVal e As System.EventArgs) Handles btnSubmit.Click


    End Sub
End Class
```

When a browser requests the Web Form, the page file and the code-behind file are combined and compiled into a single executable Page class file. It is this Page class that intercepts and processes incoming requests. After processing the incoming request, the Page class dynamically creates and sends an HTML response stream back to the browser. Because the Page class is compiled code, execution is much faster than previous technologies, which relied on interpreting script. The Internet Information Services (IIS) Web server is also able to cache the execution code in memory to further increase performance.

Web Server Control Fundamentals

The .NET Framework provides a set of Web server controls specifically for hosting within a Web Form page. Developers work with these various controls using the familiar object model associated with Windows Form controls. The types of Web server controls available include common form controls such as a TextBox, Label, and Button, as well as more complex controls such as a Table and a Calendar. The Web server controls abstract out the HTML coding from the developer. When the Page class sends the response stream to the browser, the Web server control is rendered on the page using the appropriate HTML. The HTML sent to the browser depends on such factors as the browser type and the control settings that have been made.

The following code is used to place a TextBox Web server control in the Web Form:

```
<asp:textbox id="txtName" runat="server" ForeColor="#ff0066" BorderStyle="Dashed">
</asp:textbox>
```

The control is then rendered in Internet Explorer (IE) 6.0 as the following HTML code:

```
<input name="txtName" type="text" id="txtName" style="color:#FF0066;
    border-style:Dashed;" />
```

If the `TextMode` property of the TextBox control is set to `MultiLine`, the code in the Web Form is altered to reflect the property setting:

```
<asp:textbox id="txtName" runat="server" ForeColor="#ff0066" BorderStyle="Dashed"
    TextMode="MultiLine"></asp:textbox>
```

Although the change in the code for the Web server control was minimal, the HTML code rendered to the browser changes to a completely different HTML control:

```
<textarea name="txtName" id="txtName" style="color:#FF0066;
        border-style:Dashed;"></textarea>
```

Web Forms and Web server controls offer Web programmers many advantages, including a familiar event-driven object model, automatic browser detection with dynamic rendering, data binding capabilities, and automatic control state maintenance, just to name a few.

Understanding Web Form and Web Server Control Inheritance Hierarchy

At the top of the Web Form interface code contained in the `.aspx` file is the following page directive:

```
<%@ Page Language="vb" AutoEventWireup="false" Codebehind="WebForm1.aspx.vb"
        Inherits="WebDemoCh11.WebForm1"%>
```

This code reveals that the Web Form interface code inherits from the Web Form code-behind class located in the `.aspx.vb` file. The code-behind class in turn inherits from the `Page` class located in the `System.Web.UI` namespace:

```
Public Class WebForm1
    Inherits System.Web.UI.Page
```

The `Page` class exposes important functionality needed to program a Web application and interact with the Web server. For example, it enables access to the `Application`, `Session`, `Response`, and `Request` objects. The `Application` object enables sharing of global information across multiple sessions and requests within the Web application. The `Request` object enables the reading of values sent by a client during a Web request. The `Page` class also exposes functionality such as working with `Postback` events initiated by client script, initiating page-level validation, and registration of hidden fields required by server controls.

If you trace the inheritance chain of the Web Form further, you discover that the Page class inherits functionality from the TemplateControl class. This class adds support for loading user controls, which are custom controls commonly created to partition and reuse user interface (UI) functionality in several Web Form pages. User controls are created in .ascx files and are hosted by the Web Forms. Along with managing the user controls inserted into a Web Form, the TemplateControl class adds transactional support and error handling functionality to the Page class.

The TemplateControl class inherits from the Control class. The Control class exposes much of the functionality needed by all sever controls. This class includes important properties such as the ID and Page properties. The ID property gets and sets the programmatic identifier of a control, and the Page property gets a reference to the Page object that contains the control. The Control class exposes methods for rendering the HTML code for the control and any child controls. There are methods for handling and raising events such as the Load, Unload, and PreRender events. The Control class also exposes the functionality needed to add data binding support to Web server controls. Figure 11-2 shows the hierarchy chain of a Web Form in the Object Browser.

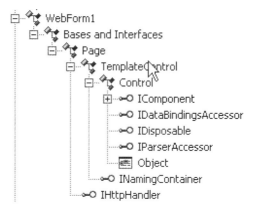

Figure 11-2. Hierarchy chain of a Web Form

Tracing the hierarchy chain of a Web server control—for example, a TextBox control—reveals that they also gain much of their functionality from the Control class. When you place a TextBox server control on a Web Form, at runtime it instantiates an object instance of the TextBox class, which is part of the System.Web.UI.WebControls namespace. This class exposes properties, methods, and events needed by a TextBox. For example, it defines such properties as the Text, ReadOnly, and Wrap properties. The TextBox class also adds functionality for raising and handling the TextChanged event.

All Web server control classes inherit common functionality from the
WebControl class. The WebControl class provides properties that control the look
of the control when it gets rendered in the browser. For example, the ForeColor,
Backcolor, Height, and Width properties are defined in the WebControl class. It
also defines properties that control the behavior of the control such as the
Enabled and TabIndex properties. The WebControl class inherits from the Control
class discussed previously. Figure 11-3 shows the hierarchy chain of a TextBox
Web server control in the Object Browser.

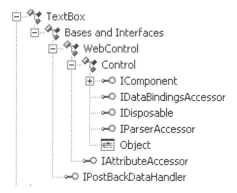

Figure 11-3. TextBox Web control hierarchy

Using the Visual Studio Web Form Designer

The Visual Studio Integrated Development Environment (IDE) includes an excellent Web Form Designer. The Web Form Designer makes designing Web Forms
similar to designing traditional Windows Forms. Using the designer you can drag
and drop controls onto the Web Form from the Toolbox and set control properties using the Properties window. Figure 11-4 shows a Web Form being designed
in Visual Studio.

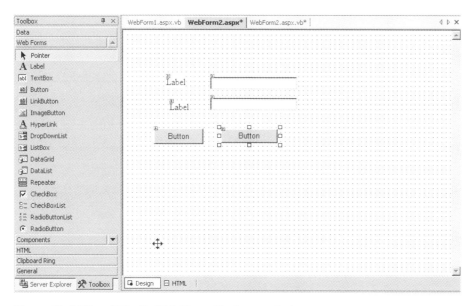

Figure 11-4. Visual Studio Web Form Designer window

Unlike the Windows Form Designer, the Web Form Designer contains two tabs at the bottom of the window. These tabs switch the view in the window from a visual representation of the Web Form to the HTML code view. The HTML view shows the tag markup code used to render the page and allows you to insert client-side script into the page. Figure 11-5 shows a Web Form displayed in the HTML view of the designer.

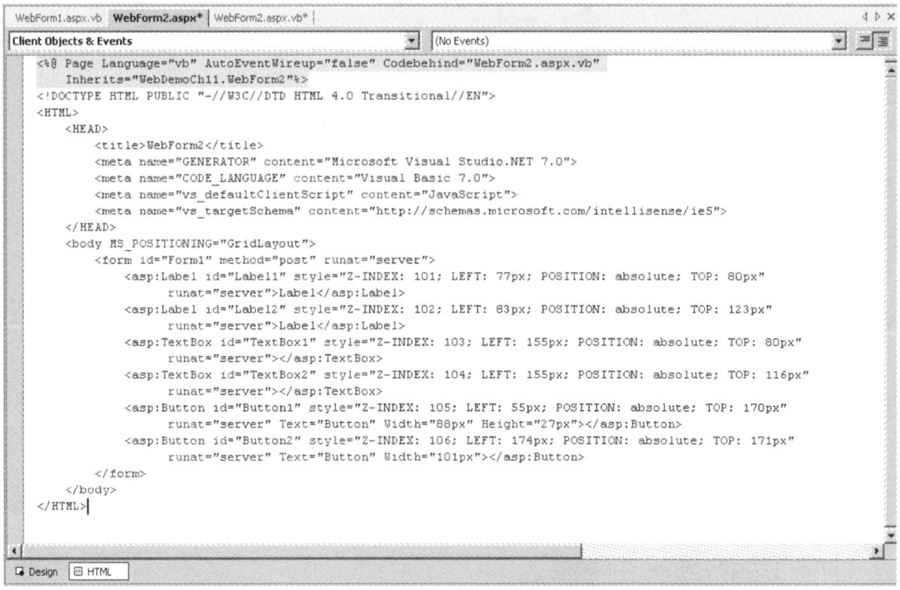

Figure 11-5. Visual Studio Web Form Designer in the HTML view

As mentioned previously, the code-behind page contains the code for handling events and adding methods that will be executed on the server before the page is rendered or when it gets posted back to the server. You use the code editor to add the server-side processing code to the Web Form class. Figure 11-6 shows the code editor displaying the code for a Web Form class.

Figure 11-6. Code editor displaying the code-behind file

Looking at the Web Form class code in the code-behind file reveals a code structure similar to the code in a Windows Form class. This includes a Web Form Designer–generated region and a class-level declaration of the Web server controls added to the Web Form page. These controls have been declared using the WithEvents keyword, which is used to allow the creation of class-level event handler methods for events raised by the controls. By default an event handler method for the Page class's Lode event is added to the code-behind class file.

Handling Web Form and Control Events

Just like their Windows Graphical User Interface (GUI) counterparts, Web Forms and controls interact with users based on an event-driven model. When an event occurs on the client—for example, a button click—the event information is captured on the client and the information is transmitted to the server via a Hypertext Transfer Protocol (HTTP) post. On the server, the event information is intercepted by an event delegate object, which in turn informs any event handler methods that have subscribed to the invocation list. Although this sounds complicated, the .NET Framework classes abstract and encapsulate most of the process from you.

Adding Page and Server Control Event Handlers

The easiest way to add a Web Form (Page) event handler is to use the drop-down list boxes at the top of the code editor. In the left drop-down box, choose the (Base Class Events) option. In the right drop-down list, select the event you want to handle, as shown in Figure 11-7.

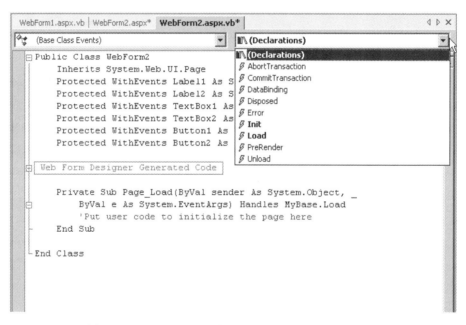

Figure 11-7. Adding a Page *event handler*

Because of the overhead of handling events through postbacks requiring a roundtrip from the browser to the server, only a limited set of events are exposed by Web Forms and server controls. Events that can occur frequently such as mouse movement and keypress events are not supported through server-side event handlers. (These events are supported through client-side event handlers written in script.)

After choosing the Page event, the code editor inserts an event handler method. The following code shows the event handler method inserted for the Page_Load event:

```
Private Sub Page_Load(ByVal sender As System.Object, _
    ByVal e As System.EventArgs) Handles MyBase.Load
    If Not IsPostBack Then
        'Initialize controls
    End If
    'Retrieve control values posted back.
    Session("UserName") = TextBox1.Text
End Sub
```

The Page_Load event occurs at the beginning of a page request after the controls in the Page have been initialized. This event is often used to read data from and load data into the server controls. The IsPostBack Page property is interrogated to determine if the page is being viewed for the first time or in response to a Postback event.

You can add Web server control event handlers in a similar fashion. Select the control in the left drop-down list and the event to handle in the right drop-down list, as shown in Figure 11-8.

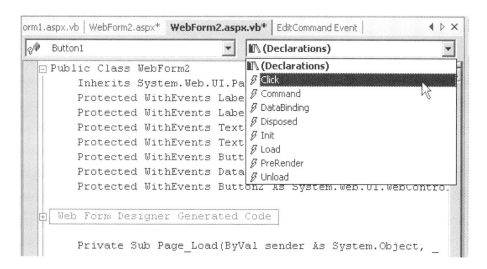

Figure 11-8. Adding a button-click event handler

By convention, the name of the event handler method is the name of the object issuing the event followed by an underscore character and the name of the event (which is similar to Windows Form event handling). The actual name of the event handler, however, is unimportant. It is the handles keyword that adds this method to the invocation list of the event's delegation object.

All event handlers must provide two parameters that will be passed to the method when the event is fired. The first parameter is the sender, which represents the object that initiated the event. The second parameter, e of type System.EventArgs, is an object used to pass any information specific to a particular event. For example, the EditCommand event is raised when the Edit button for an item in a DataList control is clicked. The event argument e is used to pass information about the item being edited in the DataList control. The following code checks to see if the item selected in the DataList is enabled:

```
Private Sub DataList1_EditCommand(ByVal source As Object, _
    ByVal e As System.Web.UI.WebControls.DataListCommandEventArgs)   _
    Handles DataList1.EditCommand
    If e.Item.Enabled Then
        'code here
    End If
End Sub
```

Server-Side Event Processing

Because of the overhead of raising events on the browser and handling them on the server, the .NET Framework supports two types of events for server controls. Postback events will cause the immediate posting back of the event to the server for processing. The button-click event is an example of a Postback event. Non-postback events do not get immediately posted back to the server for processing. Instead the event message is cached locally until a Postback event occurs. The server then processes the cached events after which the Postback event is processed. The TextChanged event of a TextBox control and the CheckedChanged event of the CheckBox control are examples of Non-postback events. You can override this behavior by setting the AutoPostBack property of the control to true in which case the event will cause an immediate postback to the server.

Table 11-1 summarizes the common page processing events that occur when a page is requested or posted back to the browser.

Table 11-1. Web Form Page Processing Events

EVENT	TYPICAL USES
Page_Init	The ASP.NET Framework uses this event to restore control properties and postback data.
Page_Load	Performs initial data binding. Read and update control properties when postback occurs.
Non-postback	Any non-postback that has been stored in the queue is processed. This processing will occur randomly and does not reflect the order that they occurred in the browser.
Postback	The event that caused the postback is processed.
Page_Unload	Performs any cleanup code. Close files and database connections. Discards object instances.

Understanding Application and Session Events

Along with the Page and control events, the .NET Framework provides the ability to intercept and respond to events raised when a Web session starts or ends. A Web session starts when a user requests a page from the application and ends when the session is abandoned or it times out. In addition to the session events, the .NET Framework exposes several application-level events. The Application_Start event occurs the first time anyone requests a page in the Web application. Application_BeginRequest occurs when any page or service is requested. There are corresponding events that fire when ending requests, authenticating users, raising errors, and stopping the application. The session-level and application-level event handlers are placed in the code-behind file of the Global.asax page. Figure 11-9 shows the Global.asax.vb code-behind file in the code editor.

Figure 11-9. The Global.asax.vb *file open in the code editor*

Notice at the top of the file that the code in the Global.asax.vb file creates a Global class that inherits from the HttpApplication class in the System.Web namespace. This class exposes and defines the methods, properties, and events common to all application objects within an ASP.NET application. A detailed explanation of the HttpApplication class is beyond the scope of this book. For more information, see the HttpApplication object in the help files.

ACTIVITY 11-1. WORKING WITH WEB FORMS AND SERVER CONTROLS

In this activity you will become familiar with the following:

- Creating a Web Form–based GUI application

- Working with page and server control events

Creating the Web Application

To create the Web application, follow these steps:

1. Start Visual Studio. On the File menu, choose New ➤ Project.

2. Choose an ASP.NET Web Application under the Visual Basic Projects folder. You should notice that by default most of the files created in the Web application are placed in a directory under the `Inetpub` directory on your computer. Change the path of the location to `http://localhost/Act11_1`. Figure 11-10 shows the New Project dialog box for creating a Web application.

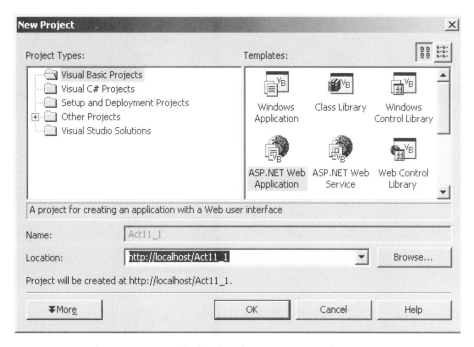

Figure 11-10. The New Project dialog box for creating a Web application

3. Click the OK button in the New Project dialog box. A message box is displayed indicating that the Web application files are being created on the Web server (see Figure 11-11). The files are transferred using FrontPage Server Extensions, which must be installed and enabled on the Web server.

Figure 11-11. Web creation message box

4. After the Web application and default files are created, you are presented with the Web Form Designer. The Toolbox displays the Web Forms tab, which contains the various ASP.NET server controls that can be hosted on the Web Form (see Figure 11-12).

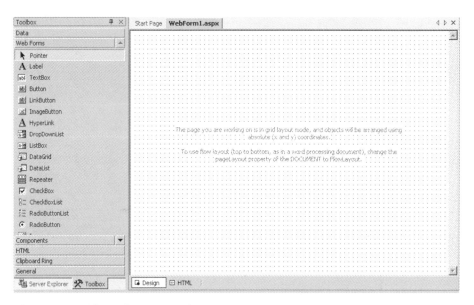

Figure 11-12. The Web Form Designer

5. Add the controls (located under the Web Forms tab in the Toolbox) in Table 11-2 to the Web Form and set the properties of the controls using the Properties window. Figure 11-13 shows the completed form in the Web Form designer.

Table 11-2. Web Form and Control Properties

CONTROL	PROPERTY	VALUE
Label	id	lblMessage
	Text	Hello Stranger
	Font-Size	X-Large
Label	id	Label1
	Text	Enter your name:
TextBox	id	txtName
	Text	[Blank]
Button	id	btnSubmit
	Text	Submit

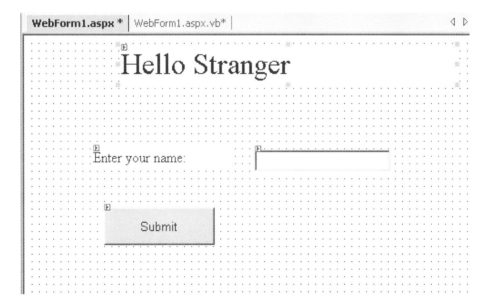

Figure 11-13. The completed Web Form

6. Click the HTML tab at the bottom of the Web Form Designer. The tags used to render the page are displayed in the designer. Notice the various ASP.NET controls you added to the form contain an asp prefix. They also contain a runat server attribute.

7. Press **F5** to launch the page in the debugger. When the page launches, enter your name in the TextBox and click the Submit button. The page will post to the server and redisplay in your browser. Because ASP.NET controls maintain their view state by default, your name will still be displayed in the TextBox after the post.

8. In the browser choose View ➢ Source. The source code for the page is displayed in Notepad. Notice that the ASP.NET controls have been rendered using standard HTML tags. A hidden control named "_VIEWSTATE" has also been inserted to track the view state information of the controls on the form.

9. Close the browser window and Notepad.

Creating Server-Side Control Event Handlers

To create server-side control event handlers, follow these steps:

1. In the Solution Explorer select the WebForm1.aspx node. At the top of window, select the View Code button to display the code-behind class for the page (see Figure 11-14).

Figure 11-14. Viewing the code-behind class of the Web Form

2. In the code editor there is a `Page_Load` event handler method added by default. In this event handler procedure check to see if the page request is the result of a postback. If it is, change the *lblMessage* text to say **hello** using the text contained in the txtName control:

```
Private Sub Page_Load(ByVal sender As System.Object, _
    ByVal e As System.EventArgs) Handles MyBase.Load
        If IsPostBack Then
            lblMessage.Text = "Hello " & txtName.Text
        End If
End Sub
```

3. Press F5 to launch the page in debug mode. When the page is displayed in the browser, enter your name and click the Submit button. Verify that the page is redisplayed and your name is included in the *Hello . . .* message. After testing, close the browser.

4. Code placed in the `Page_Load` event handler will execute every time there is a `Postback` event. To demonstrate this, switch to the Form Designer and click the Design tab at the bottom of the window. Add another ASP.NET Button server control to the form. Change the `ID` property of the button to **btnCancel** and the `Text` property to **Cancel**.

5. Press F5 to launch the page in debug mode. When the page is displayed in the browser, enter your name and click the Cancel button. Verify that the page is redisplayed and your name is included in the *Hello . . .* message. After testing, close the browser.

6. Switch to the code editor for WebForm1. Remove the code in the `Page_Load` event handler. In the left drop-down list at the top of the code editor, select the btnSubmit control. In the right drop-down list, select the Click event (see Figure 11-15).

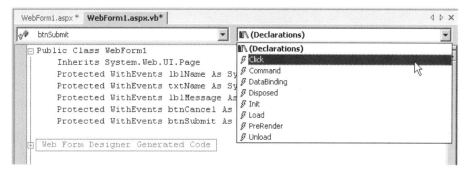

Figure 11-15. Adding the button-click event handler

7. Add code to display the user's name in the message when the Submit button is clicked:

```
Private Sub btnSubmit_Click(ByVal sender As Object, _
ByVal e As System.EventArgs) _
        Handles btnSubmit.Click
            lblMessage.Text = "Hello " & txtName.Text
    End Sub
```

8. Add code to display an abort message and clear the txtName text when the Cancel button is clicked:

```
Private Sub btnCancel_Click(ByVal sender As Object, ByVal e As _
        System.EventArgs) _
        Handles btnCancel.Click
            lblMessage.Text = "Login Canceled"
            txtName.Text = ""
    End Sub
```

9. Press F5 to launch the page in debug mode. When the page is displayed in the browser, enter your name and click the Submit button. Verify that the page is redisplayed and your name is included in the *Hello . . .* message. Now click the Cancel button. Verify that the page is redisplayed with the cancel message and the text in the txtName control is cleared. After testing, close the browser.

Creating Non-Postback Server Control Events

To create non-postback server control events, follow these steps:

1. Switch to the Form Designer for the WebForm1.aspx page. Add
   a RadioButtonList control to the form. Change the ID property to
   rblFontColor. Click the Items collection in the Properties window to display the ListItem Collection Editor dialog box. Add a Black item and
   a Red item to the list (see Figure 11-16).

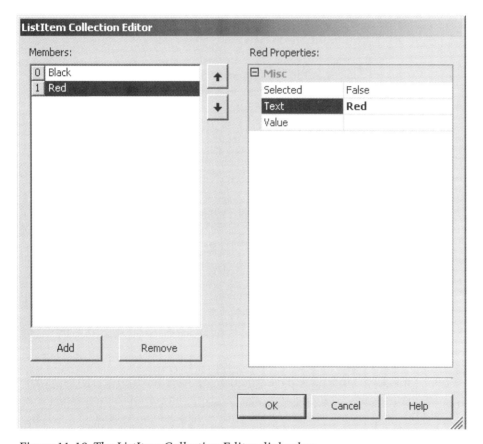

Figure 11-16. The ListItem Collection Editor dialog box

2. Switch to the code editor for WebForm1. In the left drop-down list at the
   top of the code editor, select the rblFontColor control. In the right drop-
   down list, select the SelectedIndexChanged event. Add the following
   code to change the font color of the lblMessage control in the event
   handler:

```
Private Sub rblFontColor_SelectedIndexChanged(ByVal sender As Object, _
    ByVal e As System.EventArgs) Handles rblFontColor.SelectedIndexChanged
        If rblFontColor.SelectedItem.Text = "Red" Then
            lblMessage.ForeColor = Color.Red
        Else
            lblMessage.ForeColor = Color.Black
        End If
End Sub
```

3. Press F5 to launch the page in debug mode. When the page is displayed in the browser, click the Red radio button. Notice that the event does not cause a postback to occur. This event will get queued until an AutoPostBack event gets initiated.

4. Enter your name in the txtName control and click the Submit button. When the postback is processed, the SelectedIndexChanged event of rblFontColor is processed, and then the Click event of the Submit button is processed. After testing, close the browser.

5. Exit Visual Studio.

> **NOTE** *This chapter has explored only server-side event handling. If the browser supports client-side scripting and Dynamic HTML, you can add code to .aspx pages to take advantage of the client-side processing capabilities.*

Storing and Sharing State in a Web Application

Web applications use a stateless protocol (HTTP) to communicate between the browser and the server. In most Web applications, however, some sort of state maintenance needs to exist during a user's session. Traditionally, maintaining state efficiently has been challenging for Web programmers. To help alleviate the challenge of state management, the .NET Framework provides several options to manage state on both the client and the server.

Maintaining View State

One type of state management that needs to occur in a Web application is the preservation of control property values when a form gets posted back to the client. Because a Web page is re-created and destroyed each time the page is requested, any changes to control made by the client are lost when the page is posted back. For example, any information entered into a TextBox control would be lost when posted back. To overcome this type of state loss, the server controls have a `ViewState` property, which provides a dictionary object used to retain the value of the control between postbacks. When a page is processed, the current state of the page and the controls are hashed into a string and saved as a hidden field on the page. During a postback, the values are retrieved and restored when the controls are initialized for rendering of the page back to the browser. The following code shows the ViewState hidden control that gets rendered to the browser:

```
<input type="hidden" name="__VIEWSTATE"
value="dDw1Njg2NjE2ODY7O2w8XNOMTowOz4+upC3lZ6nNLX/ShtpGHJAmi8mpH4=" />
```

Using Cookies

You can use *cookies* to store small amounts of data in a text file located on the client device. The `HttpResponse` class's `Cookie` property provides access to the `Cookies` collection. The `Cookies` collection contains cookies transmitted by the client to the server in the `Cookies` header. This collection contains cookies originally generated on the server and transmitted to the client in the `Set-Cookie` header. Because the browser can only send cookie data to the server that originally created the cookie and cookie information can be encrypted before being sent to the browser, it is a fairly secure way of maintaining user data. A common use for cookies is to send a user identity token to the client that can be retrieved the next time the user visits the site. This token is then used to retrieve client specific information from a database. The use of cookies is a good way to maintain client state between visits to the site. In the following code, a `Cookie` object is created to hold the date and time of the users visit. This `Cookie` object is then added to the `Cookies` collection and sent to the browser:

```
Dim VisitDate As New HttpCookie("VisitDate")
Dim CurrentDate As Date = Date.Today
VisitDate.Value = CurrentDate.ToShortDateString
VisitDate.Expires = CurrentDate.AddMonths(1)
Response.Cookies.Add(VisitDate)
```

Maintaining Session and Application State

Another type of state management often needed in Web applications is session state. *Session state* is the ability to maintain information pertinent to a user as they request the various pages within a Web application. Session state is maintained on the server and is provided by an object instance of the HttpSessionState class. This class provides access to session state values and session-level settings for the Web application. Session state values are stored in key-value dictionary structure only accessible by the current browser session. The following code uses the Session object to store a validated attribute for the current user in a session key-value pair. Notice that the intrinsic Session object exposes an object instance of the HttpSessionState class:

```
Sub cmdLogin_Click(ByVal Sender As Object, ByVal E As EventArgs)
    Dim EmployeeId As Integer
    Dim oEmployee As New Employee()
    'Attempt to Validate User Credentials
    EmployeeId = oEmployee.Login(txtUserName.Value, txtPassword.Value)

    If EmployeeId > 0 Then
        Session("isValid") = True
    Else ' Login failed
        Session("isValid") = False
        spnInfo.InnerHtml = "Login Failed!"
    End If
End Sub
```

Although session state is scoped on a per-session basis, there are times a Web application needs to share a state among all sessions in the application. You can achieve this globally scoped state using an object instance of the HttpApplicationState class. The application state is stored in a key-value dictionary structure similar to the session state except that it is available to all sessions and from all forms in the application. The first time a client requests any URL resource from the Web application, a single instance of an HttpApplicationState class is created. This instance is exposed through the intrinsic Application object. The following code uses the Application object to store a connection string attribute for a SqlConnection object:

```
Dim PubsConnectionString As String
PubsConnectionString = "Integrated Security=SSPI;Initial Catalog=pubs;" _
        & "Data Source=localhost"
Application("PubsConnectionString") = PubsConnectionString
```

> **NOTE** *Application state can also be stored in cache using the* Cache *class in the* System.Web.Caching *namespace.*

Data Binding in Web Form-Based GUIs

Just as with traditional Windows Form–based GUIs, programs developed using a Web Form–based GUI need to interact with data. Users of business applications need to view, query, and update data held in a backend data store. The .NET Framework exposes the functionality needed to implement data binding in Web Forms. Although the end result of data binding in Web Forms and Windows Forms looks similar, the mechanisms for achieving the data binding are not.

There are two types of data binding you can use in Web Forms: simple binding or complex binding. Controls such as the TextBox, Label, and CheckBox are used for simple binding and display one value from one record at a time. Controls such as the Repeater, DataList, and DataGrid are used for complex binding and are designed to display multiple fields of multiple records at the same time. Because of the nature of the Web it is not practical to use simple data binding to bind fields to a data source and then loop through the records using command buttons (see Figure 11-17).

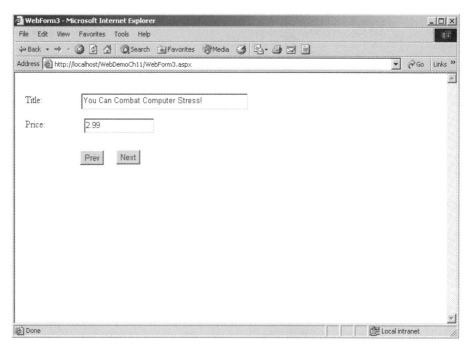

Figure 11.17. Simple data binding Web server controls.

In this scenario, moving between records would cause a Postback event to occur. During this postback the DataSet needs to be regenerated, which is not an efficient way to view data over a Web connection.

Multivalue Data Binding

The DataGrid, DataList, and Repeater Web server controls have been specially designed to efficiently perform data binding in Web Forms. The DataGrid control displays the records of a data source as an HTML table. To bind data for display in the DataGrid, the DataSource property is set to the object containing the data. The object containing the data can be of any type that supports the IEnumerable interface, such as a DataTable, DataView, DataRow, ArrayList, DataReader, Collection, or an ArrayList. If the DataSource is a DataSet that contains more than one DataTable, the DataMember property of the DataGrid is set to the name of the table to bind to. Once the DataSource and DataMember properties are set, the DataBind method of the DataGrid is called. The following code demonstrates binding a DataGrid to a DataTable in a DataSet. Figure 11-18 shows the table displayed in IE 6.0.

```
Private Sub Page_Load(ByVal sender As System.Object, _
        ByVal e As System.EventArgs) Handles MyBase.Load
    BindGrid()
End Sub
Private Sub BindGrid()
    Dim odbPubs As New dbPubs()
    dgPublishers.DataSource = odbPubs.GetPublisherInfo
    dgPublishers.DataBind()
End Sub
```

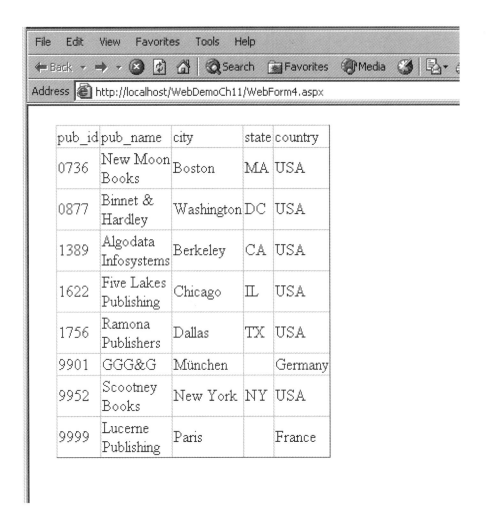

Figure 11-18. Using a DataGrid control to display data

The appearance of the DataGrid control is highly customizable; you have the ability to change the color, font, and alignment of the rows. You can add a header and footer to the DataGrid as well as control the appearance of alternating and selected rows in the grid. Figure 11-19 shows the same DataGrid displayed in Figure 11-18 with custom formatting applied.

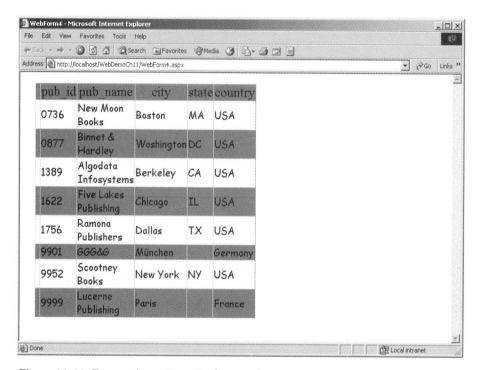

Figure 11-19. Formatting a DataGrid control

Updating Data in a DataGrid Control

To allow users to update data in the DataGrid control, you add a special EditCommandColumn that contains an edit Button control (see Figure 11-20).

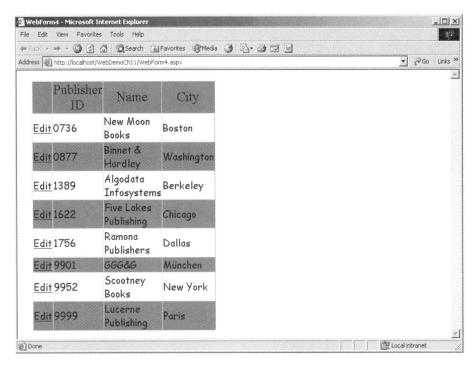

Figure 11-20. Adding editing capabilities to a DataGrid control

When the user clicks on the button, the DataGrid posts back and issues a DataGrid `EditCommand` event. In the event handler for the event, the `EditItemIndex` property for the DataGrid is set to the `ItemIndex` of the row selected in the grid:

```
dgPublishers.EditItemIndex = e.Item.ItemIndex
dgPublishers.DataBind()
```

The grid is rebound and sent back down to the browser. The values in the row are then displayed in updateable TextBox controls and an Update and a Cancel LinkButton control is displayed (see Figure 11-21).

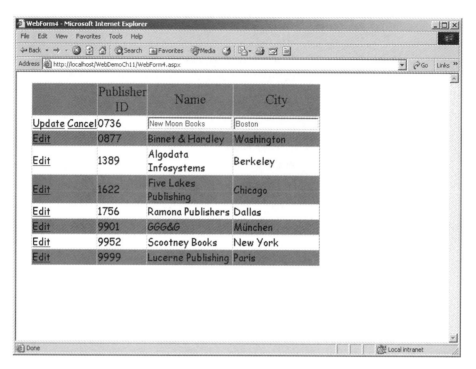

Figure 11-21. Adding updating and canceling capabilities to a DataGrid control

The user can then edit the values in the TextBox control and click on the Update button that posts the data back and fires the UpdateCommand event of the DataGrid. In the event handler of the event, the value is retrieved from the control used to update the cell in the DataGrid. By default this is a TextBox control, but this can be overridden. This value is then sent to the data source for updating, and the grid is rebound:

```
Private Sub dgPublishers_UpdateCommand(ByVal source As Object, _
    ByVal e As System.Web.UI.WebControls.DataGridCommandEventArgs) _
    Handles dgPublishers.UpdateCommand
  Dim odbPubs As New dbPubs()
  Dim nameText As TextBox = CType(e.Item.Cells(2).Controls(0), TextBox)
  odbPubs.UpdatePublisherInfo(e.Item.Cells(1).Text, nameText.Text)
  dgPublishers.EditItemIndex = -1
  BindGrid()
End Sub
```

The user can also select the Cancel button, in which case the EditItemIndex of the DataGrid is set to –1 and the grid is rebound:

```
Private Sub dgPublishers_CancelCommand(ByVal source As Object, _
        ByVal e As System.Web.UI.WebControls.DataGridCommandEventArgs) _
        Handles dgPublishers.EditCommand
    dgPublishers.EditItemIndex = -1
    BindGrid()
End Sub
```

ACTIVITY 11-2. BINDING A DATAGRID IN A WEB FORM

In this activity you will become familiar with the following:

- Investigate data binding to a DataGrid server control

- Implement data updating using a DataGrid server control

Displaying Data in an ASP.NET DataGrid Control

To display data in an ASP.NET DataGrid control, follow these steps:

1. Start Visual Studio. On the File menu, choose Open ➤ Project.

2. Navigate to the Act11_1.sln file and click Open.

3. Right-click on the Act11_1 project node in the Solution Explorer. In the pop-up menu that appears, choose Add ➤ Add Web Form. In the Add New Item dialog box, name the Web Form to **AuthorInfo.aspx** and click Open. Using the Web Form Designer add a DataGrid control to the form from the Web Forms tab of the Toolbox. Using the Properties window, change the ID property of the DataGrid to **dgAuthorInfo**.

4. Add a new class to the project called **dbAuthorInfo** that will encapsulate the retrieval of author information from the Pubs database. Add the following function to the class that returns a DataSet to the client containing author information:

```
Public Function GetAuthorInfo() As DataSet
    Dim cn As New SqlClient.SqlConnection _
        ("User ID=sa;Data Source=localhost;Initial Catalog=pubs")
    Dim da As New SqlClient.SqlDataAdapter _
        ("Select au_id, au_lname, au_fname, contract from authors", cn)
    Dim ds As New DataSet()
    da.FillSchema(ds, SchemaType.Source, "authors")
    da.Fill(ds, "Authors")
    Return ds
End Function
```

5. View the code-behind class for the AuthorInfo Web Form in the code editor. At the top of the class code after the dgAuthorInfo declaration, declare a private class-level DataSet variable:

```
Private ds As DataSet
```

6. Add the following method to bind the dgAuthorInfo control to the DataSet. Place the method after the Page_Load event handler:

```
Private Sub BindGrid()
    dgAuthorInfo.DataSource = ds
    dgAuthorInfo.DataMember = "Authors"
    dgAuthorInfo.DataBind()
End Sub
```

7. Add the following code to retrieve the DataSet and call the BindGrid method added in step 6:

```
Private Sub Page_Load(ByVal sender As System.Object, _
    ByVal e As System.EventArgs) Handles MyBase.Load
        'Put user code to initialize the page here
        Dim oAuthor As New dbAuthorInfo()
        ds = oAuthor.GetAuthorInfo
        BindGrid()
End Sub
```

8. Build the project and fix any errors.

9. Right-click the AuthorInfo.aspx node in the Solution Explorer and choose Set as Start Page.

10. Press the F5 key to run the project in the debugger. After the page loads in the browser, you should see the author information displayed in an HTML table (see Figure 11-22).

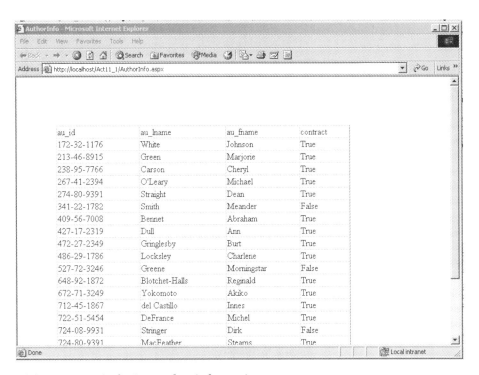

Figure 11-22. Displaying author information

11. After testing, close the browser.

Updating Data Using the ASP.NET DataGrid Control

To update data using the ASP.NET DataGrid control, follow these steps:

1. Right-click the AuthorInfo.aspx node in the Solution Explorer and choose View Designer.

2. In the Properties window, select the dgAuthorInfo. In the Columns property, click the ellipses (. . .), which launches the DataGrid Properties dialog box (see Figure 11-23).

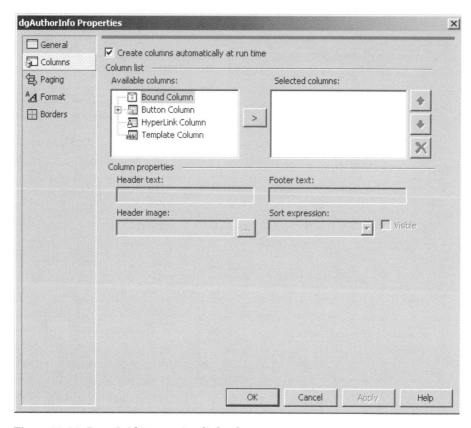

Figure 11-23. DataGrid Properties dialog box

3. Uncheck Create Columns Automatically at Runtime.

4. Expand the Button Column node in the Available Columns list. Select the Edit, Update, Cancel column and add it to the Selected Columns list. Change the Button Type drop-down list to PushButton (see Figure 11-24).

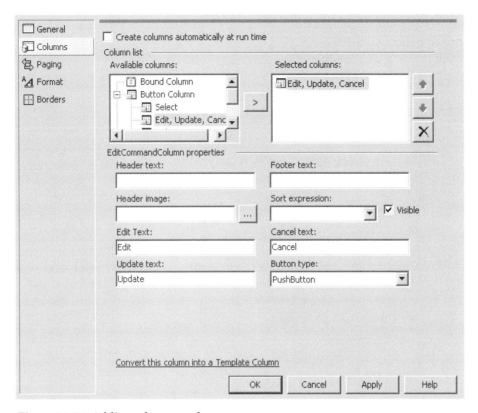

Figure 11-24. Adding a button column

5. In the Available Columns list, select the Bound Column node and add it to the Selected Columns list. Set the Bound Properties of the column to the values in Table 11-3.

Table 11-3. Bound Property Values

PROPERTY	VALUE
Header text	Author ID
DataField	au_id
Read Only	checked

6. Repeat step 5 to add another Bound column with the properties in Table 11-4.

Table 11-4. The Next Bound Property Values

PROPERTY	VALUE
Header text	Last Name
DataField	au_lname
Read Only	unchecked

7. Close the DataGrid Properties editor and press F5 to view the page in the browser. You should see the dgAuthorInfo grid with Edit buttons displayed in the first column. After viewing the grid, close the browser.

8. Right-click the AuthorInfo.aspx node in the Solution Explorer and choose View Code. Using the drop-down lists at the top of the code editor, select the EditCommand event handler for the dgAuthorInfo control. Add the following code to the event handler to set the EditItemIndex of the grid to the selected row. The DataGrid is then rebound and the page is rendered in the browser:

```
Private Sub dgAuthorInfo_EditCommand(ByVal source As Object, _
    ByVal e As System.Web.UI.WebControls.DataGridCommandEventArgs) _
    Handles dgAuthorInfo.EditCommand
        dgAuthorInfo.EditItemIndex = e.Item.ItemIndex
        BindGrid()
End Sub
```

9. Alter the Page_Load event handler so that the DataSet retrieved from the dbAuthorInfo class is held in session state. The DataSet can then be retrieved from session state when a Postback event occurs:

```
Private Sub Page_Load(ByVal sender As System.Object, _
    ByVal e As System.EventArgs) Handles MyBase.Load
        'Put user code to initialize the page here
        If Not IsPostBack Then
            Dim oAuthor As New dbAuthorInfo()
            ds = oAuthor.GetAuthorInfo
            BindGrid()
            Session("ds") = ds
        Else
            ds = CType(Session("ds"), DataSet)
        End If
End Sub
```

10. Press F5 to view the page in the browser. You should see the dgAuthorInfo grid with Edit buttons displayed in the first column. Click the Edit button. The page will repost and display the row with an Update and Cancel button. The last name column contains an editable TextBox control (see Figure 11-25). After testing, close the browser.

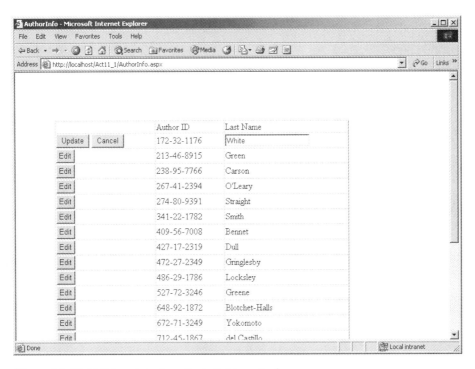

Figure 11-25. Editing data in a DataGrid control

11. Right-click the AuthorInfo.aspx node in the Solution Explorer and choose View Code. Using the drop-down lists at the top of the code editor, select the UpdateCommand event handler for the dgAuthorInfo control. Add the following code to the event handler to retrieve the updated value from the TextBox and updated the DataSet. The DataGrid is then rebound with an EditItemIndex of –1 and the page is rendered in the browser:

```
Private Sub dgAuthorInfo_UpdateCommand(ByVal source As Object, _
    ByVal e As System.Web.UI.WebControls.DataGridCommandEventArgs) _
    Handles dgAuthorInfo.UpdateCommand
```

```
                        Dim LNameTextBox As TextBox = CType(e.Item.Cells(2).Controls(0),
                         TextBox)
                        Dim au_id As String = e.Item.Cells(1).Text
                        Dim au_lname As String = LNameTextBox.Text
                        Dim PKValue As Object = CType(au_id, Object)
                        Dim dr As DataRow = ds.Tables("Authors").Rows.Find(PKValue)
                        dr.BeginEdit()
                        dr("au_lname") = au_lname
                        dr.EndEdit()
                        ds.AcceptChanges()
                        dgAuthorInfo.EditItemIndex = -1
                        BindGrid()
          End Sub
```

12. Using the drop-down lists at the top of the code editor, select the
    CancelCommand event handler for the dgAuthorInfo control. Add the fol-
    lowing code to the event handler. The DataGrid is rebound with an
    EditItemIndex of –1 and the page is rendered in the browser:

```
Private Sub dgAuthorInfo_CancelCommand(ByVal source As Object,      _
        ByVal e As System.Web.UI.WebControls.DataGridCommandEventArgs)  _
        Handles dgAuthorInfo.CancelCommand
            dgAuthorInfo.EditItemIndex = -1
            BindGrid()
    End Sub
```

13. Press F5 to view the page in the browser. You should see the
    dgAuthorInfo grid with Edit buttons displayed in the first column. Click
    the Edit button. Change the last name value and click Update. After test-
    ing, close the browser.

NOTE *The data source has not been updated. The changes made to the*
DataSet *are retained only until the session ends. The exercise of updating*
the data source is left to the reader.

Creating the OSO Application's Web Form-Based GUI

Now that you have a basic understanding of how Web Forms and server controls are used to construct a Web-based GUI, you are ready to review the user interface for the Office-Supply Ordering (OSO) application.

Displaying Products

The first goal of the user interface is to present information about the products that can be ordered. The product information is presented in a DataGrid Web server control. The user will view products in a particular category by selecting the category in a DropDownList server control. Figure 11-26 shows the OSO Web order form with the controls added. OrderForm.aspx hosts the Web Form and server controls.

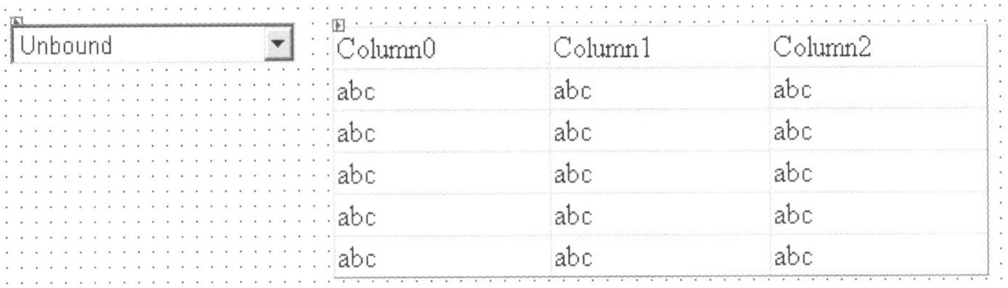

Figure 11-26. The OSO Web order form

The properties of the server controls are set as shown in Table 11-5.

Table 11-5. Server Control Property Values

CONTROL	PROPERTY	VALUE
DropDownList	id	ddlProductCategories
	AutoPostBack	True
	runat	server
DataGrid	id	dgProducts
	runat	server
	AutoGenerateColumns	False

Table 11-6 shows the properties to which the DataGrid columns are set.

Table 11-6. Column Property Values

COLUMN	PROPERTY	VALUE
0	Type	ButtonColumn
	Text	Add to Order
	ButtonType	PushButton
	CommandName	Select
1	Type	BoundColumn
	DataField	ProductID
	HeaderText	Product ID
2	Type	BoundColumn
	DataField	Name
	HeaderText	Name
3	Type	BoundColumn
	DataField	Descript
	HeaderText	Description
4	Type	BoundColumn
	DataField	UnitCost
	HeaderText	Unit Cost

You use a Page_Load event handler to create an instance of the ProductCatalog class. The GetProductInfo method loads a local DataSet object. This DataSet is also saved in a Session variable, which is retrieved when a Postback event occurs:

```
Private Sub Page_Load(ByVal sender As System.Object, _
    ByVal e As System.EventArgs) Handles MyBase.Load
        If Not IsPostBack Then
            Dim oProductCatalog As New ProductCatalog()
            dsProducts = oProductCatalog.getProductInfo
            Session("dsProducts") = dsProducts
            BindList()
            BindGrid()
        Else
            dsProducts = CType(Session("dsProducts"), DataSet)
        End If
End Sub
```

A BindList method is called to bind the DropDownList to the Category DataTable of the DataSet. The DataTextField property of the DropDownList is set to the Name column of the Category table contained in the DataSet. The DataValueMember is set to the CatID column:

```
Private Sub BindList()
        ddlProductCategories.DataSource = dsProducts
        ddlProductCategories.DataMember = "Category"
        ddlProductCategories.DataValueField = "CatID"
        ddlProductCategories.DataTextField = "Name"
        ddlProductCategories.DataBind()
End Sub
```

A BindGrid method is called to bind the DataGrid to a DataView created by filtering the Product DataTable by the currently selected item in the DropDownList:

```
Private Sub BindGrid()
    Dim dv As New DataView(dsProducts.Tables("Product"))
    dv.RowFilter = "CatID = " & _
        ddlProductCategories.Items.Item _
        (ddlProductCategories.SelectedIndex).Value
    dgProducts.DataSource = dv
    dgProducts.DataBind()
End Sub
```

Figure 11-27 shows how the page will be displayed in the browser (IE6).

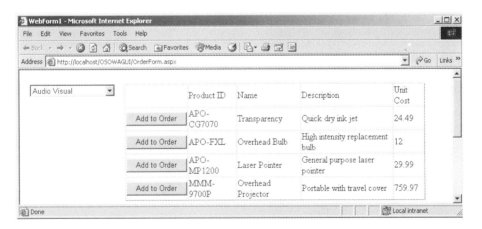

Figure 11-27. Filtering products by category

When a new category is selected in the DropDownList, a postback occurs. On the server an event handler for the SelectedIndexChanged event of the DropDownList calls the BindGrid method, which filters the DataView to the currently selected CatID:

```
Private Sub ddlProductCategories_SelectedIndexChanged _
    (ByVal sender As Object, ByVal e As System.EventArgs) _
    Handles ddlProductCategories.SelectedIndexChanged
        BindGrid()
End Sub
```

Initiating an Order

When a user clicks on the Add to Order button, a postback occurs and a server-side ItemCommand event handler executes. It checks to see if the value of the Session("EmployeeID") has been set.Iif not it redirects them to a login page.

```
If IsNothing(Session("EmployeeID")) Then
    Response.Redirect("Login.aspx")
  . . .
```

> **NOTE** *This functionality could also be implemented using the Forms Authentication service of ASP.NET.*

Validating Employees

To implement the employee login functionality, the user is presented with
a login.aspx page (see Figure 11-28).

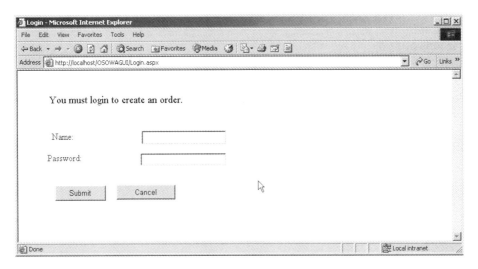

Figure 11-28. The login.aspx *page*

The properties of the Web Form controls have been set to the values shown
in Table 11-7.

Table 11-7. Control Property Values

CONTROL	PROPERTY	VALUE
Label	id	lblMessage
	Text	You must login to create an order.
Label	id	Label1
	Text	User Name:
Label	id	Label2
	Text	Password:
TextBox	id	txtUserName
	Text	[Blank]
TextBox	id	txtPassword
	Text	[Blank]
	TextMode	Password
Button	id	btnSubmit
	Text	Submit
Button	id	btnCancel
	Text	Cancel

In the btnSubmit_Click event handler, the Login method of the Employee object is called for verification. If the employee is validated, the Session("EmployeeID") value is set and the user is redirected back to the OrderForm.aspx:

```
Private Sub btnSubmit_Click(ByVal sender As System.Object, _
    ByVal e As System.EventArgs) Handles btnSubmit.Click
        Dim oEmployee As New Employee()
        Dim strUserName As String
        Dim strPassword As String
        Dim EmployeeID As Integer

        strUserName = txtUserName.Text
        strPassword = txtPassword.Text
        EmployeeID = oEmployee.Login(strUserName, strPassword)
        If EmployeeID > 0 Then
```

```
            Session("EmployeeID") = EmployeeID
            Response.Redirect("OrderForm.aspx")
        Else
            lblMessage.Text = "You could not be verified. Please try again."
        End If
End Sub
```

Adding Order Items

A Button, Label, and DataGrid ASP.NET control are added to the `OrderForm.aspx` page. The properties of the server controls are set as shown in Table 11-8.

Table 11-8. Server Control Property Values

CONTROL	PROPERTY	VALUE
Button	id	btnPlaceOrder
	Text	Place Order
	Enabled	False
Label	id	lblMessage
	Text	[Blank]
DataGrid	id	dgOrder
	runat	server
	AutoGenerateColumns	False

The properties of DataGrid columns are set as shown in Table 11-9.

Table 11-9. DataGrid Column Property Values

COLUMN	PROPERTY	VALUE
0	Type	BoundColumn
	DataField	ProductID
	HeaderText	Product ID
1	Type	BoundColumn
	DataField	UnitPrice
	HeaderText	Unit Price
2	Type	BoundColumn
	DataField	Quantity
	HeaderText	Quantity
3	Type	ButtonColumn
	Text	Delete Item
	ButtonType	PushButton
	CommandName	Delete

When a user clicks the Add to Order button after logging in, an Order object is created. The item selected is added to the OrderItem collection of the Order object. And the dgOrder DataGrid is bound to the OrderItem collection, as shown in Listing 11-1.

Listing 11-1. Adding an Order Item

```
Private Sub dgProducts_ItemCommand(ByVal source As Object, _
    ByVal e As System.Web.UI.WebControls.DataGridCommandEventArgs) _
    Handles dgProducts.ItemCommand
        If IsNothing(Session("EmployeeID")) Then
            Response.Redirect("Login.aspx")
        End If

        If Not IsNothing(Session("Order")) Then
            oOrder = CType(Session("Order"), Order)
        Else
            oOrder = New Order()
        End If
```

```
        Dim ProductIDCell As TableCell = e.Item.Cells(1)
        Dim UnitPriceCell As TableCell = e.Item.Cells(4)
        Dim ProductID As String = ProductIDCell.Text
        Dim UnitPrice As String = UnitPriceCell.Text

        oOrder.AddItem(New OrderItem(ProductID, CDbl(UnitPrice), 1))
        BindOrderGrid()
End Sub
Private Sub BindOrderGrid()
        dgOrderItems.DataSource = oOrder.OrderItems
        dgOrderItems.DataBind()
        Session("Order") = oOrder
        If oOrder.OrderItems.Count > 0 Then
            btnPlaceOrder.Enabled = True
        Else
            btnPlaceOrder.Enabled = False
        End If
End Sub
```

Figure 11-29 shows the Web order form with order items in the grid.

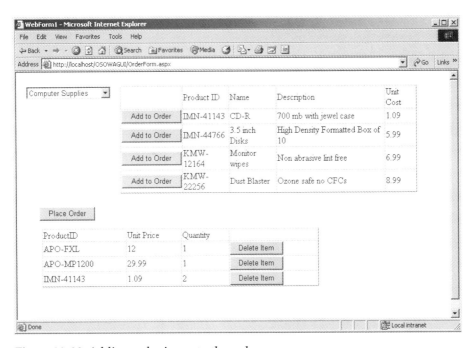

Figure 11-29. Adding order items to the order

> **NOTE** *When the Add to Order button is clicked again for the same product, the quantity is incremented by one.*

Removing Items

When a user clicks the Delete Item button in the dgOrder DataGrid, the following event handler passes the Product ID of the item to the RemoveItem method of the Order object. This method removes the OrderItem from the OrderItem array and rebinds the dgOrder DataGrid:

```
Private Sub dgOrderItems_DeleteCommand(ByVal source As Object, _
    ByVal e As System.Web.UI.WebControls.DataGridCommandEventArgs) _
    Handles dgOrderItems.DeleteCommand
        oOrder = CType(Session("Order"), Order)
        Dim ProductIDCell As TableCell = e.Item.Cells(0)
        Dim ProductID As String = ProductIDCell.Text
        oOrder.RemoveItem(ProductID)
        BindOrderGrid()
End Sub
```

Placing an Order

When a user is ready to place an order, the btnPlaceOrder_click event handler runs. This method calls the PlaceOrder method of the Order object and displays the OrderNumber returned to the user:

```
Private Sub btnPlaceOrder_Click(ByVal sender As System.Object, _
    ByVal e As System.EventArgs) Handles btnPlaceOrder.Click
        oOrder = CType(Session("Order"), Order)
        If oOrder.OrderItems.Count > 0 Then
            lblMessage.Text = oOrder.PlaceOrder(Session("EmployeeID")).ToString
        Else
            lblMessage.Text = "There are no items in the order."
        End If
End Sub
```

ACTIVITY 11-3. TESTING THE OSO WEB GUI

In this activity you will become familiar with the following:

- Testing the OSO Web GUI

To test the OSO Web GUI, follow these steps:

1. Start Visual Studio.

2. On the File menu, choose New ➢ Project.

3. Choose an ASP.NET Web Application under the Visual Basic Projects folder. In the New Project dialog box, change the path of the location to **http://localhost/Act11_3** and click OK.

4. Right-click the WebForm1.aspx node in the Solution Explorer and choose Delete.

5. Right-click the Act11_3 project node in the Solution Explorer and choose Add ➢ Add Existing Item. In the Add Existing Item dialog box, navigate to the BusinessClasses folder in the Act11_3Starter folder.

6. The folder contains the OSO business logic classes developed in Chapter 9, "OSO Application Revisited: Implementing the Business Logic." Select the dbOrder.vb, Order.vb, Employee.vb, and ProductCatalog.vb files and click Open.

7. Right-click the Act11_3 project node in the Solution Explorer and choose Add ➢ Add Existing Item. In the Add Existing Item dialog box, navigate to the WebForms folder in the Act11_3Starter folder. Change the File Type drop-down list to All Files.

8. The folder contains the Web Forms and code-behind classes for the OSO Web UI. Select the Login.aspx, Login.aspx.vb, OrderForm.aspx, and OrderForm.aspx.vb files and click Open.

9. Right-click the OrderForm.aspx node in the Solution Explorer and choose Set as Start Page. Press the F5 key to launch the debugger. Verify that the product information is updated in the grid when the category is changed in the drop-down list.

10. Click the Add to Order button. You should be redirected to the `Login.aspx` page. Enter a user name of **jsmith** and a password of **js**. You should be validated as an employee and redirected back to the `OrderForm.aspx` page.

11. Test adding and deleting items in the order.

12. Place an order and verify that the order number is returned.

13. After testing the OSO Web GUI, stop the debugger and exit Visual Studio.

Summary

In this chapter you did the following:

- Worked with Web Forms and ASP.NET server controls

- Looked at the inheritance hierarchy of Web Forms and Web controls

- Responded to Page and server-side control events

- Worked with data binding of Web Form controls

- Reviewed and tested the OSO application's Web GUI layer

In this chapter you looked at implementing the interface tier of an application using a Web Form–based front end. Along the way you took a closer look at the classes and namespaces of the .NET Framework that are used to implement Web Forms–based user interfaces. You were also exposed to data binding Web server controls, in particular, the DataGrid control. This concludes the OSO case study. You have seen how an application evolves from the initial design stages to implementing the class structure that encapsulates the business logic of the application. You used ADO.NET to store and retrieve data to and from a SQL Server database. Finally, you implemented a user interface for the application, both for Windows and for the Web.

CHAPTER 12

Wrapping Up
and Reviewing

IF YOU HAVE MADE IT THIS FAR, take a moment and pat yourself on the back. You have come a long way from the day you first cracked open the cover of this book. You have gained valuable skills needed to successfully program using the .NET Framework and Visual Basic .NET. These include an understanding of the following:

- The importance of the application design cycle

- The Unified Modeling Language and how it can help facilitate the analysis and design of object-oriented programs

- The Common Language Runtime

- The structure of the .NET Framework

- Creating and using class structures and hierarchies

- Implementing inheritance, polymorphism, and interfaces

- Object interaction and collaboration

- Event-driven programming

- Structured error handling

- Working with data structures and data sources using ADO.NET

- Using the features of the Visual Studio integrated development environment to increase productivity and facilitate debugging

- Implementing a Windows Form–based graphical user interface

- Implementing a Web Form–based graphical user interface

Congratulations! You can now call yourself a Visual Basic .NET programmer (albeit a neophyte). But do not get too high on yourself. If your goal is to become a professional Visual Basic .NET programmer, your journey has just begun. The next stage of your development is to gain experience. In other words, design and code, and then design and code some more. If you are designing and coding Visual Basic .NET at work, this will be easy. (Although it will be stressful if you are expected to be the expert after two weeks and that three-day course they sent you to!) If you are learning on your own, you will have to find time and projects on which to work. This is easier than you might think. Commit to an hour a day and come up with an idea for a program. For example, you could design a program that converts recipes into Extensible Markup Language (XML) data. The XML data could then generate a shopping list. Heck, if you really want to go all out, incorporate it with an inventory tracking system that tracks ingredients you have in stock. However you go about gaining experience, remember the important adage: Use it or lose it!

The following sections highlight some other important things to consider as you develop your programming skills.

Improving Your Object-Oriented Design Skills

Object-oriented analysis and design is one of the hardest tasks you will perform as a programmer. This is not a skill that comes easily for most programmers. It is, however, one of the most important skills you should strive to master. It is what separates what I call a *programmer* from a *coder*. If you talk to most Chief Information Officers and programming managers, finding coders is easy; it is the programmer they are after.

Remember that there is not one "true" methodology, but, rather, several I consider equally valid. A good starting point for investigating the various methodologies is `www.cetus-links.org`. This Web site contains an index of Internet addresses relating to object orientation and component orientation.

Investigating the .NET Framework Namespaces

The .NET Framework contains a vast number of classes, interfaces, and other types aimed at optimizing and expediting your development efforts. The various namespaces that make up the .NET Framework Class Library are organized by functionality. It is important you take the time to become familiar with the capabilities provided by these namespaces. Start out with the namespaces that incorporate functionality you will use most often. For example, the root namespace `System` and the `System.Windows.Forms` namespace, which provides the functionality required to create Windows-based graphical user interfaces (GUIs). After you become familiar with the more common namespaces, start exploring some of the more obscure ones. For example, `System.Security.Cryptography` provides cryptographic services such as data encoding, hashing, and message authentication. You will be amazed at the extent of the support provided by the framework. You can find a wealth of information on the members of the various namespaces in the Visual Studio .NET integrated documentation.

Becoming Familiar with ADO.NET

Data is fundamental to programming. You store, retrieve, and manipulate data in every program you write. The data structure a program works with during execution is *nondurable* data—it is held in RAM. When the application terminates, this data is lost and has to be re-created the next time the application is started. *Durable data* is data that is maintained in a permanent data structure such as a file system or a database. Most programs need to be able to retrieve data from and persist data to some sort of durable data storage. This is where ADO.NET steps in. ADO.NET refers to the namespaces that contain the functionality for working with durable data. (It also contains functionality for organizing and working with nondurable data in a familiar relational database or XML-type structure.) Although I have introduced you to ADO.NET, this is such an important topic that it deserves a book devoted solely to working in the ADO.NET. (Do not worry— there are many!) This is definitely an area where you need to devote further study.

Moving Toward Component-Based Development

After you have mastered object-oriented development and the encapsulation of your programming logic in a class system, you are ready to move toward component-based development. *Components* are assemblies that further encapsulate the functionality of your programming logic. Although the Office-Supply Office (OSO) application's business logic tier is logically isolated from the user interface tier, physically they reside in the same assembly. You can increase code maintenance and reuse by compiling the business logic into its own assembly. You should start moving to a Lego approach of application development. This is where your application is comprised of a set of independent pieces (assemblies) that can be snapped together and work in conjunction to perform the necessary services. You can find more information on component-based development at `www.cetus-links.org`.

Finding Help

An enormous amount of information is available on the .NET Framework and Visual Basic .NET. The help system provided with Visual Studio is an excellent resource for programmers. Get in the habit of using this resource religiously. Another extremely important resource is www.msdn.microsoft.com. This Web site provided by Microsoft for developers contains a wealth of information, including white papers, tutorials, and Webcast seminars. Quite honestly, this is one of the most informative sites in the industry. If you are developing using Microsoft technologies, visiting this site should be as routine as reading the daily paper.

Joining a User Group

Microsoft is investing a lot of support for the development of local .NET user groups. The user groups consist of members with an interest in .NET programming. The user groups provide a great avenue for learning, mentoring, and networking. There is a listing of .NET user groups available at www.msdn.microsoft.com. If you do not find one in your area, heck, why not start one?

Getting Certified

Microsoft has an extensive certification program. There are two certifications available for application developers. The Microsoft Certified Application Developer (MCAD) is aimed at programmers who develop test and deploy Web and Windows applications. The Microsoft Certified Solution Developer incorporates the MCAD certification and extends it to include analysis and design of enterprise-level applications.

Obtaining these certifications is beneficial for two reasons. First, it verifies that you have the skills needed to successfully develop and architect applications using the .NET Framework. Employers are increasingly using these certifications as a verifiable method of measuring abilities. Second, it provides you with a well-focused path for learning the .NET Framework, Visual Basic .NET, and application analysis and design. Be forewarned, however: The certification process is not to be taken lightly. Microsoft is committed to maintaining high standards for the certifications. You can find more information on these certifications at www.msdn.microsoft.com.

Please Provide Feedback

Although every effort has been made to provide you with an error-free text, it is inevitable that some mistakes will make it through the editing process. I am committed to providing updated errata at the Apress Web site (`www.apress.com`). I cannot do this without your help. If you have come across any mistakes while reading this text, please report them to me through the Apress site. I am also planning to post some additional case studies on this site. If you have an idea for a case study, I would love to hear from you.

Thank You and Good Luck

I sincerely hope you found working your way through this text an enjoyable and worthwhile experience. I want to thank you for allowing me to be your guide on this journey. Just as your skills as a developer increased as a result of reading this book, my skills as a developer have increased immensely as a result of writing it. My experience of teaching and training for the past 18 years (in a previous life I was a physics teacher) has been that you really do not fully comprehend a subject until you can teach it to someone else. So, again, thank you and good luck!

APPENDIX A

Fundamental Programming Concepts

THE FOLLOWING INFORMATION IS for readers who are new to programming and need a primer on some fundamental programming concepts. If you have programmed in another language, chances are the concepts presented in this appendix are not new to you. You should, however, review the material briefly to become familiar with the Visual Basic syntax used.

Working with Variables and Data Types

Variables in programming languages store values that can change while the program executes. For example, if you wanted to count the number of times a user tries to log in to an application, you can use a variable to track the number of attempts. The variable is a memory location where the value is stored. Using the variable your program can read or alter the value stored in memory. Before you use a variable in your program, however, you must declare it. When you declare a variable, you use the keyword Dim to reserve memory space for the variable:

```
Dim Counter
```

The compiler also needs to know what kind of data will be stored at the memory location. For example, will it be numbers or letters? If the variable will store numbers, how large can a number be? Will the variable store decimals or only whole numbers? You answer these questions by assigning a *data type* to the variable. A login counter, for example, only needs to hold whole positive numbers. The following code demonstrates how you declare a counter in Visual Basic with an Integer data type:

```
Dim Counter as Integer
```

Specifying the data type is referred to as *strong typing*. Strong typing results in more efficient memory management, faster execution, and compiler type checking, which reduces runtime errors.

Once you declare the variable, you can assign an initial value to the variable. You can also do this at the same time as the declaration statement. For instance, the following code:

```
Dim Counter as Integer = 1
```

is equivalent to this:

```
Dim Counter as Integer
Counter = 1
```

If you do not explicitly assign a variable an initial value when it is declared, the compiler will implicitly assign numeric data types to 0, Boolean data types to false, character data types to empty (""), date data types to 1/1/0001, and object data types to null (which is an empty reference pointer). The following sections further describe these various data types.

Understanding Elementary Data Types

Visual Basic supports elementary data types such as numeric, character, and date.

Integral Data Types

Integral data types represent whole numbers only. Table A-1 summarizes the integral data types used in Visual Basic.

Table A-1. Integral Data Types

DATA TYPE	STORAGE SIZE	VALUE RANGE
Byte	8-bit	0 through 255
Short	16-bit	–32,768 through 32,767
Integer	32-bit	–2,147,483,648 through 2,147,483,647
Long	64-bit	–9,223,372,036,854,775,808 through 9,223,372,036,854,775,807

Obviously, memory size is important when choosing a data type for a variable. A less obvious consideration is how easily the compiler works with the data type. The compiler performs arithmetic operations with integers more efficiently than the other types. Often it is better to use integers as counter variables even though a Byte or Short type could easily manage the maximum value reached.

Non-Integral Data Types

If a variable must store numbers that include decimal parts then the non-integral data types are used. Visual Basic supports the non-integral data types listed in Table A-2.

Table A-2. Non-Integral Data Types

DATA TYPE	STORAGE SIZE	VALUE RANGE
Single	32-bit	–3.4028235E+38 through –1.401298E–45 for negative values; 1.401298E–45 through 3.4028235E+38 for positive values
Double	64-bit	1.79769313486231570E+308 through –4.94065645841246544E–324 for negative values; 4.94065645841246544E–324 through 1.79769313486231570E+308 for positive values
Decimal	128-bit	0 through +/–79,228,162,514,264,337,593,543,950,335 with no decimal point; 0 through +/–7.9228162514264337593543950335 with 28 places to the right of the decimal

The Decimal data type holds a larger number of significant digits than the Single and the Double and is not subject to rounding errors. It is usually reserved for financial or scientific calculations that require a higher degree of precision.

Character Data Types

Character data types are for variables that hold characters used in the human language. For example, a character data type holds letters such as *a* or numbers used for display and printing such as *2* apples. The character data types in Visual Basic are based on Unicode, which defines a character set that can represent characters found in all the various human languages. Visual Basic supports two character data types: Char and String. The Char data type holds single (16-bit) Unicode character values such as *a* or *B*. The String data type holds a sequence of Unicode characters. It can range from zero up to about two billion characters.

Boolean Data Type

The Boolean data type holds a 16-bit value that is interpreted as True or False. It is used for variables that can be one of only two values—for example, yes or no, or on or off.

Date Data Type

Dates are held as 64-bit integers where each increment represents a period of elapsed time from the start of the Gregorian calendar (1/1/0001 at 12:00 a.m.).

Object Data Type

An Object data type is a 32-bit address that points to the memory location of another data type. It is commonly used to declare variables where the actual data type they refer to cannot be determined until runtime. Although the Object data type can be a catch-all to refer to the other data types, it is the most inefficient data type when it comes to performance and should be avoided unless absolutely necessary.

Introducing Composite Data Types

Combining elementary data types creates composite data types. Structures, arrays, and classes are examples of Composite data types.

Structures

Structures are useful when you want to organize and work with related information. A single variable works with the information. For example, the following code demonstrates creating an Employee structure used to organize employee information:

```
Structure Employee
    Dim LastName As String
    Dim EmpID As Integer
    Dim HireDate As Date
End Structure
```

Once you define the structure, you can declare a variable of the structure type.

```
Dim aEmployee As Employee
```

Arrays

Although structures organize data of different data types together as a unit, *arrays* are often used to organize and work with groups of the same data type. You declare an Array by placing parentheses after the variable name:

```
Dim Names() As String
```

To limit the number of elements of the array, you indicate the size of the array between the parentheses. Because the elements of the array are referenced by a zero-based index, the following array holds five elements:

```
Dim Names(4) As String
```

Visual Basic supports multidimensional arrays. When you declare the array, you separate the size of the dimensions by commas. The following declaration creates a two-dimensional array of integers with five rows and four columns:

```
Dim Names(4,3) As String
```

You access elements of the array using the variable name of the array followed by the index of the element in parentheses. For example, `Name(2)` references the third element of the `Names` array declared previously.

Classes

Classes are used extensively in object-oriented programming languages. The rest of this book covers the topic of creating and working with classes. At this point it is suffice to say that classes define a complex data type definition for an object. They contain information about how an object should behave, including its name, methods, properties, and events. The .NET Framework contains many predefined classes with which you can work. You can also create your own class type definitions. A variable defined as a class type contains a 32-bit address pointer to the memory location of the object. The following code declares an object instance of a `Clipboard` class defined in the .NET Framework:

```
Dim oClipboard As Clipboard
```

Looking at Literals, Constants, and Enumerations

Although the value of variables change during program execution, literals and constants contain items of data that do not change.

Literals

Literals are fixed values implicitly assigned a data type and are often used to initialize variables. The following code uses a literal to add the value of 2 to an integer value:

```
Count = Count + 2
```

By inspecting the literal, the compiler assigns a data type to the literal. Numeric literals without decimal values are assigned the Integer data type. Numeric literals with a decimal value are assigned as Double. The keywords True and False are assigned the Boolean data type. If the literal is contained in quotes, it is assigned as a String data type. In the following line of code, the two string literals are combined and assigned to a string variable:

```
FullName = "Bob" & "Smith"
```

Enclosing the literal in between pound symbols creates a Date literal:

```
#12/25/02#
```

It is possible to override the default data type assignment of the literal by appending a type character to the literal. For example, a value of 12.25 would be assigned the Double data type but a value of 12.25S would assign it the Single data type.

Constants

Many times you have to use the same *constant* value repeatedly in your code. For example, a series of geometric calculations may need to use the value of pi. Instead of repeating the literal 3.14 in your code, you can make your code more readable and maintainable by using a declared constant. You declare a constant using the Const keyword followed by the constant name and the data type:

```
Const pi As Single = 3.14159265358979323846
```

The constant is assigned a value when it is declared and this value cannot be altered or reassigned.

Enumerations

You often need to assign the value of a variable to one of several related predefined constants. In these instances you can create an *enumeration* type to group together the values. Enumerations associate a set of integer constants to names that can be used in code. For example, the following code creates an Enum type of Manager used to define three related manager constants with names of DeptManager, GeneralManager, and AssistantManager with values of 0, 1, and 2, respectively:

```
Enum Manager
    DeptManager
    GeneralManager
    AssistantManager
End Enum
```

A variable of the Enum type can be declared and set to one of the Enum constants:

```
Dim MgrLevel As Manager = Manager.AssistantManager
```

> **NOTE** *The .NET Framework provides a variety of intrinsic constants and enumerations designed to make your coding more intuitive and readable. For example, the* StringAlignment *enumeration specifies the alignment of a text string relative to its layout rectangle.*

Exploring Variable Scope

Two important aspects of a variable are its scope and lifetime. The *scope* of a variable refers to how the variable can be accessed from other code. The *lifetime* of a variable is the period of time when the variable is valid and available for use. A variable's scope and lifetime are determined by where it is declared and the access modifier used to declare it.

Block-Level Scope

A code block is a set of grouped code statements. Examples of code blocks include code organized in If-Else, Do-Loop, or For-Next statements. Block-level scope is the narrowest scope a variable can have. A variable declared within a block of code is available only within the block it is declared. In the following code, the BlockCount variable can only be accessed from inside the If block. Any attempt to access the variable outside the block will generate a compiler error:

```
If iCount > 10 Then
    Dim BlockCount As Integer
    BlockCount = iCount
End If
```

Although the scope of the variable is limited to the block, the lifetime of the variable is for the entire procedure where the block exists. You will probably find block-level scope to be too restrictive in most cases and instead use procedure scope.

Procedure Scope

Procedures are blocks of code that can be called and executed from other code. There are three types of procedures supported in Visual Basic: Sub, Function, and Property. Variables declared outside of a code block but within a procedure have procedure-level scope. Variables with procedure scope can be accessed by code within the same procedure. In the following code, the counter is declared with procedure scope and can be referenced from any where within the procedure block:

```
Sub counter()
    Dim iCount As Integer

    Do While iCount < 10
        iCount = iCount + 2
    Loop
    MessageBox.Show(iCount.ToString)
End Sub
```

The lifetime of a procedure scope variable is limited to the duration of the execution of the procedure.

Module Scope

Variables with *module scope* are available to any code within the module, class, or structure. To have module scope, the variable is declared in the general declaration section (outside of any procedure blocks) of the module, class, or structure. To limit the accessibility to the module where it is declared, you use the Private access modifier keyword. In the following code, the iCount variable can be accessed by both procedures defined in the class:

```
Public Class Class1
    Private iCount As Integer
    Sub IncrementCount()
        Do While iCount < 10
            iCount = iCount + 2
        Loop
    End Sub
    Sub ReadCount()
        MessageBox.Show(iCount.ToString)
    End Sub
End Class
```

The lifetime of the variable declared with module scope is the same as the lifetime of the object instance of the class or structure in which it is declared. The lifetime of module scope variables declared within a module is for the lifetime of the application.

> **NOTE** *There are several additional variations of scope addressed in the main body of the book.*

Understanding Data Type Conversion

During program execution there are many times when a value must be converted from one data type to another. The process of converting between data types is referred to as *casting* or *conversion*.

Implicit Conversion

The Visual Basic compiler will perform some data type conversions for you automatically. For example, if a value of a numeric variable is assigned to a string variable for display, the compiler will perform an implicit conversion. In the following code, an Integer data type is implicitly converted to a String data type:

```
Dim iCount As Integer
Dim strCount As String
Do While iCount < 10
    iCount = iCount + 2
Loop
strCount = iCount
MessageBox.Show(strCount)
```

Although allowing the compiler to perform implicit conversion can make coding easier, it can cause inefficient code execution and introduce unintended results such as data truncation and runtime errors. In the following code, the value of the text contained in a textbox, which is a String data type, is converted into an Integer data type:

```
Dim Count As Integer
Count = txtCount.Text
Count = Count + 1
```

This code executes fine as long as the user enters an integer into the textbox. However, if a character text is entered into the textbox, a runtime exception will occur.

Explicit Conversion

Explicit conversion is when you use a type conversion keyword. The following code is the same as the preceding example except that explicit conversion converts the String type to an Integer type. This results in faster code execution:

```
Dim Count As Integer
Count = CInt(txtCount.Text)
Count = Count + 1
```

> **NOTE** *To convert between various composite data types, use the* CType *conversion keyword.*

Widening and Narrowing Conversions

Widening conversions occur when the data type converted to can accommodate all the possible values contained in the original data type. For example, an Integer data type can be converted to a Double data type without any data loss or overflow. Data loss occurs when the number gets truncated. For example, 2.54 gets truncated to 2 if it is converted to an Integer data type. Overflow occurs when a number is too large to fit in the new data type. For example, if the number 50000 is converted to a Short data type, the maximum capacity of the Short data type is exceeded, causing the overflow error. *Narrowing conversions*, on the other hand, occur when the data type being converted to cannot accommodate all the values that can be contained in the original data type. For example, when the value of a Double data type is converted to a Short data type, any decimal values contained in the original value will be lost. In addition, if the original value is more than the limit of the Short data type, a runtime exception will occur. You should be particularly careful to trap for these situations when implementing narrowing conversions in your code.

Working with Operators

An *operator* is a code symbol that tells the compiler to perform an operation on a value. The operation can be arithmetic, comparative, or logical.

Arithmetic Operators

Arithmetic operators perform mathematical manipulation to numeric types. Table A-3 lists the commonly used arithmetic operators available in Visual Basic.

Table A-3. Arithmetic Operators

OPERATOR	DESCRIPTION
=	Assignment
*	Multiplication
/	Division
+	Addition
-	Subtraction
^	Exponential

The following code increments the value of an Integer data type by one:

```
Count = Count + 1
```

Visual Basic also supports shorthand assignment operators that combine the assignment with the operation. The following code is equivalent to the previous code:

```
Count += 1
```

> **NOTE** *String data type values are combined using the concatenation operator (&).*

Comparison Operators

A comparison operator compares two values and returns a Boolean value of True or False. Table A-4 lists the common comparison operators used in Visual Basic.

Table A-4. Comparison Operators

OPERATOR	DESCRIPTION
<	Less than
<=	Less than or equal to
>	Greater than
>=	Greater than or equal to
=	Equal to
<>	Not equal to

You use comparison operators in condition statements that determine if a block of code executes. The following If-Then block checks to see if the number of invalid login attempts is greater than three before ending the application:

```
If InvalidAttempts > 3 Then
    Application.Exit()
End If
```

> **NOTE** *Two special case comparison operators are* Like *and* Is. *The* Like
> *comparison operator is for string pattern matching. The* Is *operator is to*
> *compare two object references.*

Logical Operators

Logical operators combine the results of conditional operators. The three commonly used logical operators are And, Or, and Not. The And operator combines two expressions and returns True if both expressions are true. The Or operator combines two expressions and returns True if either one is true. The Not operator switches the result of the comparison. A value of True returns False and a value of False returns True. The following code checks to see if the logged-in user is a manager or assistant manager before loading an instance of a form:

```
If CurrentUserLevel = UserLevel.Manager Or _
    CurrentUserLevel = UserLevel.AssistantManager Then
        oEmployeeInfoForm.Show()
End If
```

> **NOTE** *The first line of the* If *block uses the line continuation character*
> *(_). This enables you to wrap long lines of code for easier viewing.*

Introducing Decision Structures

Decision structures allow conditional execution of code blocks depending on the evaluation of a condition statement. The If-Then statement evaluates a Boolean expression and executes the code block if the result is True. The Select-Case statement checks the same expression for several different values and conditionally executes a code block depending on the results.

If-Then Statements

To execute a code block if a condition is true, use the following structure:

```
If condition Then
    Code statements
End If
```

To execute a code block if a condition is true and an alternate code block if it is false, add an `Else` block:

```
If condition Then
    Code statements
Else
    Code staments
End If
```

To test additional conditions if the first evaluates to `False`, add an `ElseIf` block:

```
If condition Then
    Code statements
ElseIf condition then
    Code staments
Else
    Code staments
End If
```

You can have multiple `ElseIf` blocks. If a condition evaluates to `True`, the corresponding code statements are executed, after which execution jumps to the `End If` statement. If a condition evaluates to `False`, the next `ElseIf` condition is checked. The `Else` block is optional but if included must be last. The `Else` block has no condition check and executes if all other condition checks have evaluated to `False`. The following code demonstrates using the `If-Then` statement to evaluate a series of conditions. It checks a performance rating to determine what bonus to use. It includes a check to see if the employee is a manager to determine the minimum bonus:

```
If Performance = 1 Then
    Bonus = Salary * 0.1
ElseIf Performance = 2 Then
    Bonus = Salary * 0.08
ElseIf EmployeeLevel = "mgr" Then
```

```
     Bonus = Salary * 0.05
Else
     Bonus = Salary * 0.03
End If
```

Select-Case Statements

Although the Select-Case statement is similar to the If-ElseIf statement, it is used to test a single expression for a series of values. The structure of the select case is as follows:

```
Select Case [Test Expression]
    Case [expression list]
          Code statements
    Case [expression list]
          Code statements
    . . .
    Case Else
          Code statements
End Select
```

You can have multiple Case blocks. If the test expression value matches the expression list, the code statements in the Case block executes. After the Case block executes, execution jumps to the End Select statement. If the test expression does not match the expression list, execution jumps to the next Case block. The Case Else block does not have an expression list. It executes if no other Case blocks are executed. The Case Else block is optional but if used it must be last. The following example uses a Select Case to evaluate a performance rating to set the appropriate bonus rate:

```
Select Performance
    Case 10
        BonusRate = 0.1
    Case 8,9
        BonusRate = 0.08
    Case 5 To 7
        BonusRate = 0.05
    Case Is < 5
        BonusRate = 0.02
    Case Else
        BonusRate = 0
End Select
```

Using Loop Structures

Looping structures repeat a block of code until a condition is met. Visual Basic supports the following looping structures.

While Statements

The While statement repeats the execution of code while a Boolean expression remains True. The following code executes until the counter is greater than 10:

```
Dim Counter As Integer
 While Counter > 10
      'code statements
      Counter = Counter + 1
 End While
```

Do-Loop Statements

Do-Loop statements repeat the execution of code until a Boolean expression evaluates to either True or False depending on the Do statement. The condition can also be evaluated before or after the loop executes. The following Do While-Loop is similar to the previous While statement. It executes until the counter is greater than 10:

```
Dim Counter As Integer
 Do While Counter > 10
      'code statements
      Counter = Counter + 1
 Loop
```

The Do While-Loop repeats until the test expression returns False. A Do While-Loop will repeat until the test expression returns True:

```
Dim Counter As Integer = 20
 Do Until Counter < 10
      'code statements
      Counter = Counter - 1
 Loop
```

Both of the previous Do-Loop statements evaluate the test expression at the beginning of the code block. If the evaluation needs to occur at the end of the code block, a Do-Loop Until or Do-Loop While statement can be used. The following Do-Loop Until statement repeats until the test expression evaluates to True:

```
Dim Counter As Integer = 20
 Do
      'code statements
      Counter = Counter - 1
 Loop Until Counter < 10
```

For-Next Statements

For-Next statements loop through a code block a specific number of times based on a built-in counter. They are a better choice when you know the number of times the loop needs to execute at design time. You use Do-Loop statements when the number of iterations can vary depending on the condition. The following code block will repeat five times:

```
Dim Count as integer
For Count = 1 to 5
    'code statements
Next
```

The counter is automatically incremented as the loop iterates. By default the increment is one, but it can be changed using the Step keyword. The counter can also be decremented by using a negative Step value. The following code will start with a counter value of 100 and loop until the counter has a value of 20. After each iteration, the counter is decreased by a value of 10:

```
Dim Count as integer
For Count = 100 to 20 Step -10
    'code statements
Next
```

For Each-Next Statements

The For Each-Next statement loops through code for each item in a collection. A *collection* is a group of ordered items; for example, the controls placed on a Windows Form are organized into a `Controls` collection. To use the `For Each-Next` statement, you first declare a variable of the type of items contained in the collection. This variable is set to the current item in the collection. The following `For Each-Next` statement loops through the controls in the form's control collection and resets the text property to the default value:

```
Dim oControl As Control
For Each oControl In Me.Controls
    oControl.ResetText()
Next
```

Introducing Procedures

Procedures are blocks of code that can be called and executed from other code. Breaking an application up into discrete logical blocks of code greatly enhances code maintenance and reuse. Visual Basic supports `Sub` procedures and `Function` procedures. The main difference between the two is `Functions` return a value to the calling code but `Sub` procedures do not. When you declare a procedure, you specify an access modifier, the procedure type, and the name of the procedure. The `End` keyword followed by the procedure type designates the end of the procedure block. The following code declares a `Sub` procedure used to encapsulate and reuse the previous `For Each-Next` loop:

```
Private Sub ResetControls()
    Dim oControl As Control
    For Each oControl In Me.Controls
        oControl.ResetText()
    Next
End Sub
```

You can declare procedures with a parameter list that defines arguments that must be passed to the procedure when it is called. The following code defines a `Function` procedure that encapsulates the calculation of a bonus rate. The calling code passes an Integer type value to the function and receives a Single type value back:

```
Private Function GetBonusRate(ByVal Performance As Integer) As Single
    Dim BonusRate As Single
    Select Case Performance
        Case 10
            BonusRate = 0.1
        Case 8, 9
```

```
            BonusRate = 0.08
        Case 5 To 7
            BonusRate = 0.05
        Case Is < 5
            BonusRate = 0.02
        Case Else
            BonusRate = 0
    End Select
    Return BonusRate
End Function
```

The following code demonstrates how the function is called:

```
Dim Salary As Double
Dim QuarterPerformance As Integer
Dim Bonus As Double
'Retrieve salary and performance from database
'  ...
Bonus = GetBonusRate(QuarterPerformance) * Salary
```

If the access modifier of the procedure is private, it is only accessible from code within the same class or module. If the procedure needs to be accessed by code in other classes or modules, then either the Public or Friend access modifier is used.

APPENDIX B

Exception Handling in VB .NET

THE TOPICS DISCUSSED IN THIS appendix are an extension of the exception handling topics covered in Chapter 8, "Implementing Object Collaboration." It is assumed you have thoroughly reviewed Chapter 8 prior to reading this appendix. The focus of this appendix is to review Microsoft's recommendations for exception management and the exception classes provided by the .NET Framework.

Managing Exceptions

Exceptions are generated when the implicit assumptions made in your programming logic are violated. For example, when a connection is made to a database, it is assumed that the database server is up and running on the network. If the server cannot be located, then an exception is generated. It is important that your application gracefully handles any exceptions that may occur. If an exception is not handled, your application will terminate.

You should incorporate a systematic exception handling process in your methods. To facilitate this process, the .NET Framework makes use of structured exception handling through the Try, Catch, and Finally code blocks. The first step is to detect any exceptions that may be thrown as your code executes. To detect any exceptions thrown, place the code within the try block. When an exception is thrown in the try block, execution transfers to the catch block. You can use more than one catch block to filter for specific types of exceptions that may be thrown. The finally block performs any cleanup code. The code in the finally block executes regardless of whether an exception is thrown. Listing B-1 demonstrates reading a list of names from a file using the appropriate exception handling structure.

Listing B-1. Adding Exception Handling to a Code Block

```
Function GetNames(ByVal FileName As String) As ArrayList
    Dim Names As New ArrayList()
    Dim Stream As System.IO.StreamReader

    Try
        Stream = System.IO.File.OpenText(FileName)
        While Stream.Peek > -1
            Names.Add(Stream.ReadLine())
        End While
    Catch fnfExcep As System.IO.FileNotFoundException
        'Could not find the file
    Catch flExcep As System.IO.FileLoadException
        'Could not open file
    Catch IOExcep As System.IO.IOException
        ' Some kind of error occurred. Report error.
    Finally
        If Not IsNothing(Stream) Then
            Stream.Close()
        End If.
    End Try

        Return Names
End Function
```

After an exception is caught the next step in the process is to determine how to respond to the exception. You basically have two options: either recover from the exception or pass the exception to the calling procedure. The following code demonstrates recovering from a DivideByZeroException by setting the result to zero:

```
 . . .
Try
    Z = x / y
Catch dbzEx As DivideByZeroException
    Z = 0
End Try
 . . .
```

An exception is passed to the calling procedure using the `Throw` statement. The following code demonstrates throwing an exception to the calling procedure where it can be caught and handled:

```
Catch fnfExcep As System.IO.FileNotFoundException
    Throw fnfExcep
```

As exceptions are thrown up the calling chain, the relevance of the original exception can become less obvious. To maintain relevance, you can wrap the exception in a new exception containing additional information that adds relevancy to the exception. The following code demonstrates wrapping a caught exception in a new exception and then passing it up the calling chain:

```
Catch flExcep As System.IO.FileLoadException
    Throw New Exception("GetNames function could not open file", flExcep)
```

You preserve the original exception by using the `InnerException` property of the `Exception` class.

Implementing this exception management policy consistently throughout the various methods in your application will greatly enhance your ability to build successful, flexible, and highly maintainable applications.

Looking at the .NET Framework Exception Classes

The Common Language Runtime has a set of built-in exception classes. The CLR will throw an object instance of the appropriate exception type if an error occurs while executing code instructions. All .NET Framework exception classes derive from the `SystemException` class, which in turn derives from the `Exception` class. These base classes provide functionality needed by all exception classes.

Each namespace in the framework contains a set of exception classes that derive from the `SystemException` class. These exception classes handle common exceptions that may occur while implementing the functionality contained in the namespace. To implement robust exception handling, it is important you are familiar with the exception classes provided by the various namespaces. Table B-1 summarizes the exception classes in the `System.IO` namespace.

Table B-1. Exception Classes in the `System.IO` *Namespace*

EXCEPTION	DESCRIPTION
`IOException`	The base class for exceptions thrown while accessing information using streams, files, and directories
`DirectoryNotFoundException`	Thrown when part of a file or directory cannot be found
`EndOfStreamException`	Thrown when reading is attempted past the end of a stream
`FileLoadException`	Thrown when a file is found but cannot be loaded
`FileNotFoundException`	Thrown when an attempt to access a file that does not exist on disk fails
`PathTooLongException`	Thrown when a path or filename is longer than the system-defined maximum length

All exception classes contain the properties listed in Table B-2 to help you identify information about where the exception occurred and the cause of the exception.

Table B-2. Exception Class Properties

PROPERTY	DESCRIPTION
`Message`	Gets a message that describes the current exception
`Source`	Gets or sets the name of the application or the object that causes the error
`StackTrace`	Gets a string representation of the frames on the call stack at the time the current exception was thrown
`InnerException`	Gets the Exception instance that caused the current exception
`HelpLink`	Gets or sets a link to the help file associated with this exception

In addition, the `ToString` method of the exception classes provides summary information about the current exception. It combines the name of the class that threw the current exception, the message, the result of calling the `ToString` method of the inner exception, and the stack trace information of the current exception.

You will find that the exception classes in the .NET Framework provide you with the capabilities to handle most exceptions that may occur in your applications. In cases where you may need to implement custom error handling, you can create your own exception classes. These classes need to inherit from `System.ApplicationException`, which in turn inherits from `System.Exception`. Creating custom exception classes is an advanced topic beyond the scope of this text. For more information on this topic, consult the .NET Framework documentation.

Index

A

Abstract class
    creating, 163–164
    defined, 157, 165
Abstraction (in OOP), discussed, 7
Access database, ConnectionString for,
       228
Access modifiers, using in base classes,
       158–159
Account class
    creating, 159–160
    overriding, 169
Activate method (Form class), 270
Activations of an object (in sequence
       diagram), 44
Activities
    identifying, 64–65
    verb phrases as, 65
Activity diagram designer, 67
Activity diagrams, 16, 61–70
    activity ownership, 63–64
    branching condition, 69
    decision points, 62
    generic, 62
    guard conditions, 62
    GUI modeling with, 71–72
    objects and activities, 64–65
    parallel processing in, 62–63
    for user login, 91, 96
    using UML modeler, 66–70
    for viewing products (OSO
       application), 97
Activity graph, 66
Activity ownership, 63–64
Actor classes, 86
Actor shape (in use case diagram), 25
AddEmployee method (OSO
       application), 145–146
AddHandler method, 195–196, 199
ADO.NET, 107, 225–226
    becoming familiar with, 369
    classes and object model, 107
    disconnected model, 226
    tight integration with XML, 108,
       245

Aggregation
    defined, 30
    depicting, 31
    discussed, 9
And operator, 385
API (Application Programming
       Interface) functions, 104
Application closing dialog box, creating,
       298–299
Application deployment (.NET
       Framework), 105
Application design phases, 224
Application design process, 224–225
Application object, 224, 320, 340
Application object model, 224
Application prototyping (GUI design),
       75
Application state, maintaining in Web
       applications, 340–341
Application_BeginRequest event, 329
Application-level events, 329
Applications for the Web, developing,
       317–366
Applications (Windows), developing,
       269–315
Application_Start event, 329
Apress Web site, providing feedback to,
       371
Architectural structure, logical vs.
       physical, 225
Arithmetic operators, 383–384
ArrayList class, 257
ArrayList variable, creating, 236
Arrays, declaring, 377
ASP.NET, 108
ASP.NET DataGrid control
    displaying data in, 347–349
    updating data using, 349–354
Assemblies
    building and executing in VS,
       124–125
    business logic in, 369
    defined, 109
    private or shared, 109
    referencing, 110

AssemblyInfo.vb file, 116
Assignment operators, shorthand, 384
Associations (between classes), 29–32,
    88–90
AsyncCallBack class, 214–215
AsyncCallback delegate, 214
AsyncCallback variable, 214, 218–219
Asynchronous calling of a method,
    218–219
Asynchronous messaging, 46, 213–219
Attributes
    adding to classes, 86–88
    explained, 136
    identifying, 32–33
Auto hide feature (VS IDE), 120–122
Auto Hide (thumbtack) icon, 120–122
Auto syntax check features (VS IDE),
    124
AutoPostBack event, 338
Average monthly balance, getting, 167

B
Base form, 287
Base form access modifiers, 287
BeginInvoke method, 214–215, 219
Behaviors
    explained, 136
    modeling for OSO classes, 90–95
Binary Association dialog box,
        Properties tab, 36
BindGrid method, 357
BindingContext object, 300–301
BindList method, 357
BlockCount variable, 380
Block-level variable scope, 380
Boolean data type, 376
Bound controls
    implementing complex, 304–305
    implementing simple, 302–304
Branching
    in activity diagrams, 69
    in collaboration diagrams, 60
    in sequence diagrams, 49
Breakpoint Condition dialog box
        (VS), 129
Breakpoint Properties dialog box
        (VS), 128
Breakpoints
    removing, 127
    setting, 125–126
    setting conditional, 128–131
Breakpoints window (VS), 128
Broadcast messaging, defined, 190
Bubble sort, 201
Build errors, locating and fixing in VS,
    131–132

Business logic
    in its own assembly, 369
    for OSO application, 223–267
Business logic class diagram (OSO
        application), 262
Business logic tier
    in application design, 225
    in OSO application, 253–266
Button click event handler methods, 303
Button click event handlers, 197, 281,
        310–312, 327, 336
Button click event procedure, 250,
        264–265
Button click events, 236, 250, 286–287
Button click routine, 202
Button control (VS IDE), 122, 124
Byte data type, 374
ByVal keyword, 189

C
C# (C-sharp) language, 4
Callback method, 214, 218
Case blocks, 387
CASE (Computer-Aided Software
        Engineering) tools, 23
Case study (ordering system). *See* OSO
        application
Casting (data type conversion), 381–383
Catch block, 204–205, 212, 393
Certifications (Microsoft), 370
Char data type, 375
Character data types, 375
Checked property of a control, 284
CheckingAccount class, creating,
        156–157
Child table, 242
Class associations, 29–32, 88–90
Class attributes, 136
    adding to classes, 86–88
    identifying, 32–33
Class behaviors, 90–95, 136
Class constructors. *See* Constructors
Class definition file, event messaging in,
        192–194
Class diagrams, 28–38
    adding a class shape, 35
    adding methods, 55–59
    defined, 15
    indicating multiplicity in, 29
    for OSO application, 86, 95, 253, 262
    for OSO Purchase Request, 95
    using UML Modeler for, 34–38
Class hierarchies, creating, 155–186
Class library (.NET Framework), 107
Class list candidate classes (OSO appli-
        cation), 85

Class methods. *See* Methods
Class node (VS IDE), 117
Class properties. *See* Properties
Class shape, adding to a class diagram, 35
Class structure
    identifying, 13–39
    modeling for OSO application, 84–86
Class View (VS IDE), 117–120
Classes, 28
    adding attributes to, 86–88
    creating, 135–153, 159–160, 184
    creating abstract, 163–164
    defining base and derived, 179
    explained, 136, 377
    identifying, 32–33
    inheriting from other classes, 89
    self-associating, 30
    testing, 142, 160–161
    using access modifiers in, 158–159
Class-level scoped variables, 243, 307
CLI (Common Language Infrastructure), 104
Click event handler, 197, 310, 311–312, 327, 336
Click event handler methods, 303
Click event procedure, 250, 264–265
Click events, coding, 286–287
Client code, defined, 137
Client-server applications, two-tier, 225
Close method of Connection object, 228
CLR built-in exception classes, 395
CLR (Common Language Runtime), 104, 106–107
CLS (Common Language Specification), 104
Code access, 106
Code editor (VS)
    event code in, 142
    using to set a breakpoint, 126
Code identity, 106
Code selection drop-down list (VS IDE), 119
Code-behind class of Web Form, viewing, 334
Code-behind file extension (.aspx.vb), 318
Code-behind file (Web Forms), 319
    defined, 318
    in Web Form Designer, 325
Code-behind page, 324
Coder, vs. programmer, 368
Collaboration diagrams, 59–61
    defined, 15
    generic, 59
Collaboration (object), 187–220

Collect method, of GC system class, 144
Collection, defined, 389
Collection class
    creating, 179
    using, 181
ComboBox control, 305–306, 308
Command object, 229
    CommandText property, 229–230
    CommandType property, 230
    ExecuteReader method, 231
    ExecuteScalar method, 235
    methods, 229
    Parameters collection, 230, 244
    SelectCommand property, 241
    using to execute a stored procedure, 238–240
CommandBuilder class, 245
Commands, executing, 229
Compare method, 119–120, 209
Comparison operators, 384–385
Complex bound controls
    implementing, 304–305
    properties, 304
Complex data binding, 301, 341
Component objects. *See* Controls
Component tray (VS IDE), 282
Component-based development, 369
Components, defined, 369
Composite data types, 376–377
Conceptual design phase, 224
Conditional breakpoints, setting in VS, 128–131
Conditional constraints (collaboration diagram), 61
Conditional constraints (message), 48
Connection object, 227, 243
    Close method, 228
    ConnectionString property, 235
    Open method, 228
ConnectionString property
    for Access database, 228
    for Connection object, 235
    for SQL Server database, 227
    for SqlConnection object, 340
Const keyword, 378
Constants, explained, 378–379
Constraints (in collaboration diagrams), 60–61
Constraints (message), 48
Constructors
    creating, 235
    creating and overloading, 147–148
    form, 275
    overloading, 146
    testing, 149–150
    using, 143

Container control, defined, 270
Container object, 275
ContainerControl class, 270
Context object, 214
Control class, 270, 321
Control event handlers, 280–281
Controls collection, 390
Controls (Windows Forms), 270
    simple-bound, 301
    synchronizing to a data source, 300
Cookies, 339
Counter, incrementing, 207, 389
Crosshairs pointer, 121
Cryptographic services, 369
Ctype conversion keyword, 382
CurrencyManager collection, 300

D

Data
    durable vs. nondurable, 369
    editing in a DataSet, 243–245
    and .NET Framework, 107–109
    retrieving using DataAdapter object,
        232–234
    retrieving using DataReader object,
        231–232, 236–238
Data binding
    complex, 301, 341
    defined, 300
    multivalue, 342–344
    simple, 341
    in Web Form-based GUIs, 341–354
    in Windows Form-based GUIs,
        300–305
Data encapsulation, 137
Data exchange, proprietary methods of,
    226
Data Link Properties dialog box (VS),
    263
Data loss, in data type conversion, 383
Data providers
    Microsoft support for, 107–108
    working with, 226–240
Data referential integrity, 242
Data source, synchronizing controls to,
    300
Data storage, 225
Data stores, 225
Data structures, 369
Data tier (application design), 225
Data type conversion, 381–383
Data types
    assigning to a variable, 373
    elementary, 374–376
DataAdapter object, 240
    creating and setting up, 244–245

Fill method, 241
SelectCommand property, 233, 247,
    251
    Update method, 243, 249
    using to retrieve data, 232–234
Database diagram for OSO application,
    254
Database References node (Solution
    Explorer), 263
DataColumn objects, 242
DataGrid control, 305–306, 308, 343
    adding a button column, 351
    bound to a data source, 301
    custom formatting of, 344
    DataMember property, 301
    displaying data in, 347–349
    EditCommand event, 345
    editing capabilities for, 345
    editing data in, 353
    EditItemIndex event, 346–347
    UpdateCommand event, 346
    updating data in, 344–347, 349–354
DataGrid Properties dialog box, 350
DataList control, 328
DataReader object, 238
    Close method, 231
    Read method, 231
    using to retrieve data, 231–232
    using to retrieve records, 236–238
DataRelation object, 242, 304–305
DataSet objects and XML files, convert-
    ing between, 245–246
DataSet/Dataset object, 232–233
    creating, 248, 252
    defined, 240
    editing data in, 243–245
    editing and updating SQL Server
        database, 249–250
    filling, 247
    GetChanges method, 250
    populating, 240
    populating from SQL Server data-
        base, 241–242, 246–248
    ReadXML method, 245
    Relations collection, 242
    relationships between tables in, 242,
        250-253
    returning to the client, 251–252
    updating, 243
    ways to create, 240
    working with, 240–253
    WriteXML method, 245
DataTable relations, establishing, 242
DataUpdate event message, 199
Date data type, 376
Date literal, 378

DateTimePicker control, 300
DbOrder class (OSO application), 259–260
DCL (Data Control Language) statements, 229
DDL (Data Definition Language) statements, 229
Debug toolbar (VS), 126–127
Decimal data type, 375
Decision points (activity diagram), 62
Decision structures, 385–387
Delegate, creating, 213, 218
Delegate class, 197
Delegated methods, 197–202
Delegated method signature, 197–198
Delegation, 197–203, 278
Derived class, 156, 164–165, 179
Derived forms, 287–288
Derived method, overloading, 176
Design pitfalls (OOP), avoiding common, 99–100
Design process (application), 224–225
Design process phases, 224
Designing OOP solutions, 41
    case study, 77–98
    class structure, 13–39
    object interaction, 41–75
Destructors, using, 144–145
Dialog boxes
    creating and using, 290–299
    examples of, 290–291
    vs. forms, 290
DialogResult enumeration, 292–293
Dim keyword, 131, 373–374
Disconnected model (ADO.NET), 226
Dispose method
    of a control, 278
    custom, 144–145
    of a form, 294
DivideByZeroException, recovering from, 394
DLL files, 109
DML (Data Manipulation Language) statements, 229
Do While-Loop statements, 388
Documenting inheritance, 30
Do-Loop statements, 388–389
Double data type, 375
Durable data, 369

E
EditCommandColumn (DataGrid), 344
Elementary data types, 374–376
Else blocks, 386
Else-If blocks, 386

EMCA (European Computer Manufacturers Association), 104
Employee class (OSO application), 260–261
    creating, 140–142
    testing, 142, 149–150
Encapsulation (in OOP), discussed, 7–8
End keyword, 390–391
EndInvoke method, 214–215, 219
Enum type, 379
Enumerations, explained, 379
Event code, in the code editor, 142
Event handler method names, 280, 327
Event handler parameters, 328
Event handlers, 278
    for form controls, 280–281
    for forms, 279–280
    multiple for the same event, 289
    for server-side control, 334–336
    using delegation for, 199
    Web Form server-side, 325–338
Event messages. *See* Messages
Event messaging. *See* Messaging
Event procedure, Public Overridable, 288–289
Event-driven applications, 278
Event-driven programming, 190–197
Events
    filtering in client class, 202–203
    form, 270
    handling multiple with one method, 196–197
    receiving in client class, 194–196
Exception class, 395
Exception classes, 204, 395–397
    creating custom, 397
    properties of, 396
    in System.IO namespace, 396
    ToString method, 396
Exception handling
    adding to a code block, 394
    nesting, 207
    in .NET Framework, 203–207
    structured, 211–212
    in VB .NET, 393–397
Exceptions
    explained, 203
    filtering, 205, 212–213
    managing, 393–395
    passing to calling procedure, 395
    recovering from, 394
    throwing, 204–206
    wrapping in other exceptions, 395
EXE files, 109
ExecuteNonQuery method, 229

ExecuteReader method, 229, 231
ExecuteScalar method, 229, 235
Expanded nodes in main explorer window, 58
Explicit data type conversion, 382
Extending use cases, 82–83
Extensibility, of .NET Framework, 104
Extension (in use case diagram), 20

F
Feedback, request to provide, 371
FileStream object, 210, 216
Final class, defined, 158
Finally block, 205–206, 393
Flat file system, 225
Flat message type, 46
Flight Booking class diagram, 32
Flight class diagram, 28
For Each-Next statements, 389–390
Foreign key, 242
Form class, 116, 237, 270, 275
Form components, initializing, 276–278
Form constructor, 275
Form controls, explained, 270
Form Designer (VS IDE), 271–278
Form event handlers, 279–280
Form events, explained, 270
Form methods, explained, 269
Form properties, explained, 269
Form-based inheritance, 287–290
Form_Load event, 280
Form_Load event handler, 303, 305, 307
Forms (see also Web Forms; Windows Forms)
    choosing controls for, 300
    creating inherited, 295–298
    defined, 269
    vs. dialog boxes, 290
For-Next statements, 389
Friend keyword, 276, 287
Function procedures, 390
Functions, defined, 4

G
GAC (Global Assembly Cache), 105, 109
GC (Garbage Collector), 106, 144
Get block, 137
Get Started tab (VS IDE), 113
GetChanges method of DataSet object, 250
GetData method, 243, 248, 251–252
GetMinBalance method
    overriding, 165–166
    testing, 174–175
Global.asax.vb file, in Web Form Designer, 330

Guard conditions (activity diagram), 62
GUI class diagrams, 74
GUI design, 71–75
GUI modeling with an activity diagram, 71–72
GUI sketch, 73
GUIs (graphical user interfaces), 71–75, 108–109

H
Handles keyword, 195, 280, 328
Help, with .NET Framework and VB .NET, 370
Help system (VS), 370
Hierarchical textual file structure, 225
HTML code, for Web server controls, 319–320
HTTP (Hypertext Transfer Protocol), 107–108, 226
HTTP post request, 326
HTTP (XML over), 226
HttpApplication class, 330
HttpApplicationState class, 340
HttpResponse class, Cookie property, 339
HttpSessionState class, 340

I
IAccount interface
    defining, 180, 184
    implementing, 180
IAsyncCallBack object, 215
IAsyncResult interface, 214–215, 218–219
IDE (Integrated Development Environment), 10, 111
IDE (VB), 10
IDE (VS). See VS IDE
IDL (Interface Definition Language) files, 110
IEnumerable interface, 342
If block, 380
If-Then statements, 385, 386–387
IIS (Internet Information Server) Web server, 319
IList interface, 301
Implements keyword, 178
Implicit data type conversion, 381–382
Imports statement, 110, 210, 216, 235, 243
Inclusion (in use case diagram), 20
Industry standards, .NET Framework support of, 104
Inheritance, 30, 156–164
    defined, 155
    discussed, 9

documenting, 30
form-based, 287–290
implementing polymorphism using,
    181–182
Inheritance hierarchy for Windows
    Forms, 270–271
Inheritance Picker dialog box, 296
Inherited form,creating, 295–298
Inherits statement, 218
InitializeComponent sub procedure,
    275–276
InnerException property of Exception
    class, 395
Integer data type, 374
Integer values
    comparing, 197
    converting to Strings, 382
    sorting, 198
Integral data types, 374–375
InterestCheckingAccount, creating, 173
Interface definition, declaring, 177
Interface flow diagrams (GUI design),
    73–74
Interface prototyping (GUI design), 73
Interfaces
    defining, 180, 184
    implementing, 177–178, 180
    implementing polymorphism using,
      184
    main advantage of using, 178
Interoperability, explained, 226
Interpretability (ADO.NET), 226
ISE (Interactive Software Engineering),
    104
Iteration
    in collaboration diagrams, 60
    explained, 47
Iterative message, 47–48

J

JIT (Just-In-Time) compiler, 111
Join method, 203

L

Label control (VS IDE), 121–122, 288
Languages (programming)
    .NET Framework-supported, 105
    .NET platform-supported, 111
    for server-side code, 108
Lifeline of an object (in sequence dia-
    gram), 44
Lifetime of a variable, 379
ListBox control, 125, 301
ListItem Collection Editor dialog box,
    337
Literals, explained, 378

Load List (VS), 129
Locals window (VS), 129–130
Logger class, 216
    LogRead method, 214, 217–218
    LogWrite method, 211
Logger form, 210, 216
Logical application design, three tiers of,
    225
Logical design phase, 224
Logical operators, 385
Logical vs. physical architectural struc-
    ture, 225
Login Failed message, 212
Login form, 193, 309
Login method, 139, 141–142
Login process, in sequence diagram, 92
Login scenarios, in activity diagram, 91
Login screen prototype for OSO, 96
Login use case for OSO, 82
Login.aspx page, 359
LoginDialog custom dialog box, 293
LoginInfo structure, creating, 294
LogRead method of Logger class, 214,
    217–218
LogReadCallBack method, 218–219
LogReader delegate
    BeginInvoke method, 219
    EndInvoke method, 219
LogReader variable, declaring, 218
LogWrite function, shared, 210
LogWrite method of Logger class, 211
Long data type, 374
Loop structures, 388–390

M

MainMenu control, 282–283
Managed code, compiling and execut-
    ing, 110–111
Managed heap, defined, 144
Managed providers, 107
Manifests, 105, 109
MCAD (Microsoft Certified Application
    Developer), 370
Me qualifier, 166, 167
Memo viewer interface
    creating, 282–286
    menu items, 283
    properties, 282
Memory leaks, 105
Memory management (.NET
    Framework), 105–106
Menu click events, coding, 286–287
MenuStart event, 270
Message branching (sequence diagram),
    49
Message constraints, 48

Message iteration, 47–48
Message layout, in sequence diagram, 54
Message order, in collaboration diagrams, 60
Message types, 46
MessageBox class, 291–292
MessageBox result, retrieving, 292
Messages
 nesting, 60
 recursive, 47
 using verb phrases to identify, 50
Messaging, 187–190
 asynchronous, 46, 213–219
 broadcast, 190
 in class definition file, 192–194
 subscription-based, 190
 synchronous, 46, 213
Metadata, stored in a manifest, 105
Method signatures, 145, 188
Methods
 adding to a class diagram, 55–59
 calling asynchronously, 214, 218–219
 creating, 139–140, 161–162
 delegated, 197–202
 explained, 3, 136
 for handling multiple events, 196–197
 overloading, 145–152, 176
 overriding, 164–175
 shadowing, 176–177
 shared, 207–213
 testing, 162–163, 170–172, 174–175, 185
Microsoft
 certifications, 370
 data access technologies, 225
 support for data providers, 107–108
Microsoft Certified Application Developer (MCAD), 370
Microsoft Certified Solution Developer, 370
Module scope, variables with, 381
MouseDown event handler, 280
MouseHover event handler, 288
MouseHover event of a Label or TextBox, 281
Movie Rental example, 42–75
 activity diagram, 61–70
 adding methods, 55–59
 collaboration diagram, 59–61
 GUI design, 71–75
 scenario, 50–51
 sequence diagram, 45, 51–55
 use case, 42–43
MSIL code, converted as-needed, 111

MSIL (Microsoft Intermediate Language) format, 110–111
Multicasting, 289
Multidimensional arrays, 377
Multiple inheritance, 178
Multiplicity (in a class diagram), 29
Multitier Web-based applications, 225
Multivalue data binding, 342–344
MustInherit keyword, 157, 163, 165
MustOverride keyword, 165, 182
My Profile tab (VS IDE), 113
MyBase qualifier, 168, 171–172
MyClass qualifier, 167, 173

N

Name property of a form, 284
Namespaces (.NET Framework), 368–369
 defined, 110
 Imports statement for, 243
 referencing, 110
Narrowing conversions, explained, 383
Nesting messages, 60
.NET Framework
 application deployment, 105
 base class library, 107
 components of, 106–109
 data and XML classes, 107–109
 exception classes, 204, 395–397
 exception handling, 203–207
 extensibility, 104
 getting help with, 370
 goals of, 103–106
 hierarchical structure, 110
 language integration support, 111
 memory management, 105–106
 namespaces, 110, 243, 368–369
 security model, 106
 support of industry standards, 104
 support for Web Services, 108
 support for Windows Forms, 109
 unified programming models, 104-105
.NET provider classes, 226
.NET user groups, 370
New constructor method, 143
New Project window (VS IDE), 114–115, 290, 331
Nondeterministic finalization, 105–106, 144
Nondurable data, 369
Non-integral data types, 375
Non-postback server control events, 337–338
Not operator, 385
NotInheritable keyword, 157–158

NotOverridable keyword, 164
Noun phrases, using to identify objects, 50, 65
NumberList (VS), 130
Numeric literals, 378

O

Object attributes
  adding to classes, 86–88
  explained, 136
  identifying, 32–33
Object Browser window (VS IDE), 119–120
Object collaboration, 187–220
Object communication through messaging, 187–190
Object data type, 376
Object independence, 207
Object instances
  added to sequence diagram, 52
  and shared variables, 207
Object interaction, modeling, 41–75
Object layout, in sequence diagram, 53
Object methods. *See* Methods
Object properties. *See* Properties
Objects
  defined, 3, 28
  discussed, 6
  identifying, 64–65
  using nouns to identify, 50, 65
Office-Supply Ordering application. *See* OSO application
OLEDB data provider, 107–108, 226
OOP design
  case study, 77–98
  class structure, 13–39
  object interaction, 41–75
OOP design pitfalls, avoiding common, 99–100
OOP (Object-Oriented Programming), 3–4, 135
  advantages of, 187
  benefits of, 5–6
  characteristics of, 6–9
  history of, 3
  objects and classes in, 135
  overview of, 3–11
  reasons for using, 4–6
Open method of Connection object, 228
OpenFileDialog properties, 285
Operation dialog box, 56
Operators, 383–385
Options dialog box (VS IDE), 113–114
Or operator, 385
Order class (OSO application), 257–259, 265–266

Order Item dialog box, 311–313
Order request screen prototype (OSO application), 98
OrderItem class (OSO application), 255–257, 311
OSO (Office-Supply Ordering) application, 77–98
  activity diagram of login scenarios, 91
  adding attributes to classes, 86–88
  adding order items, 311–313, 361–364
  business logic, 223–267
  business logic class diagram, 262
  business logic tier, 225, 253–266
  candidate classes for purchase requests, 85
  case study background, 77–78
  class attributes list, 87
  class diagram, 253
  class inheriting from another class, 89
  class list candidate classes, 85
  class structure associations, 89
  creating the SRS, 78–79
  creating the Web Form-based GUI, 354–364
  database diagram, 254
  DataGrid column property values, 356, 362
  dbOrder class, 259–260
  developing use cases, 79–81
  diagramming use cases, 81–83
  displaying products, 306–309, 355–358
  Employee class, 260–261
  filtering products by category, 357
  identifying class associations, 88–90
  initiating an order, 358
  Login dialog form, 309
  Login dialog form property values, 310
  Login screen prototype, 96
  Login use case, 82
  modeling class behaviors, 90–95
  modeling the class structure, 84–86
  Order class, 257–259
  order form, 306
  order form and control property values, 307
  order panel control, 308
  order panel control property values, 309
  Order request screen prototype, 98
  OrderItem class, 255–257
  placing an order, 314, 364
  preliminary class diagram, 86
  preliminary use case diagram, 81

OSO (Office-Supply Ordering)
application (*continued*)
ProductCatalog class, 254–255
Purchase Request class diagram, 95
Purchase Request class diagram with
associations, 90
Purchase Request class diagram with
attributes, 88
Purchase Request sequence diagram,
94
Purchase Request use case diagrams,
83
removing order items, 313, 364
sequence diagram of login process,
92
sequence diagram for View Supply
Catalog, 93
server control property values, 355,
361
setting up the database, 262–263
testing the business logic, 263–265
testing the Web GUI, 365–366
testing the Windows GUI, 314
user interface model design, 95–98
user login activity diagram, 96
validating employees, 309–311,
358–361
View Products activity diagram, 97
View Products screen prototype, 98
Web Form control property values,
360
Web order form, 355
Windows Form-based GUI, 306–315
Output window (VS IDE), 124
Overflow, in data type conversion, 383
Overloaded Update method, testing,
151–152
Overloading, explained, 8
Overloading of constructors, 146–149
Overloading of methods, 145–152, 176
Overridable keyword, 164
Overrides procedure, 288–289
Overriding of methods, 164–175

P

Page class, 321
Page class file (Web Forms), 319
Page class IsPostBack property, 327
Page event handler, 326
Page file extension (.aspx), 318
Page file (Web Forms), 318–319
Page_Load event, 327
Page_Load event handler, 335
Parallel processing (in activity diagram),
62–63
Parameter dialog box, 57

Parameter object, 244
Parameters
passing, 188–189
passing by reference, 189
passing by value, 189
Parameters collection, 230, 238, 244, 249
Parent table, 242
Permissions, 106
Physical design phase, 224
Physical vs. logical architectural struc-
ture, 225
Polymorphic method, testing, 182–183,
185
Polymorphism, 178–185
defined, 155
discussed, 8
implementing using inheritance,
181–182
implementing using an interface, 184
PositionChanged event, 300
Postback events, 320, 327, 335
Presentation tier (application design),
225
Primary key, 242
Private assembly, 109
Private instance variables, 141
Private keyword, 136, 158, 381
Private method, 147
Private variable, declaring, 235
Procedural scoped variables, 236, 380
Procedures, 4, 380, 390–391
Process Movie Rental example. *See*
Movie Rental example
ProductCatalog class (OSO application),
254–255
Programmer
vs. coder, 368
designing and coding practice, 368
gaining experience, 368
Programming concepts, 373–391
Project node (VS IDE), 116
Properties
creating, 136–138
explained, 136
restricting access to, 138
shared, 207–213
Properties Editor (UML Modeler), 24
Properties of a form, explained, 269
Properties window (VS IDE), 122–123
Property Pages window (VS IDE),
116–117
Protected instance variable, 159
Protected keyword, 158
Protected method, creating, 161–162
Public enumeration, creating, 200
Public keyword, 136, 158

Public Overridable event procedure, 288–289
Public properties, 141
Purchase Request (OSO application)
    class diagram with associations, 90
    class diagram with attributes, 88
    class diagrams, 88, 90, 95
    sequence diagram, 94
    use case diagrams, 83

R
RaiseEvent statement, 190
RDBMS (relational database management system), 225, 240
ReadLog method, 218
ReadOnly keyword, 138
Read-only property, 138
ReadXML method (DataSet object), 245
Recursion, explained, 47
Recursive messages, 47
Reference type, 107
References node (VS IDE), 116
Referential integrity between tables, 242
Relations collection of DataSet object, 242
Request object, 320
Reserve Seat use case diagram, 19
ResumeLayout method, 276
Return Parameter dialog box, 58
Rights, 106
Run On dialog box (VS), 263

S
Scalability, defined, 225–226
Scenarios, 41–43
Scope of variables, 379–381
Screen prototypes
    for OSO Order Request, 98
    for OSO View Products, 98
ScrollableControl class, 270
Sealed class, defined, 158
Security model (.NET Framework), 106
Select-Case statements, 385, 387
SelectCommand property
    of Command object, 241
    of DataAdapter object, 233, 247, 251
Self-associating class, 30
Self-association, explained, 30
Self-describing code, 110
Sequence diagrams, 43–39
    activations of an object, 44
    defined, 15
    depicting login process, 92
    lifeline of an object, 44

message branching, 49
message layout, 54
object instance added to, 52
object layout, 53
Process Movie Rental example, 45
for Purchase Request, 94
using UML modeler, 51–55
for View Supply Catalog, 93
Server-side code, languages for, 108
Server-side control event handlers, 334–336
Server-side event handling (Web Form), 325–338
Server-side event processing, 328–329
Session events, 329
Session object, 340
Session state
    defined, 340
    maintaining in Web applications, 340
Set block, 137
Shadowing a method, 176–177
Shadows keyword, 177
Shared assembly, 109
Shared methods, 207–214
    client code accessing, 208
    creating, 209–211
    creating and calling synchronously, 215–218
Shared properties, 207–213
    accessing, 208
    creating in class definition, 207–208
Short data type, 374
Shorthand assignment operators, 384
ShowDialog method, 293
Simple bound controls
    defined, 301
    implementing, 302–304
    properties, 302
Simple data binding, 341
Simple data binding Web server controls, 341–342
Simple message type, 46
Single data type, 375
SOAP (Simple Object Access Protocol), 104, 108, 226
Software design, goals of, 14–15
Solution Explorer (VS IDE), 115–120
Sort class, 203
Sort form, 200
Sort function, 202
Sort method, 200–201
Sort routine, 198, 200–203
Sorting a list of words, 200–202
Split function, 203
SQL data provider, 107

SQL Server database
  ConnectionString for, 227
  editing and updating a DataSet to,
      249–250
  having appropriate rights in, 234
  populating a DataSet from, 241–242,
      246–248
SQL Server provider classes, 226
SQL statements, executing, 229
SQLClient namespace, 235
SqlCommand object, 247, 249, 251
SqlCommand variable, creating, 236
SqlConnection object, connection
      string, 340
SqlConnection variable, declaring, 235
SqlDataReader object, 231
SqlDataReader variable, creating, 236
SqlParameter object, 230
SRS (software requirement specifica-
      tion) document, 15–16
  class diagrams, 28–38
  creating for OSO application, 78–79
  defined, 15
  developing, 16
  functional requirements, 21
  identifying principal actors, 22
  identifying use cases, 22
  parts of, 15–16
  purpose of, 16
  sample, 16–17
  use cases, 17–27
Start Page (VS IDE), 112
State maintenance, in Web applications,
      338–341
StatusBar control, displaying message
      and date, 285
StatusBarPanels Collection Editor dialog
      box, 284
StatusBarPanels properties, 285
Step keyword, 389
Step Over, 127
Stored procedures
  executing, 233–234
  executing using Command object,
      238–240
  using, 230–231
StreamReader object, 216
StreamWriter object, 210
String array, declaring, 203
String data type, 375
String data type conversion to Integer, 382
StringAlignment enumeration, 379
Strings, comparing, 209
Strong typing, explained, 373
Structural programming, shortcomings
      of, 5

Structured exception handler, creating,
      211–212
Structures, explained, 376–377
Sub procedures, 390
Subscription-based messaging, 190
SuspendLayout method, 276
Swim lanes (in activity diagram), 63–64
Synchronizing controls to a data source,
      300
Synchronous calling of a shared
      method, 215–218
Synchronous messaging, 46, 213
System namespace, 110, 369
System.ApplicationException class, 397
System.Collections namespace, 257
System.Data namespace, 110, 225, 240,
      269
System.Data.OLEDB namespace,
      226–227
System.Data.SqlClient namespace, 110,
      226–227
System.EventArgs object, 280, 328
System.Exception class, 395, 397
System.IO classes, 210, 396
System.IO namespace, 216
System.IO.FileNotFoundException, 211
System.Runtime.Remoting.Messaging
      namespace, 214–215
System.Security.Cryptography name-
      space, 369
System.String class, Compare method,
      209
System.Threading namespace, 216
System.Web namespace, 330
System.Web.UI.page class, 318
System.Web.UI.WebControls name-
      space, 321
System.Windows.Forms namespace,
      110, 116, 270, 291, 369
System.Windows.Forms.Form base
      class, 117

T
Task List window (VS), 132
TemplateControl class, 321
TextBox class, 321
TextBox controls, 122–124, 300
  hierarchy of, 271, 322
  TextMode property, 320
TextBox Web server control, 319–320
Thread class, 216
Throw statement, 395
Toolbox (VS IDE), 120
ToString method of exception classes,
      396
Try block, 161, 204–207, 393

Try-catch block, 204–205, 212, 236–237
Two-dimensional arrays, 377
Two-tier client-server applications, 225
Type conversion keyword, 382
Types, defined, 107

U
UML common models, 15–16
UML Modeler
    activity diagram, 66–70
    class diagram, 34–38
    Properties Editor, 24
    sequence diagram, 51–55
    use case diagram, 23–27
UML (Unified Modeling Language),
       15–27, 136
Unicode, 375
Unified programming models (.NET
       Framework), 104–105
Update command, creating, 244
Update method, testing overloaded,
       151–152
Update method of DataAdapter object,
       243, 249
Update query, Parameters collection, 249
Use case diagram, 18
    adding an actor shape, 25
    adding a description, 26
    completed examples, 27, 38
    described, 19–20
    extension, 20
    inclusion, 20
    postconditions, 19–20
    preconditions, 19
    using UML Modeler for, 23–27
Use cases, 17–27
    defined, 15
    description for, 42
    identifying for SRS, 22
    internal processing, 43
    extending, 82–83
    for OSO application, 79–83
    for Process Movie Rental example,
       42–43
User group, joining, 370
User interface model design for OSO,
       95–98
User login activity diagram for OSO, 96

V
Value type, 107
Variable lifetime, 379
Variable scope, 307, 379–381
Variables
    assigning initial values to, 374
    with class-level scope, 307

creating, 236
declaring, 214, 373–374
defining, 243
explained, 373
shared, 207
Verb phrases
    as activities, 65
    using to identify messages, 50
View Flight Info use case, 18
View Products activity diagram (OSO),
       97
View Products screen prototype (OSO),
       98
View state, maintaining in Web appli-
       cations, 338–339
View Supply Catalog, sequence diagram
       for, 93
ViewState hidden control, 339
Visual Basic IDE, 10
Visual Basic .NET, 103–133
    exception handling in, 393–397
    getting help with, 370
Visual Basic programming, 373–391
    commenting code, 131
    expanding and viewing code, 124
    stepping through code, 125–127
    uncommenting code, 132
Visual Basic (VB), history of, 9–10
VS (Visual Studio) IDE, 111–132
    building and executing assemblies,
       124–125
    choosing a control, 279
    choosing an event, 279
    component tray, 282
    creating a new project, 114–115
    creating a Web application, 331–334
    customizing, 112–114
    Form Designer, 271–278
    help system, 370
    locating and fixing build errors,
       131–132
    sample form layout, 122
    setting conditional breakpoints,
       128–131
    Solution Explorer and Class View,
       115–120
    stepping through code, 125–127
    Toolbox and Properties window,
       120–123
    VB project templates, 115
    Web Form Designer, 322–325

W
Watch window (VS), 130–131
Web applications
    creating in VS, 331–334

Web applications (*continued*)
   developing, 317–366
   state maintenance in, 338–341
Web creation message box, 332
Web Form and control events, handling, 325–329
Web Form Designer (VS IDE), 322–325, 332
   in code editor view, 324–325
   in HTML view, 324
   tabs, 323
   window, 323
Web Form hierarchy chain, 321
Web Form (Page) event handler, 326
Web Form page processing events, 329
Web Form-based GUI
   data binding in, 341–354
   for OSO application, 354–364
Web Forms, 108, 317
   advantages of, 320
   fundamentals of, 317–319
   inheritance hierarchy, 320–321
   parts of, 318
   programming logic, 318
   visual interface, 318
Web server control event handlers, 327
Web server controls, 319–322
   advantages of, 320
   inheritance hierarchy, 321–322
Web Services, 108
Web-based applications, multitier, 225
WebControl class, 322
Web-enabled clients, 108
What's New tab (VS IDE), 113
While statements, 388
Widening conversions, explained, 383
Windows API functions, 104
Windows applications, developing, 269–315

Windows Form and control events, handling, 278
Windows Form Designer-generated code, 272–275
Windows Form-based GUI
   data binding in, 300–305
   for OSO application, 306–315
Windows Forms
   fundamentals, 269–287
   inheritance hierarchy, 270–271
   .NET Framework support for, 109
Windows GUI application, building, 109
Withdraw method, 171–172
   creating, 162
   overriding, 169
   testing, 162–163, 170–172
WithEvents keyword, 191, 194, 276, 325
WriteLog method, 211, 213
WriteOnly keyword, 138
Write-only property, 138
WriteXML method of DataSet class, 245

X
Xcopy deployment, 105
XML classes, .NET Framework and, 107–109
XML data structure, 108
XML (Extensible Markup Language), 104, 108, 226, 245
XML files and DataSet objects, converting between, 245–246
XML format, 107–108
XML over HTTP, 226

Z
Zero-based array index, 377

apress™

books for professionals by professionals™

About Apress

Apress, located in Berkeley, CA, is a fast-growing, innovative publishing company devoted to meeting the needs of existing and potential programming professionals. Simply put, the "A" in Apress stands for *"The Author's Press*™*"* and its books have *"The Expert's Voice*™*".* Apress' unique approach to publishing grew out of conversations between its founders Gary Cornell and Dan Appleman, authors of numerous best-selling, highly regarded books for programming professionals. In 1998 they set out to create a publishing company that emphasized quality above all else. Gary and Dan's vision has resulted in the publication of over 50 titles by leading software professionals, all of which have *The Expert's Voice*™.

Do You Have What It Takes to Write for Apress?

Apress is rapidly expanding its publishing program. If you can write and refuse to compromise on the quality of your work, if you believe in doing more than rehashing existing documentation, and if you're looking for opportunities and rewards that go far beyond those offered by traditional publishing houses, we want to hear from you!

Consider these innovations that we offer all of our authors:

- **Top royalties with *no* hidden switch statements**
  Authors typically only receive half of their normal royalty rate on foreign sales. In contrast, Apress' royalty rate remains the same for both foreign and domestic sales.

- **A mechanism for authors to obtain equity in Apress**
  Unlike the software industry, where stock options are essential to motivate and retain software professionals, the publishing industry has adhered to an outdated compensation model based on royalties alone. In the spirit of most software companies, Apress reserves a significant portion of its equity for authors.

- **Serious treatment of the technical review process**
  Each Apress book has a technical reviewing team whose remuneration depends in part on the success of the book since they too receive royalties.

Moreover, through a partnership with Springer-Verlag, New York, Inc., one of the world's major publishing houses, Apress has significant venture capital behind it. Thus, we have the resources to produce the highest quality books *and* market them aggressively.

If you fit the model of the Apress author who can write a book that gives the "professional what he or she needs to know™," then please contact one of our Editorial Directors, Gary Cornell (gary_cornell@apress.com), Dan Appleman (dan_appleman@apress.com), Peter Blackburn (peter_blackburn@apress.com), Jason Gilmore (jason_gilmore@apress.com), Karen Watterson (karen_watterson@apress.com), or John Zukowski (john_zukowski@apress.com) for more information.